THE SOVIET COMES OF AGE

THE SOVIET COMES OF AGE

BY

TWENTY-EIGHT OF THE FOREMOST CITIZENS
OF THE U.S.S.R.

With a FOREWORD
by
SIDNEY and BEATRICE WEBB

Essay Index Reprint Series

BOOKS FOR LIBRARIES PRESS, INC.
FREEPORT, NEW YORK

First Published 1938
Reprinted 1968

PUBLISHERS' NOTE (1938)

This book is not concerned with the merits or demerits of the ideology of the Soviet Union, but represents an attempt to record the progress and achievements of what is, after all, the greatest social experiment in the history of the world. It is, as it were, the balance sheet of the U.S.S.R. on the occasion of its attaining its majority.

It was obvious that a survey which would include the social, cultural and economic aspects of a country as vast as the U.S.S.R. could not be undertaken by one person, if it were to be done adequately, and it was for this reason the Publishers commissioned the 28 essays which form this book.

Though everything has been done to make the work as impartial as possible, it is but natural that the expression of a very understandable national pride should manifest itself now and again. This is *not* a propaganda book, but has been commissioned in the normal way of business, and the Publishers hope that the public will accept it as neither "pro" nor "con," but as a report on their stewardship by some of the leading protagonists in this mighty enterprise.

LIBRARY OF CONGRESS CATALOG CARD NUMBER:
68-20337

PRINTED IN THE UNITED STATES OF AMERICA

FOREWORD

This series of separate studies by distinguished Russian scientists and administrators, of what has happened in Soviet Russia since the Revolution of November, 1917, published in celebration of the 21st anniversary of this world-shaking event, will be of great value to the serious student of Soviet Communism.

There is no emotional self-glorification; no abuse of the capitalist system. We find page after page of sober narrative about the political geography of this vast territory, extending from the Polar regions to the sub-tropics, from the Atlantic of Europe and America to the Pacific of Asia and the U.S.A. We are told about thc 60 or more separate races, ranging from accomplished citizens to the wildest nomads, all alike enjoying, under the Stalin Constitution, not only complete identity of legal and political rights, but also the same freedom in economic and social relations. There follows an explanation of the peculiar and intricate economic structure, to which we shall presently refer; the methods of transport and communication; the creation of a great army and air force, and the beginnings of a navy.

Most interesting, perhaps, to the general reader, are the chapters describing the amazing developments in the public health service and in the universal education of all the inhabitants, from the infant crèche to the university and the research laboratory, together with the always increasing circulation of the classics of all countries, and the provision of newspapers, all published by public authorities whether political, economic or cultural. There is a special section on *Science* and its application, not only to external nature but to the mind and behaviour of man. Fastidious readers will delight in criticizing the chapters on *Contemporary Music* and *Literature, Present Day Art, The Cinema,* and *The Theatre,* describing, from the standpoint of communist philosophy, the change over from concentration on the psychology, conscious and sub-conscious, of the individual man, cut off from the masses of the people, such as the works of Joyce and Proust, of J. B. Priestley and Virginia Woolf, to what they call socialist realism, with its overwhelming optimism and its meticulous descriptions of the life and work of peasants, wage-earners, salaried managers and specialists, which seem boresome to the select few who live above the crowd. "Soviet literature is," we are told, "essentially concerned with everyday life. The Revolution gave power to a new class of people—workers, peasants, toiling intelligentsia—all of them strong and enterprising men and women, believing in reality, seeking their happiness on earth and devoting their common efforts to its creation."

The most important sections of this series of reports are, however, those relating to the economic structure of Soviet Russia: for instance, the description of the substitution of planned production for community consumption, for capitalist enterprise, involving the penalization of the profit-making motive, throughout the whole realm of the U.S.S.R. We have a section on *Industries,* on *The Railways, Mercantile Fleet and Inland Waterways* and *Civil Aviation,* describing the transformation of Russia from a backward agrarian country into a great industrial power, which in its productivity is second only to the U.S.A. Another source of success is the enormous development of electric power.

To the socialist and trade union readers the most significant section is that on *Labour*. "Work in the U.S.S.R. is the honourable duty of every able-bodied citizen in the land. The right to work is secured in the constitution and guaranteed by the socialist organization of national economy, the steady growth of the productive powers of society and the absence of economic crises and unemployment." It is needless to say that unemployment does not exist in the U.S.S.R. What some readers will welcome and other readers will deplore is the dominance of the trade union movement, with its 22 million members, both in regard to the administration of various departments of social insurance, the money being provided by the state, and above all its undisputed control of the rates of wages. The General Council of Trade Unions who take an active part in state planning, and are the supreme authority for settling wage rates, know that the amount available each year for wages and salaries will be estimated according to the past productivity of the workers by hand and brain. Hence the trade unions have started what is called "socialist competition"; each individual in each plant competes with other individuals and other plants in seeking to produce more commodities for the wages received. They are all equally anxious to use any method of remuneration, or to introduce any machinery, lessening effort and increasing productivity. What is even more surprising is the device of "patronage." If one factory has beaten another factory in the race for increased production, it is in honour bound to send its best men and even provide machines, to bring the other factory up to the level of production. This sounds romantic. But the amount to be distributed depends on the total production during the past year of all the workers in all the plants, so it is in the interests of each plant to increase the productivity of every other plant.

As might be expected, the section on *Agriculture* is perhaps the most controversial, seeing that it is in this direction that there has been the most complete revolution in economic structure. This revolution did not take place until 1928 when Stalin introduced collectivization of agriculture on a large scale, and it has been practically accomplished within ten years. On page 60 we are given the following statistics:—

The Proportion of the Various Categories of Agricultural Economy in the Total Acreage under Crop

	1928	1937
State farms - - - - - - - - -	1.5	9.0
Collective farms - - - - - - -	1.2	89.4
Individual peasant farms - - - - - -	97.3	0.8
Small holdings of workers and employees for their own personal needs - - - -	—	0.8
	100.0	100.0

The greatly increased expenditure on consumable commodities and the substantial deposits in the State Savings Bank, by collective farmers, prove conclusively that the collectivization of agriculture has been an outstanding success.

Then we have one section on *Soviet Trade* and another on *Foreign Trade,* describing the regulation and direction of imports and exports by a single national economic plan which, of course, involves state monopoly, and which makes the economic structure of the U.S.S.R. wholly independent of the vagaries of international finance, whether created by tariffs or by differential wage rates, or by the manipulation of currency. "The principle of the state monopoly of foreign trade is a vital part of the economic plan adopted for the country. The details of the various trading operations, i.e., the nature and quantities of the commodities and goods to be exported from the country and to be imported in lieu, are determined in advance in conformity with that part of the economic plan applicable to the space of time in question."

In the section on *Finance and Money* we find an illuminating explanation of the financial system of Soviet Communism, and the subordinate part played by currency—whether domestic or foreign. (We may recall, by the way, that the U.S.S.R. is to-day second only to the Transvaal in its production of gold, and that its government is piling up a large reserve of this over-rated metal for possible contingencies.) "The revenues of all state-owned property accrue to the national exchequer and provide the main source of its income. The revenues of the co-operative and collective undertakings, on the other hand, belong solely and wholly to the latter, after payment of the statutory taxes of the state exchequer. Taxation is in the form of income tax. . . . The private ownership permitted by law is limited to individual peasants and handicraftsmen and must be based entirely on personal labour. At the present time it plays a negligible part in the life of the country and its sole relation to the national financial organization is represented by the payment of income tax to the state and agricultural tax to the local authorities. . . . The fourth source of direct taxation is that provided by the private earnings of citizens which are subject to income tax on their salaries or wages from state-owned undertakings or co-operative undertakings, as well as on their share of profits as members of the latter. . . . Of these four sources of national revenue, the first is by far the greatest, as the whole revenue of the state-owned property of the country goes to the national exchequer where it constitutes the actual basis of the fiscal system, whereas the other three sources of revenue merely serve to supplement the national income to a very limited extent."

We have not the space to indicate all the contents of this remarkable report, such as the sections on *Housing Construction, Sports and Athletics, The Position of Women* and *The Judicial System*. In conclusion, we single out as of immediate interest, the section entitled *The U.S.S.R. and the External World,* in short, foreign policy. When it is remembered that Russia was more despoiled by the war than any of the great powers, and that her territory was invaded during the war by the Germans and after the war by the Allies, it is certainly remarkable that they have no desire to revenge themselves and retake what they have lost. Of all the great powers the U.S.S.R. has proved itself to be the most determined advocate of collective security. "The Soviet Union stands for the consolidation of all the peace forces in the world under the banner of the League of Nations; for it is convinced that aggressors will not dare to attack peaceful states if they all stand together." Recent history has proved that it was only the government of the U.S.S.R. who has stood out against the aggressors, the breakers of the Covenant, the defaulters from the League of Nations, whether in Manchuria, Abyssinia, Spain, China, and in recent days Austria and Czechoslovakia. Whether the betrayal of the League of Nations and collective security will lead to the Soviet Union withdrawing silently and unobtrusively from European politics, is an interesting question, not dealt with in this essay on Soviet foreign policy, which, it is needless to observe, was written before the crisis of September, 1938.

SIDNEY AND BEATRICE WEBB.

Passfield Corner,
Liphook, Hants.

November, 1938.

CONTENTS

CONTENTS

MAPS

LIST OF ILLUSTRATIONS

LIST OF ILLUSTRATIONS

I

THE LAND OF THE SOVIETS

By Professor L. Ziemann
of the State University of Moscow

The U.S.S.R. extends over the eastern half of Europe and over two-thirds of Asia. The area of the U.S.S.R. —about 21 million square kilometres (8,241,673 square miles)—is approximately equal to one-sixth of the inhabited surface of the earth. Its frontiers have a total length of over 60,000 kilometres (37,300 miles) or one and a half times that of the equator. Practically three-quarters of these frontiers are represented by sea coast. Fourteen seas wash the shores of the U.S.S.R., six of them forming part of the Arctic Ocean (the White, Barents, Kara, Laptev, Eastern Siberian and Tchoukhotsk Seas), three being part of the Pacific Ocean (the Bering and Okhotsk Seas and that of Japan), three belonging to the Atlantic Ocean (the Baltic, Black and Azov Seas) and two being inland seas—the Caspian and Aral—the last named being wholly located within the Union.

The total length of the country from west to east is over 8000 kilometres (5000 miles) and express trains take 10 days to cover the distance from Minsk on the western border of the Union to Vladivostok on the Pacific. When it is 8 a.m. in Byelorussia, it is already 6 p.m. in the Tchoukhotsk District.

The most northerly of the islands of the Soviet Arctic

Regions—Rudolf Island—is in the latitude of 82° N. and is barely 1000 kilometres (621 miles) from the North Pole. The most southerly point of the country, the town of Koushka on the Afghanistan frontier, lies in the latitude of 35° N.—being farther south than Gibraltar.

The immense stretch of territory between these two extreme points in the north and south is subjected to wide variations of climate, including sub-tropical conditions.

The country at the extreme north of the Union is a region of eternal snows. Polar nights and days are three to four months long in these parts, but even this harsh land is not devoid of natural wealth. Fish, seals, walruses, whales and polar bears attract fishermen and hunters to the extreme north during the summer months.

The whole of the mainland of this northern territory and some of the islands are covered by the barren wilderness of the tundra, which actually extends over nearly one-sixth of the total surface of the country. Here the soil never thaws and the severe winter lasts for eight or nine months. The flora consists of mosses, lichens and berry-bearing shrubs of various kinds. Coarse grass and flowers cover large areas during the summer. The fauna comprises reindeer, arctic foxes and ermine, with polar bears on the sea coast. The breeding of reindeer has, from time immemorial, been one of the principal means of livelihood of the inhabitants of the tundra. In recent years various forms of agriculture have been successfully introduced—such as the growing of potatoes and vegetables.

South of the tundra, and covering an area equal to half that of the entire Union, lies a belt of coniferous forests—the taiga in the north, which changes into a zone of mixed forests in the south. Nearly half the total area of the coniferous forests of the entire world—about 500 million hectares or 1,900,000 square miles—is situated in the country. Pines, firs, spruce and larch yield valuable timber in these regions and the fauna is remarkably abundant in fur-bearing animals, such as squirrels, foxes, sable, ermine, &c.

South of the forest belt are the steppes—extending from the western border of the U.S.S.R. to the Altai Mountains. The zone of steppes covers about 12% of the territory of the Union. Most of the soil is black earth remarkable for its fertility. The U.S.S.R. possesses the greatest area of black earth in the world. At the present time almost the whole of the steppes have been ploughed up and brought under cultivation. There are practically no forests in the steppes and the wild fauna is limited to birds and rodents.

The regions situated east of the Caspian and Aral Seas are partly desert, including the sandy wastes of Kara Kum and Kizil Kum. In vivid contrast to their aridity is the profuse sub-tropical flora of the Central Asiatic oases, where wide tracts of country are covered with American and valuable Egyptian cotton, alternating with rice fields, vineyards, mulberry groves and luxuriant gardens; apples and pears, peaches, apricots and almonds are also grown here.

The diligent labour of Soviet scientists in improving means for bringing the desert under cultivation and the extensive construction of a system of irrigation in Central Asia, are causing the deserts to shrink and to give place to the flowering gardens and cultivated fields of the collective farms.

The flora of the sub-tropical regions of the Black Sea and part of those west of the Caspian, is even richer and every year sees an increase in the area of the tea plantations, orange and lemon groves and of the land under sub-tropical crops designed to meet the requirements of industry. Palm trees of various kinds, eucalyptus, magnolia, bamboo thickets and bananas have been successfully grown here in increasing quantities.

Colchis, that legendary land of the Argonauts on the Caucasian shore of the Black Sea, was formerly a country of marshes and a source of malaria. It is only under Soviet rule that the systematic drainage of Colchis has been taken in hand and the marshes are being replaced by orange and lemon groves.

In 1931 J. V. Stalin, in one of his reports, pointed out that the rapid development of industry "required, above all, an adequate extent of *natural resources* in the country—iron ore, coal, oil, corn and cotton. Are these things available in our country? They are, and in quantities greater than in any other country. In the Urals alone there is a combination of natural riches such as is not to be found anywhere else. There is iron ore, coal, oil, corn—practically everything! Our country has everything except, perhaps, rubber, but in a couple of years' time we hope to have rubber also. As regards natural resources, we have an abundance of everything—more, in fact, that we need for ourselves."[1]

The mineral wealth of the U.S.S.R. is very great and varied. Its oil fields are the most extensive in the world. At the Seventeenth International Geological Congress held in Moscow in the summer of 1937, it was shown

[1] Stalin, *Questions of Leninism,* 10th edn., pp. 440-441.

JOSEPH STALIN

that the *proved* reserves of crude oil available in the country amounted to 3877 million tons, which is more than half the total oil supply of the entire world. The reserve supplies (those which have been insufficiently investigated) are estimated at 2499 million tons. In Tsarist Russia there was a partial exploitation of the oil fields at Baku and Grozny in the Caucasus, and at Emby on the Caspian. At the present time about 45 separate oil fields are being exploited and about 80 more are being investigated by deep boring. The Soviet Union obtains oil in Bashkiria, Sakhalin, the Urals, Georgia, Daghestan and the Volga regions. Her geologists have found oil in the Far East, the Ukraine, in far-off Yakutsk and even in the Arctic (on the Nordvik Peninsula).

The geological coal resources of the country are estimated at 1653 million tons (second only to those of the U.S.A.). The principal coalfields are those of the Donetz (in the Ukraine), of Kuznetsk (Siberia), Karaganda (Kazakhstan) and Moscow.

Systematic research work has produced abundant results in regard to other minerals. The supplies of iron ore have increased from 2 to 10.6 million tons. The results of intensive prospecting for copper ore have enabled the supplies of copper—calculated in terms of the smelted metal—to be increased from 627,000 tons in 1913 to 17,072,000 in 1937, viz., more than 27 times the original figure. There has been a large increase in the proved supplies of zinc and lead ore in the U.S.S.R.

The Union possesses the world's greatest store of peat. Prior to the Revolution practically no peat was cut, whereas now scores of our largest electric power stations erected near the peat bogs around Leningrad, Moscow,

Ivanovo, Gorky and other great industrial centres supply electric current derived from peat as fuel to industry and means of transport.

A large range of new minerals has been discovered in the territories of the Union. Before the World War Germany was considered to be the only country possessing natural supplies of feldspar, but Soviet scientists have now discovered immense supplies of this chemical material in the Northern Urals (at Solikamsk) and in Western Kazakhstan, the extent of which is far greater than those of Western Europe. In the Arctic Circle the existence of huge deposits of another valuable mineral—apatite—has been established and its exploitation has already begun. Tsarist Russia had no native phosphates, whereas the U.S.S.R. now disposes of supplies one and a half times as great as those of all other countries put together.

Soviet geologists have also developed sources of supply for the basic materials for the aluminium industry by finding and working bauxite near Leningrad, in the Urals, and in the Ukraine, for the nickel industry, in the Urals and on the Kola Peninsula, for the tin and wolfram industries.

The Government assigns huge sums of money for research work and thousands of geologists, engineers, metallurgists and ordinary workers are constantly engaged in prospecting for minerals in their country.

A Union of 60 Nations, Peoples and Races

The inhabitants of the U.S.S.R. number over 170 millions. The country is situated at the junction of Western Europe and the Asiatic East and a series of complicated historical processes has resulted in the evolution of a large number of different nationalities among the population of the Union. The total number of these nationalities, national groups and peoples is about 60.

The largest group in point of numbers are the Russians (some 90 millions), then come the Ukrainians (over 35 millions), and Byelorussians (over 5 millions). There are between three and five million Kazakhs, Uzbegs, Tartars and Jews; between one and three million Georgians, Azerbaijanians, Armenians, Mordvins, Chuvashes, Tadjiks and Germans; about one million Turkomans and Kirgizes.

Tsarist Russia was rightly described as the prison of the peoples. The majority of the nationalities were forcibly russified and their culture was suppressed, while others died out. The Revolution has completely altered the national policy of the country and has changed the nature of its social and economic structure.

The First Article of the Constitution, adopted on 5th December, 1936, and called after its creator the Stalin Constitution, states: "The Union of the Soviet Socialist Republics is a socialist state of workers and peasants." The Constitution then goes on to say that "the economic foundation of the U.S.S.R. is the socialist system of economy and the socialist ownership of the implements and means of production firmly established as a result of the liquidation of the capitalistic system of economy, the abolition of private property in the implements and means of production and the abolition of the exploitation of man by man."

The reconstruction of all social relations also involved the abolition of all oppressive legislation directed against separate nationalities and promised the economic and cultural growth of all the peoples inhabiting the vast country.

Article 123 of the Stalin Constitution states: "The equality or the equal rights of citizens of the U.S.S.R., irrespective of their nationality and race, in all spheres of the economic, state, cultural, social and political life, is an indefeasible law.

"Any direct or indirect restriction of rights, or, conversely, any kind of direct or indirect privileges, for citizens on account of their race or nationality, as well as the advocacy of racial or national exclusiveness or hatred and contempt, is punishable by law."

The national policy of the Government is reflected in the administrative structure of the country.

At the present time the Union consists of 11 united republics. The largest of these is the Russian Soviet Federative Socialist Republic (the R.S.F.S.R.) with a population of some 110 million inhabitants, the Ukrainian S.S.R. has over 30 million inhabitants, the Kazakh, Byelorussian and Uzbeg S.S.R.s have each a population of six to seven millions, the Azerbaijan and Georgian S.S.R.s have each three million inhabitants, while the Tadjik, Kirgiz, Turkoman and Armenian S.S.R. have each one to one and a half million inhabitants.

Of these 11 united republics six include other autonomous republics and regions. The R.S.F.S.R. comprises 17 autonomous republics and six autonomous areas. Among these, for example, the Tartar and Bashkir A.S.S.R.s have each a population of three millions and the Mordovsk about one and a half millions.

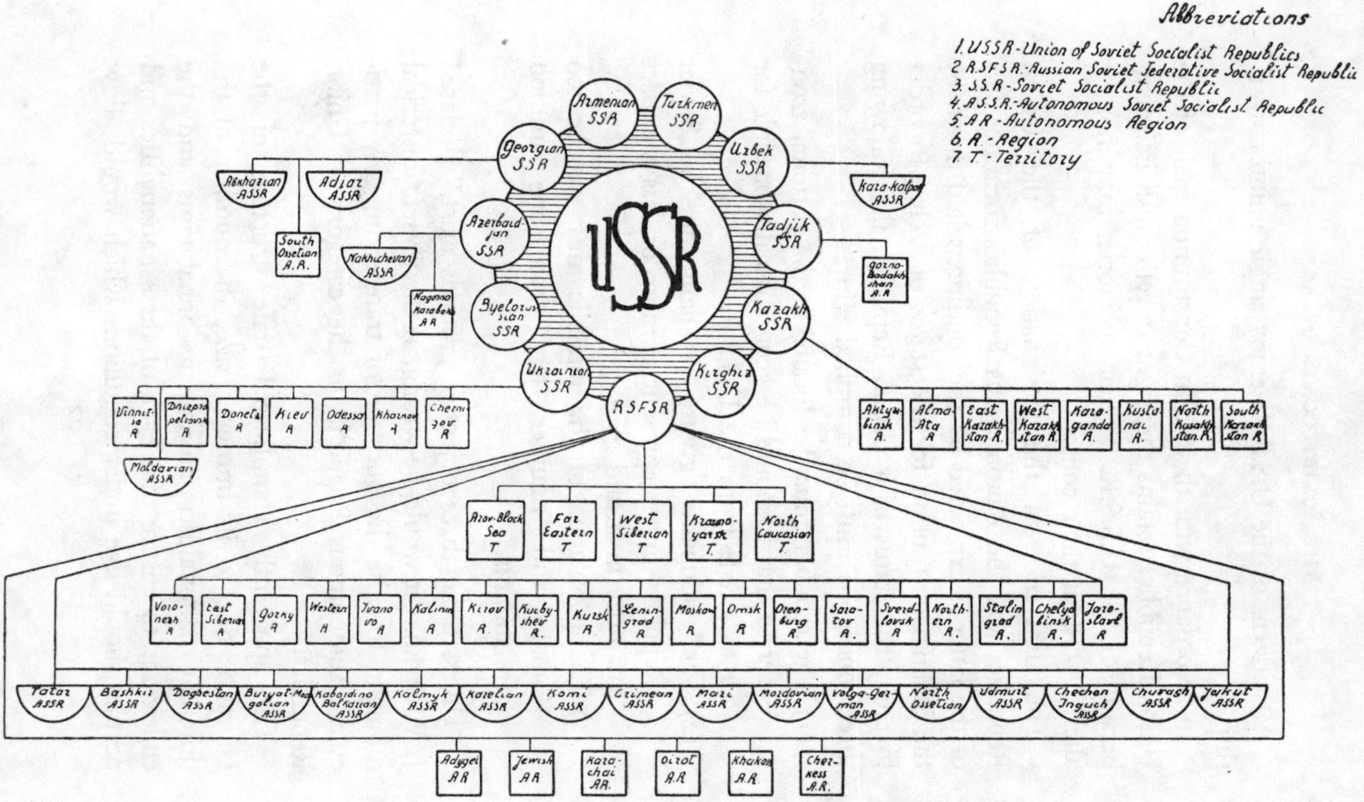

The composition of the Union

All citizens of the U.S.S.R. enjoy single union citizenship.

In accordance with the Stalin Constitution each of the Union Republics retains the right to relinquish its membership of the U.S.S.R. Their territories may not be altered without their consent.

The difference in the designation of the Union Republics and the Autonomous Republics forming part of the latter is explained by the conditions laid down by the Stalin Constitution for the status of each. In order to enjoy the status of a Union Republic, the following three conditions must be complied with:—

(1) The republic must be located at the national frontier so that it should be geographically possible for it to secede from the U.S.S.R.

(2) The nationality giving its name to the Soviet Republic must represent a more or less compact majority in it and

(3) The population of the republic must not be too small and number less than one million inhabitants.

"Unless these three objective grounds exist," declared J. V. Stalin, "it would be wrong, at the present historical moment, to raise the question of transferring any particular Autonomous Republic to the category of Union Republics."

The apparently complicated state structure of the Union is due to its immense size, the number of the different nationalities among its inhabitants and the endeavour to ensure that each of these nationalities and peoples should live under conditions which would allow unhampered development of economic and cultural resources to be effected.

The highest organ of state authority in the Union is the Supreme Soviet of the U.S.S.R., consisting of two chambers—the Council of the Union and the Soviet of Nationalities. This system of two chambers has been established because the U.S.S.R. is not a single national state. The Council of the Union is the supreme authority of the U.S.S.R. in regard to the common interests of all the inhabitants of the country, irrespective of their nationality, whereas the National Council of the U.S.S.R. is essentially concerned with matters of national interest to the various peoples and nationalities of the Union.

The Supreme Soviet, like all other legislative organs of the Soviet Government, is elected under a system of universal and equal suffrage, by means of a direct and secret ballot.

New Distribution of Productive Forces

Before the Revolution the present territory of the U.S.S.R. had 30 cities and towns with over 100,000 inhabitants and the latter totalled one-sixteenth of the entire population of the country. During the years of the Civil War and foreign intervention many large cities lost a large number of their inhabitants and it was only in 1926-27 that their population once more reached the pre-War level. During the 10 years between 1927 and 1937 the number of large cities with a population of over 100,000 rose from 30 to 70 and their total population increased from 9½ to 23 millions. This increase in the number of great cities is one of the most remarkable features of the economic progress which has been made.

The distribution of the large towns of pre-revolutionary Russia was extremely unequal. If an imaginary line had been drawn between St. Petersburg-Kazan, Astrackan-Odessa, it would have been found that five-sixths of the total urban population of the country was concentrated on the territory enclosed by this imaginary line, although its area was less than 10% of the entire country. This was the so-called centre. This territory was surrounded on the north, east and south-east by great tracts of "border" districts inhabited by nationalities oppressed and economically backward, which acted as sources of supply for the raw materials required by the more intensively developed industry of the central regions.

Under the Soviet régime the difference between the border district and the central regions is tending to disappear. The number of great cities (with over 100,000 inhabitants) in the northern, eastern and south-eastern parts of the country had, already in 1937, risen from 9 to 30 and their population from 1½ to 7½ millions.

Before the Revolution, Archangel had about 40,000 inhabitants, while Murmansk was merely a small settlement, whereas now Archangel has 250,000 and Murmansk about 100,000 inhabitants. The former lies in a latitude of 64° 30′ N. and the latter even farther north—at 69° N. Nowhere else in the world are there cities of such size so far north, and the growth of Archangel and Murmansk proves that the policy of the authorities in developing the Arctic regions of the country has been crowned with success.

Of the 11 United Republics, eight are situated in the Caucasus and in Central Asia. The remarkable changes wrought in the economic condition of these former border

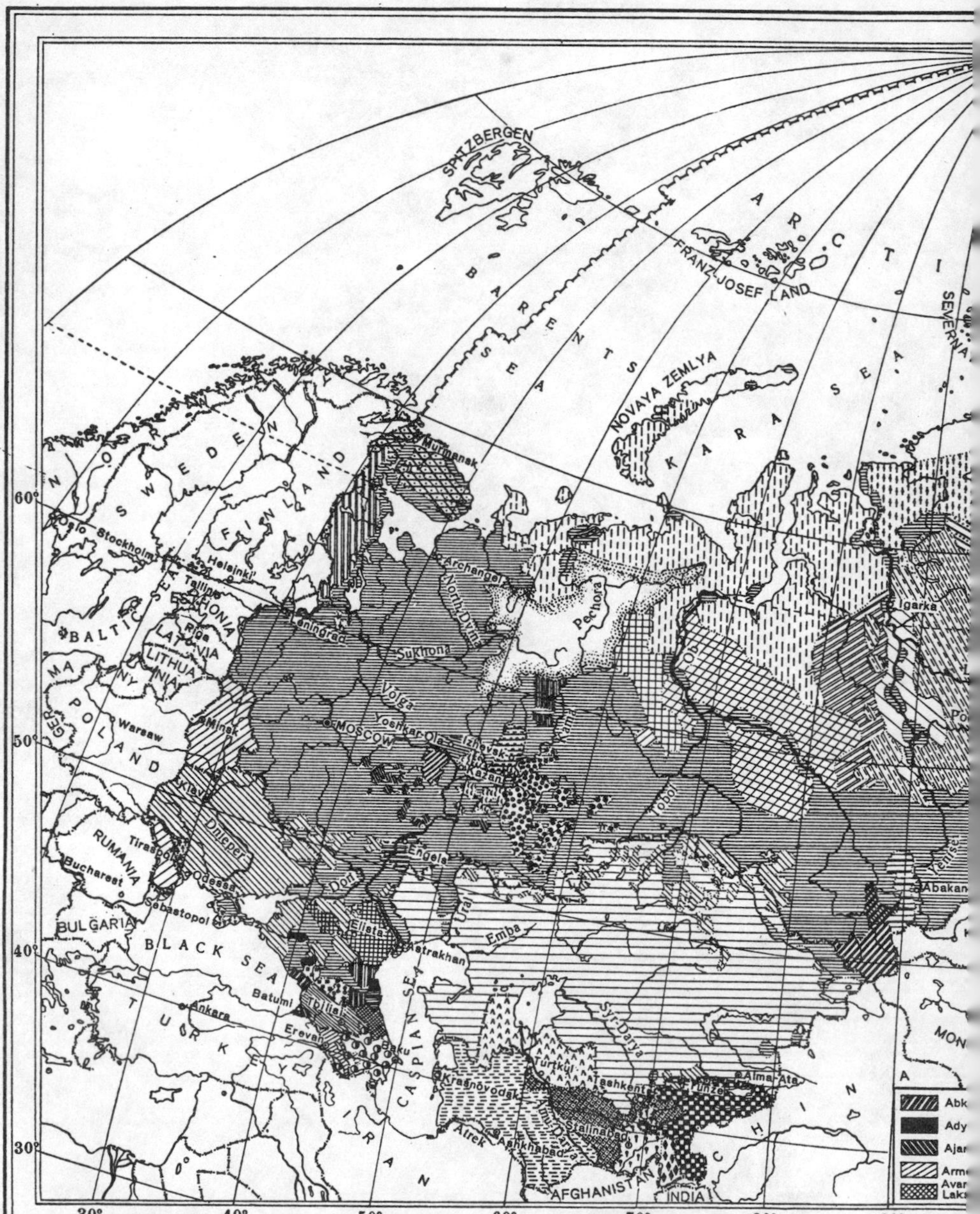

SPITZBERGEN
FRANZ JOSEF LAND
SEVERNA
A R C T I
BARENTS SEA
NOVAYA ZEMLYA
KARA SEA
NORWAY
SWEDEN
FINLAND
Murmansk
Archangel
North Dvina
Pechora
Oslo
Stockholm
Helsinki
Tallinn
ESTHONIA
BALTIC SEA
Riga
LATVIA
LITHUANIA
GERMANY
POLAND
Warsaw
Minsk
Leningrad
Sukhona
Volga
MOSCOW
Yoshkar-Ola
Izhevsk
Kazan
Kama
Tobol
Ob
Igarka
Yenisei
Abakan
Kiev
Dnieper
Tiraspol
RUMANIA
Bucharest
Odessa
Sebastopol
BULGARIA
BLACK SEA
Engels
Don
Elista
Astrakhan
Ural
Emba
Batumi
Tbilisi
Erevan
Baku
Ankara
TURKEY
CASPIAN SEA
Krasnovodsk
Atrek
Ashkhabad
IRAN
Syr-Darya
Turtkul
Tashkent
Frunze
Alma-Ata
Stalinabad
Amu-Darya
AFGHANISTAN
INDIA
CHINA
MON
Abk
Ady
Ajar
Arm
Avar
Laks
60°
50°
40°
30°
30°
40°
50°
60°
70°
80°
90°
250

USSR – ETHNOGRAPHY

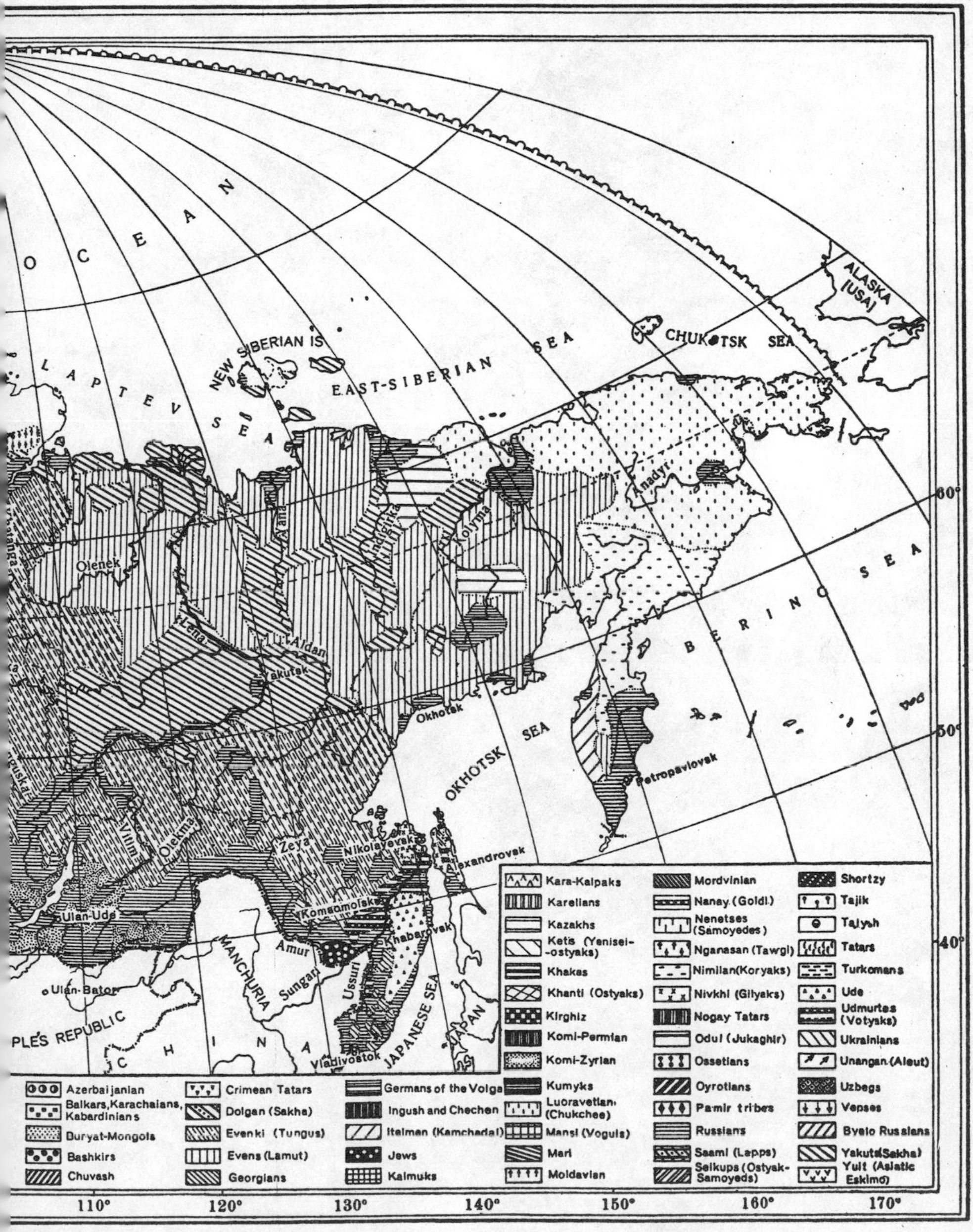

O C E A N
LAPTEV SEA
NEW SIBERIAN IS
EAST-SIBERIAN SEA
CHUKOTSK SEA
ALASKA (USA)
BERING SEA
OKHOTSK SEA
JAPANESE SEA
JAPAN
MANCHURIA
CHINA
PEOPLE'S REPUBLIC
Olenek
Lena
Yana
Indigirka
Kolyma
Anadyr
Aldan
Yakutsk
Okhotsk
Petropavlovsk
Vilim
Olekma
Zeya
Nikolaevsk
Alexandrovsk
Komsomolsk
Khabarovsk
Amur
Sungari
Ussuri
Vladivostok
Ulan-Ude
Ulan-Bator
60°
50°
40°
110°
120°
130°
140°
150°
160°
170°
750 km
Kara-Kalpaks
Karelians
Kazakhs
Kets (Yenisei-ostyaks)
Khakas
Khanti (Ostyaks)
Kirghiz
Komi-Permian
Komi-Zyrian
Kumyks
Luoravetlian (Chukchee)
Mansi (Voguls)
Mari
Moldavian
Mordvinian
Nanay (Goldi)
Nenetses (Samoyedes)
Nganasan (Tawgi)
Nimilan (Koryaks)
Nivkhi (Gilyaks)
Nogay Tatars
Odul (Jukaghir)
Ossetians
Oyrotians
Pamir tribes
Russians
Saami (Lapps)
Selkups (Ostyak-Samoyeds)
Shortzy
Tajik
Talysh
Tatars
Turkomans
Ude
Udmurtes (Votyaks)
Ukrainians
Unangan (Aleut)
Uzbegs
Vepses
Byelo Russians
Yakuts (Sakha)
Yuit (Asiatic Eskimo)
Azerbaijanian
Balkars, Karachaians, Kabardinians
Buryat-Mongols
Bashkirs
Chuvash
Crimean Tatars
Dolgan (Sakha)
Evenki (Tungus)
Evens (Lamut)
Georgians
Germans of the Volga
Ingush and Chechen
Italmen (Kamchadal)
Jews
Kalmuks

districts may be appreciated from one example—that of Kazakhstan.

Before the Revolution there was not a single town in Kazakhstan with a population of 50,000. Now Alma-Ata has over 200,000 inhabitants, Semipalatinsk and Karaganda have each 100,000, while Petropavlovsk, Chikment, Mirzoyan and Uralsk have each between 50,000 and 100,000.

The only sources of supply of coal and mineral ore in Tsarist Russia were in the south and comprised the coal-fields of the Donetz area and the iron ore mines of Krivoi Rog. One of the greatest achievements of the Five Year Plans of Stalin is the creation of an additional source of supply of coal and mineral ore in the east.

Before the Revolution the industrial undertakings in the Urals were few in number and backward in character. None of the towns there had 100,000 inhabitants. Now the Urals are unrecognizable. The original industries—iron, copper, gold and platinum—are now flourishing, while a whole series of new ones—potassium, oil, high-grade metallurgy, engineering and chemical undertakings—have been successfully developed. The geographical limits of the Urals have been extended to Magnitogorsk and even Orsk in the south and to Solikamsk in the north and numerous large cities and towns have sprung up within them.

Sverdlovsk (formerly Ekaterinburg) has increased its population from 70,000 to 400,000 and has become one of the greatest cities of the Union. It possesses a gigantic engineering works and scores of other important undertakings, together with numerous higher educational establishments and scientific institutions. The second largest city of the Urals is Cheliabinsk with a population of a quarter of a million inhabitants and huge works for the manufacture of tractors, metallurgical and abrasive products, while the third largest is Ufa, the capital of the flourishing Bashkir Republic. At Magnitogorsk there is an immense metallurgical establishment (the largest in Europe) and a new socialist city with over 150,000 inhabitants.

The growth of the Urals has been closely bound up with the industrial development of Western Siberia. The combination of the advantages provided by the exploitation of the rich iron ore fields of the Urals and the vast coalfields of the Kuznetsk region has given a great impetus to the establishment and growth of important industrial undertakings at either end of the 1000-mile axis of the Urals and Kuznetsk. Stalinsk with its huge metallurgical works and population of 150,000, Kemerovo with its chemical works and Prokopievsk, are all new socialist cities begotten by the first two Five Year Plans.

The creation of the second source of supply of coal and mineral ore in the east has not prejudiced the further development of heavy industry in the south. The growth of the industrial capacity of the Donetz and Dnieper regions is from 300 to 400%. Whereas the coal output of the mines in the Donetz region in 1913 was half that of South Wales, it is now almost three times as great.

Prior to the Revolution the Donetz region did not possess a single town of a population of more than 50-60,000 and with electric tramways and municipal drainage. Now Stalino has over a quarter of a million inhabitants, while Voroshilovgrad (formerly Lugansk)

with its great locomotive works, the port of Mariupol on the Sea of Azov and the town of Makeievka have all from 150,000 to 200,000 inhabitants. All these towns—together with many others—are provided with tramway and motor-bus services, municipal waterworks and sewage systems, numerous educational establishments, theatres and clubs.

The construction on the Dnieper of the largest hydro-electric station in Europe and the increasing development of the iron ore fields of Krivoi Rog and the manganese ore fields of Nikopol, have enabled the growth of the heavy industries of the Dnieper region to outstrip even that of the Donetz. The districts of the Don and Dnieper taken together had, in 1913, an output of pig iron equal to one-third that of Great Britain, whereas it is now one and a half times as great.

The growth of the cities of the Ukraine, more especially of those associated with the development of heavy industry, has been particularly significant. The population of Kharkov before the Revolution was 250,000, whereas it has now trebled itself and equalled that of Kiev, the capital of the Republic. The chief industrial centre of the Dnieper region, Driepropetrovsk (formerly Ekaterinoslav) has now half a million inhabitants—which is twice its pre-revolution population. Furthermore, it is surrounded by a whole number of new cities—such as Zaporoghie near the Dnieper hydro-electric station with its population of 250,000, Dnieprodzerjinsk and Krivoi Rog.

Moscow and Leningrad are the two largest cities of the Union. Before the Revolution St. Petersburg was the principal industrial centre of Russia, but its factories

and works used Cardiff coal for producing the power required to manufacture goods from imported cotton, wool, rubber and metals. The industry of Leningrad has greatly developed since the Revolution and has altered in nature as well. The hydro-electric power-stations at Svirsk and Volkhovsk and a number of great peat-burning power-houses supply electric current to Leningrad. Bauxite from Tikhvin, apatite from Khibin, Karelian wood pulp, synthetic rubber made from alcohol and other products of the surrounding districts, are playing an increasingly important part in the supply of raw material to the industry of Leningrad. Possessing a large number of workers and experts, the factories and works of Leningrad specialize in the manufacture of intricate products, in which respect they head the industry of the entire country.

Pre-revolutionary Moscow's industries were much smaller than those of St. Petersburg and were mainly concerned with textiles. At the present time the establishment of immense works for the manufacture of motor cars, electrical products, ball-bearings, machinery and chemical products has caused the textile industry to take second place to that concerned with the making of implements and means of production.

In 1913 Moscow had a population of just over one and a half millions, while it now has about four millions. The phenomenal growth of the city has not taken place at the expense of the industrial and cultural development of the surrounding country; it has, on the contrary, stimulated the latter. The exploitation of the lignite mined in the adjacent districts has resulted in the rise of the new socialist city of Stalinogorsk with gigantic

chemical works, while the town of Kashira (with its great electric power-station and works for the construction of electric locomotives) has grown enormously.

Yaroslavl, a city on the Volga, formerly possessing only one large textile mill, now boasts a huge rubber factory, a motor lorry-building works and many other first-class industrial establishments. The Moscow-Volga Canal and the direct railway line connecting Moscow with the Donetz region provide efficient communications between the capital and the country north and south of it.

Thus throughout the whole of the vast country the flourishing socialist work of development is, day by day, altering the geographical relations of its constituent parts owing to the increasing exploitation of its natural resources, giving birth to new cities and changing the whole aspect of the country.

II

THE SOVIET EAST

By Professor N. Mikhailov

Author of "A New Geography of the U.S.S.R."

The Soviet East, which covers one-third of the continent of Asia, was, prior to the October Revolution, a colony of Tsarist Russia and only differed from the colonial territories of other states in that it adjoined the metropolis. The East was a source of supply of raw material, a market for Russian products and an outlet for the peasantry of Western Russia who, before the Revolution, could not endure the oppression they suffered from the wealthy landowners, nor the generally backward state of agriculture. Geographically Western Russia was the political and economic centre, while the East was merely its colonial periphery.

The colonial conditions prevailing in the East hampered the productive resources of the country. The multifarious peoples of the East lived in a state of harsh national oppression, the greater part remaining in their original condition of patriarchal feudalism, ignorance, religious fanaticism and appalling poverty.

The Soviet régime has completely altered the social and economic conditions of the Eastern territories.

Lenin said: "We want a *voluntary* union of nations, a union which will not permit any kind of violence on the part of any one nation against another."[1]

[1] Lenin, *Works*, vol. xxiv, p. 657.

A general revision of national frontiers took place and a number of national republics and territories were set up and incorporated in the Soviet Union.

The aim of the national policy of the Soviet régime was not only juridical but actual national equality, and this could only be attained by overcoming the cultural backwardness of the peoples inhabiting the East.

Much was done to raise the cultural standard of the population of Soviet Asia and its numerous peoples were provided with educational facilities in their respective native languages in order to encourage science, literature and art.

However, something more than cultural development was called for and in 1923 Stalin said: "It is essential that, apart from the provision of schools and teaching, the proletariat of Russia should take the necessary steps to develop industries in the border republics, whose backward cultural state is not their own fault but is entirely due to their former treatment as mere sources of supply of raw materials."[2]

The development of industries in the East not only remedied the formerly backward condition of the people, but also enabled the other principles of socialist redistribution to be made effective: the greatest possible uniformity in the industrial development of every part of the country, the utilization of raw materials for manufacture at or near their sources of origin, and the bridging up of the gap which still separates the industrial advanced city from the rural countryside in technical and cultural development.

---

[2] Stalin, *Marxism and the National and Colonial Problem of 1935*, p. 117.

This was the beginning of the great historic and geographic process referred to in the Soviet Union as "the displacement of the productive resources to the East."

Until quite recently the Ukrainian coal and iron-ore fields in the south-west were the only ones in the Union. The East could only be industrialized if a second coal and iron-ore field could be made available for this purpose. The Kuznetsk region and the Urals, where the coking coal of Kuznetsk combined with the iron ore in the Urals conformed to these requirements, were accordingly developed and the present-day Ural-Kuznetsk Combine was brought into being.

The railway trucks which bring the Siberian coal to the Urals take back Ural iron ore to Siberia and at each end of the railway a large number of new metallurgical undertakings have sprung up or are under construction. In 1936 the coal output of the Ural-Kuznetsk Combine was greater than that of the whole of Russia in 1913, while the two new ironworks turned out 30% more pig iron in 1936 than the whole of Japan.

In addition to pig iron, steel and coal, the Ural-Kuznetsk Combine produces non-ferrous metals and manufactures machinery, agricultural implements and similar products. The component parts of this vast combination of undertakings have been created with the help of the older industrial regions and in its turn it is creating new industrial centres in Siberia and in the Far East.

The backbone of the Ural-Kuznetsk Combine are the Urals with their immense and varied mineral wealth. Here the Soviet régime inherited about 40 small or minute works with out-of-date plant and equipped with charcoal-fired blast furnaces of a primitive character. At

M. Litvinoff
People's Commissar for Foreign Affairs

M. I. Kalinin
President of the Supreme Soviet

V. Kachalov
People's Artist of the U.S.S.R.

V. M. Molotov
Chairman of Council of People's Commissars

the present time the best of these works have been reconditioned and rebuilt and their charcoal-fired blast furnaces now turn out high-grade steel for machine-building, while coal brought from Kuznetsk is used in the huge new ironworks at Magnitogorsk which in 1936 produced two and a half times as much pig iron as the whole of Poland.

Another great ironworks in which Kuznetsk coal will be used is in process of construction.

Numerous well-equipped new engineering works have sprung up in the Urals. They turn out metallurgical products, tractors, lathes, railway rolling stock, &c. There are also new copper and zinc-smelting works and—for the first time in the country—a nickel-smelting works. In Solikamsk, where 80% of the world's deposits of feldspar are located, the latter are being worked on a large scale. Oil is also being obtained for the first time. The entire Ural region is served by a network of high-tension electric supply cables and some hundreds of miles of railway have been electrified. The Soviet Urals have been transformed into a thoroughly modern seat of heavy industry equipped with the very latest technical appliances.

The Kuznetsk area is situated on the lower slopes of the Altai Mountains in the centre of Siberia. A recent survey of its vast mineral wealth has resulted in the location of deposits of coal of the highest grade, estimated to amount to the stupendous total of 450 thousand million tons, with seams up to 50 feet wide. The output of the new Kuznetsk coal mines is approaching that of the Donetz collieries—which were practically the sole source of supply for the whole of pre-War Russia. In Stalinsk (formerly called Kuznetsk and the place of exile of Dostoevsky) a huge new ironworks supplies ferrous metal to Siberia and other parts of the country. There is also a non-ferrous metal works in the neighbourhood and the local railways are electrified. The total population of the new towns of the Kuznetsk area—which have only sprung up in the last five to eight years—is about three-quarters of a million.

The very word *Siberia* used to be a symbol of anything that was backward and resembled penal servitude and savagery. At the present time the immense potential wealth of Siberia is being actively exploited, agriculture is being mechanized, industries have been developed and the culture of a skilled labouring community is flourishing.

South of the trunk line connecting the Urals with the Kuznetsk area is the Kazakh Soviet Socialist Republic (Kazakhstan), which is an integral part of the U.S.S.R.

Kazakhstan has an area five times that of France. The country is one huge, dry, woodless plain, with a hilly region at its central part.

Until recently the Kazakhs were nomads living in felt tents and following their herds of cattle from place to place in search of fresh pastures. If an unexpected frost occurred and covered the grass with a layer of ice, the cattle could find no food and perished, whereupon a general famine would begin.

Now the old nomadic country is unrecognizable. Permanent up-to-date settlements with hospitals and schools have been built. At certain fixed times of the year the cattle change their pasturage, but they are only accompanied by herdsmen. In the winter the cattle are kept in covered stalls. The collective farms of Kazakhstan prepare stocks of hay and grain for the winter and agriculture is rapidly increasing near the permanent settlements with the aid of modern appliances and machinery.

Prior to the Revolution there were no industries in Kazakhstan beyond a few small mines and non-ferrous metal works. Now the industries of the country are extremely important. Coal is mined in Karaganda, where a large new town has arisen, reached by a newly built railway. Coal is exported to the Southern Urals, Karaganda being the third coal-mining district of the Soviet Union.

Oil is obtained on the banks of the river Emby, whence it is conveyed through a new pipe-line to the Urals nearly 400 miles distant. The quantity of crude oil available at the Emby oilfields is enormous—a preliminary estimate places it at over 1000 million tons.

The copper-smelting works now under construction will be among the largest in the world and railways have already been built to their site. Until recently the latter could only be reached by means of a camel caravan.

The old Ridderovsk non-ferrous metal industries have been greatly extended and now enjoy the benefit of railway communication. A hydro-electric station has been built near the mines.

Formerly sugar beet was only cultivated in the distant territory of the Ukraine, whereas there are now huge plantations of sugar beet in the East—including Kazakhstan—which have created a flourishing sugar industry.

The formerly roadless country of Kazakhstan now boasts an extensive network of railways, some 2500 miles of railway having been built there under the new régime. The capital of Kazakhstan—Alma-Ata—is a garden city nestling at the foot of the Transilian Alatau. The city has many scientific institutes, higher educational establishments, theatres, &c.

The Far Eastern Territories are on the Pacific coast, where the country is mountainous and the climate subject to the monsoons. The flora and fauna of both the north and south are found here in curious combination, cedars being covered with wild vines and tigers prowling in forests inhabited by the sable.

Until quite recently the Far Eastern littoral was more or less a wilderness and practically all the necessities of life—other than timber, fish and coal—were imported from the inland regions of the country or from abroad. The few towns were surrounded by primæval forests. At the present time the Far East is being opened up and developed at a remarkable rate.

The creation in the eastern part of the country of the huge metallurgical base of the Ural-Kuznetsk Combine has facilitated the industrialization of the remote districts on the Pacific coast and their economic resources have been more fully developed. The original timber, fishing and coal-mining industries have been completely modernized. Immense and comprehensive lumber combines have been set up, motor-boats have replaced sailing boats in the fisheries and a number of fish-canning factories have been built all along the coast. The collieries have been largely mechanized.

New engineering and shipbuilding industries have sprung up. The crude oil found on the island of Sakhalin was formerly exported, while finished oil products were imported from the Caucasus. Now the production of crude oil in Sakhalin has been greatly increased and it is refined locally. New sugar, vegetable oil and clothing industries have come into being, while iron foundries are now being established.

New cities are springing up in the forest—such as Komsomolsk at the mouth of the Amur, which is connected with the general system of railways. Motor roads have been built and remote districts are in regular communication with the central region by air.

In Tsarist Russia the Jews were deliberately confined to the so-called "defined limits of settlement," and were debarred from agriculture. At the present time both the state and public opinion encourage the Jews to take up farming and in 1934 a Jewish autonomous district was set up in the Far East, at Birobidjan on the Amur. Helped by the Government, the Jewish immigrants are building new settlements, draining marshes, clearing tracts of forest, ploughing up new land and sowing crops, thereby creating a new centre of industry and culture, with newspapers and periodicals published in Yiddish, and a permanent Jewish theatre.

The forests of Siberia and the Far East are also inhabited by some 30 different—and numerically small—nationalities of the north, such as the Evenks, Tunguzes, Nanains, Golds, Nivkhians, Giliaks, Lauravetlans, Tchouckchis, &c. Before the Revolution all these peoples were in an extremely backward state of civilization. They were still using stone spearheads, bows and arrows, and their sole occupations were the breeding of reindeer after a primitive nomadic fashion, fishing and hunting. They possessed no written language. Tsarist scientists regarded these tribes as doomed to extinction and in the 10 years preceding the Revolution quite a number of them did, in fact, die out and disappear.

Under the Soviet régime *not a single* people is dying out. The economic life of these people has been radically altered. Government factories furnish the hunters and trappers with modern arms and equipment and pay them fair prices for their pelts. The collective and co-operative system has been introduced and the former exploitation by rapacious fur dealers has been eliminated. These northern tribes have, for the first time in their lives, learned to appreciate vegetables, which they now grow around their settlements, together with sown grass for their beasts. Their languages have been set down in writing and at the present time books and newspapers are printed in the tongues spoken by the northern peoples. A number of state establishments, known as "Cultural Bases," have been set up in the forests, with baths, dispensaries, schools and hostels. The appearance of their settlements has completely altered and the people are replacing their mud huts by comfortable timber-built cottages. Collective labour and the absence of exploitation by middlemen enable them to earn a good living, and whereas they were formerly on the verge of starvation, they now wear European dress and use gramophones, bicycles, chess boards and radio sets. The people of the north now have special technical colleges and institutes for training their young men and women.

Prior to 1917 labour conditions in Central Asia were those of semi-slavery and medieval despotism. At the present time these territories are populated by a free people, enjoying absolute equality in every respect with other Soviet citizens, and having mechanized and collective farming, new industries and a flourishing cultural life of their own.

Soviet Central Asia comprises four Soviet Socialist Republics forming part of the U.S.S.R.; these are the Turkoman, Uzbek, Tadjik and Kirgiz S.S. Republics.

The Turkoman S.S.R. is situated east of the Caspian Sea and 85% of it is sandy desert. New industries have, however, been established in the Turkoman towns and the capital, Askhabad, has a textile factory and a glass-works. Oil is worked near the Nebitdagh Mountains, where it has only just been located. Vast deposits of glauberite have been found on the shores of Kara-Bugoz Bay, where a new town with great chemical works has come into being.

Recent experiments conducted by the modern agricultural research stations established all over the country indicate that it may be possible to transform the Trans-caspian deserts into arable land. The immense importance of this discovery for the numerous workers' settlements which have, during the past few years, replaced the wandering bands of nomads amidst these sandy wastes, can scarcely be overestimated. The desert towns are already being surrounded with verdure and wells are being bored. Plantations and gardens are appearing in the desert.

Turkoman culture is flourishing. Formerly there were no books printed in the Turkoman tongue, whereas in 1936 over two million copies of Turkoman books were published.

Uzbekistan is situated in the heart of Central Asia and is the greatest cotton-growing region of the Soviet Union.

The present-day cotton crop of the U.S.S.R. is three times as great as that of Tsarist Russia, which had to import 50% of its requirements of cotton. That grown in the U.S.S.R. suffices for the requirements of the country. A vast new system of irrigation is in process of completion and the primitive water-wheels of Alexander the Great are being replaced by modern pumping plant. The whole of Uzbekistan cotton used formerly to be exported to Russia, but at the present time textile factories have been established in the actual cotton-growing country, in Tashkent and Ferghana, while huge hydro-electric stations are being erected on the river Cherik in order to extract nitrogen from the air by electrolysis for the fertilization of the cotton fields.

Over 18,000 tractors are at work on the collective and state farm lands of Uzbekistan and there are 26 higher educational establishments in the cities and towns, whereas previously there were none. The women have been completely emancipated and have discarded the veils with which they used to cover their faces.

The Tadjik S.S.R. lies in the sun-baked valleys of the slopes of the Pamir-Alai foothills, and here Egyptian cotton is grown in the newly irrigated fields. A new capital of the Republic—Stalinabad—has been built. The parts of the Pamirs within the borders of the Republic are traversed by a number of modern motor roads. The school attendance in Tadjikistan is nearly 500 times as great as it was prior to the Soviet régime, at which time there were, of course, no theatres in the country. Now there are six.

The Kirgiz S.S.R. is situated at the extreme east of Central Asia among the mountains of Tien-Shan. Here

A children's nursery in Tashkent—A Turkmenian family at home

textile and sugar industries have been created and coal mining has been brought up to date. Rare metals are also mined. The cultivation of sugar beet, camphor and Italian hemp is increasing, and the nomad inhabitants are beginning to live in permanent settlements. During the last 21 years the industrial output of the Kirgiz S.S.R. has multiplied itself by 95.

In the general economic progress it is worthy of note that the development of the formerly backward Eastern Territories is proceeding even more rapidly than elsewhere, thereby tending to render that of the country as a whole more uniform. For example, during the First Five Year Plan, the industrial resources of Central Russia increased by 87%, while those of Central Asia went up by 277% and those of the Urals and Western Siberia by 285%.

The whole aspect of the Eastern Territories of the U.S.S.R. has altered in the last few years and they are now in process of becoming a great country with rapidly growing industries.

III

INDUSTRIES

By A. D. Kursky
Bachelor of Economic Sciences

During the years of the Soviet régime the Soviet Union has been transformed from a backward agrarian country into a great industrial power.

The generally backward state of Tsarist Russia was largely due to the technical and economic backwardness of her industry. The gross value of the total output of Russia's large-scale industries in 1913 was 11,000 million roubles or 42% of the gross value of the country's entire production (industries and agriculture). Although one of the greatest countries in the world in size and population, pre-revolutionary Russia only occupied the fifth place in regard to the gross value of her industrial output. Her heavy industry—which constituted less than half of her entire organized industry—was very imperfectly developed and some of its essential branches were simply non-existent.

As the ruined villages ensured an abundance of cheap labour, most branches of pre-revolutionary industry utilized manual labour.

The primitive state of Russia's industries in those days accounted for the exceedingly low productivity of labour, while 10 to 11 hours a day were worked under very arduous conditions. As V. I. Lenin pointed out, the labour efficiency of industry in Tsarist Russia was 3.5 times lower than that of the U.S.A.

The economic and political backwardness of the country involved a dependence on foreign capital for its industry. The grant of enslaving concessions and the negotiation of enslaving loans reduced Tsarist Russia to a semi-colonial status. Over three-quarters of the undertakings connected with her basic heavy industries—engineering, coal mining and metallurgy—were under the sole control of foreign capital, and her industries relied on Western European capital not only for their technical equipment, but also for supplies of essential raw materials. This technical and economic backwardness of Russian industry proved disastrous at the time of the World War which dealt it a crushing blow and completely shattered it.

The Soviet authorities were faced with the urgent problem of building up industry afresh and of its radical technical reconditioning in as short a time as possible, as an essential feature of their programme of socialist reconstruction. Stalin said: "We inherited from the Old Régime a technically backward and ruined country reduced to semi-destitution. Ruined by four years of imperialist war and again by three years of civil war, a country with a semi-illiterate population, primitive means of production and small oases of industry scattered in the desert of petty peasant farmsteads—such was our inheritance from the past. We were faced with the problem of moving this country away from the path of medievalism and darkness to that of modern industry and mechanized agriculture."[1]

Those hostile to the Soviet régime declared that the

[1] Extract from Stalin's address to graduates of Red Army Academy on 5th May, 1935.

economic backwardness of the country and the absence of a powerful heavy industry would inevitably cause the programme of socialist reconstruction to break down, and endeavoured to put their plans of a restoration of capitalism in the U.S.S.R. into effect. But the Soviet Government propounded and carried out its plan for overcoming this backwardness by means of the socialist industrialization of the country.

The first essential of the policy of national industrialization was the development of heavy industry—more especially engineering—in order to re-equip the national economy and to overcome its technical and economic backwardness. "Not every development of industry," points out J. V. Stalin, "constitutes industrialization. The essential basis of industrialization consists in the development of heavy industry (fuel, metal, &c.), the building up of means of production and of our own engineering industry."[2]

Lenin and Stalin emphasized that what the U.S.S.R. required was not *any* industrialization, but the socialist industrialization which would ensure "the increasing pre-eminence of *the socialist forms of industry* over petty commercial and, with all the more reason, *capitalist* forms."[3]

The leading capitalist countries built up their heavy industry with outside help, by means of loans, robbery of other countries, colonies, &c. "We cannot tread any of these paths," remarks Stalin, "colonial robbery having no place in our policy, while nobody will grant us loans.

[2] Stalin, *The Economic Position of the Soviet Union—A Collection of Works for the Study of the History of the Communist (Bolshevik) Party of the Soviet Union*, vol. iii, pp. 57-58.

[3] Stalin, *Problems of Leninism*, 10th edn., p. 365.

The only course remaining open to us is that indicated by Lenin—the building up of our industry and its re-equipment from our own accumulated resources."[4]

Actually, the advantages possessed by the socialist system of economy rendered it possible to rely on the internal resources of the country and to accumulate the necessary means for putting the programme of national industrialization into effect.

The Communist Party "relied on the existence of the Soviet régime, the nationalization of land, industry, transport, banks and trade for the purpose of enforcing a programme of rigid economy in order to accumulate the necessary means for building up and developing heavy industry."[5]

The main feature of the socialistic method of industrialization is its unity of interests of both industrialization and the working masses and its continuous expansion of the home market, thereby creating a sound internal base for the development of industrialization.

The decisive factor in the programme of socialist industrialization was the question of the rate at which industry could be developed. The urgent nature of the problem of creating and building up a native heavy industry was due to the contrast between the technical and economic backwardness of the country and the highly modern industrial resources possessed by most of its capitalist neighbours. This problem of attaining parity with and then outstripping the leading capitalist countries in the realm of technical economy was regarded by V. I.

---

[4] Extract from Stalin's address to members of Plenary Conference of Central Committees' Executives in October, 1927.

[5] Stalin, *Problems of Leninism*, 10th edn., p. 487.

Lenin as an essential condition for the socialist reconstruction of Russia. "We have caught up with and overtaken the leading capitalist countries in regard to the establishment of a new political order—that of the Soviet. That is all right as far as it goes, but it is not enough. In order to win a final victory for socialism we must also catch up with and overtake those countries in the realm of technique and economy. Unless we can do this, we will be extinguished and this applies not only to the question of building up socialism; it is equally applicable to the maintenance of the independence of our country, surrounded as it is by capitalist powers. We cannot hope to preserve our independence unless we possess the industries required for our national defence. We cannot create these industries unless we have the technical resources for equipping them. That is why it is imperative for us to develop our industry as quickly as possible."[6]

In addition to the above considerations, the internal state of the country made it essential to hasten the process of national industrialization. The Soviet régime could not expect to endure for any length of time on a basis made up of two opposites—that of a socialist organized industry and the petty private ownership of the peasant farmsteads. "As long as we live in a country of petty peasants," said Lenin, "there will be a more solid economic foundation in Russia for capitalism than for communism."[7] In order to extirpate capitalism, it was imperative to place the whole of the country's economy —including agriculture—on the technical basis of modern

---

[6] J. V. Stalin, *Industrialization of the Country and the Right Deviation in the Communist (Bolshevik) Party of the Soviet Union*, vol. iii, p. 315.

[7] V. I. Lenin, *Collected Works*, vol. xxvi, p. 46.

large-scale industry. This again required the creation of a powerful socialist industry.

Thus it came about that history compelled the Soviet Republic to choose between the creation of a heavy industry in order to achieve a victory for socialism and a return to capitalism.

The socialist industrialization of the country could not be begun immediately after the October Revolution. In order to be in a position to start on this policy (as was done in 1926) the proletarian state had to obtain possession of the basic sources of industry by means of nationalization in order to rebuild the industries ruined by years of imperialist and civil war. This policy of socialist industrialization was first developed and put into practice by means of the First Five Year Plan. The results of the latter as regards the creation of a native industrial basis, were utilized for the realization of the Second Five Year Plan, the main object of which was the technical reconstruction of the entire national economy, of which the most important feature was the completion of the programme begun during the time of the First Five Year Plan, for the technical re-equipment of industry and the mastering of the newest methods of technical practice.

The net result of the two Five Year Plans of Stalin has been the creation in the U.S.S.R. of a first-rate and technically up-to-date socialist industry.

The value of the output of the whole of the large-scale industry of the Soviet Union in 1937 was about 95,000 million roubles or nearly nine times that of the 1913 output and more than 13 times that of the 1917 output. As regards the actual volume of the gross output of industry, the U.S.S.R. occupies first place in Europe and second place in the world.

Industry has now taken first place in national economic production, and in industry itself heavy industry comes first, more especially engineering. During the years of the two Five Year Plans a whole number of new engineering industries were established.

In pre-revolutionary Russia a few simple types of machines were manufactured, but the Soviet machine building industry is now turning out several hundred types and sizes of machines and is mastering the whole art of modern machine construction. New industries set up include the manufacture of motor cars, tractors and the most complicated agricultural machinery. Other new industries are the manufacture of power generators and equipment, factory plant for heavy and light industries and railway rolling stock. As a consequence of the immense development of the engineering industries, the U.S.S.R. has ceased to be an importing country and is now a producer of machinery and plant of every description. The import of machinery and plant in 1936 was equal to 2.5% of the country's internal consumption as against 42.4% in 1918.

The national economy is now based on home produced metallurgical supplies. The production of pig-iron in 1937 was nearly 3.5 times greater than the output in Tsarist days. To meet the growing demand of the engineering industry an almost entirely new manufacture of electric steel and high-grade rolled iron has been developed. Tsarist Russia only possessed a few small and poorly equipped copper-smelting works, whereas now

Dnieproges: the dam, and a view of the interior

the U.S.S.R. has an immense non-ferrous metal industry, producing copper, zinc, nickel, aluminium, &c.

The chemical industry has grown enormously during the years of the Soviet régime, more especially as regards basic chemical products. The 1936 output was 13.6 times that of the 1913 production, that of superphosphates being 20 times, and that of sulphuric acid 10 times the latter. The U.S.S.R. is now the largest producer of superphosphates in Europe, whereas in 1913 Tsarist Russia only occupied the thirteenth place.

The national fuel and power industries have undergone a complete reconstruction. Most of the fuel consumed in the country is now of mineral origin (coal or oil). The mining of coal as compared with 1913 has increased by 330%, the total quantity mined in 1936 being 126.4 million tons. The oil production in 1936 showed an increase of 220% on that of Tsarist Russia. The oil industry has been adapted to meet the requirements of the vast numbers of newly built auto-tractors and aircraft.

The generation of electric power is now more than 17 times as great as in pre-War Russia, being equivalent to 32,800 million k.w. hours in 1936. This immense increase in the generation of electric power is due to the systematic electrification of the country in accordance with the idea suggested by V. I. Lenin and first realized in concrete form in the State Electrification Scheme worked out in 1920 while the country was still in a condition of economic chaos. This scheme provided for the construction of 30 great generating stations with a power of 1.5 million k.w. The capacity of the generating stations in 1936 was 7.5 million k.w., or nearly seven times as great as that of the generating stations of Tsarist Russia. During the years of the Soviet régime a number of huge generating stations have been built, such as the Dneprovsk hydro-electric stations, the Zouevo and Kashira stations, the Svir hydro-electric station and others. Electric-generating stations have been erected in all the most important centres.

The creation of an up-to-date heavy industry rendered it possible to re-equip the various branches of the food industry.

During the period of the two Five Year Plans a vast new food industry was developed. The production of food in 1937 was nearly five times as great as in 1913 and thus actually greater than the entire industrial output of Tsarist Russia. The meat and bread-baking industries which in pre-revolutionary Russia were no more than handicraft trades were, in the course of the First Five Year Plan, converted into great mechanized industries. New branches of the food industry include food-canning, margarine manufacture, and factory treatment of poultry and whole milk.

The entire structure of light industry in all its branches has undergone a radical change. The clothing, boot and shoe, and knitting industries and the manufacture of educational articles have all emerged from their original status of handicrafts and are now important branches of large-scale industry.

The three great boot and shoe factories of the Soviet Union—the "Skorokhod" of Leningrad, the "Paris Commune" of Moscow, and the "Mikoyan" of Rostov turned out 30.6 million pairs of boots and shoes in 1936 or nearly four times as many as all the Russian boot and shoe factories in 1913.

The industrial undertakings established under the construction programme of socialistic industrialization laid down by the two Five Year Plans are equipped with the most modern plant.

The Moscow and Kharkov machine works, the Kharkov turbo-generator works, the Ural and Kramatorsk heavy engineering works, the Stalingrad, Kharkov and Cheliabinsk tractor works, the Rostov and Saratov agricultural machinery manufactories, the Moscow and Gorky motor-car works, the Magnitogorsk and Kuznetsk metallurgical combines, the Berezniki and Stalinogorsk chemical works, the Tashkent and Barnaoul cotton mills, the Moscow and Leningrad meat combines are only a few of the huge number of new industrial undertakings typical of present-day industry.

In 1937 the new undertakings produced 80% of the total industrial output, so that the Soviet Union disposes of the most up-to-date industrial machinery in the world.

The greatest achievement of the technical reconstruction of industry in the U.S.S.R. has been the mechanization of those of its branches which by their nature involved arduous labour conditions. Apart from the great improvement effected in respect of these, mechanization has led to a large increase in the output of the industries concerned. Coal-mining was mechanized in 1936 to the extent of 88%, the oil industry 98%, the peat industry 52%, glass manufacture 84%, and the fisheries to the extent of 67%.

The socialist industrialization of an immensely large country with vast natural resources, the urgent need for overcoming the economic and cultural backwardness of the border territories and the problem of national defence made it necessary to effect a radical change in the original distribution of industry. The backward industry of pre-revolutionary Russia was almost entirely concentrated in the central regions of the country. Only about 7% of the gross industrial output and about 11% of the total labour involved came from the East and from Central Asia.

The gigantic building programme completed during the period of the two Five Year Plans has wrought a complete change in the industrial geography of the country. There has been a general displacement of the centre of industrial development eastwards.[8]

The industrial reconstruction of the U.S.S.R. has created a working class capable of mastering new methods of production, the cultural standard of which has been raised to such a degree that the mastering of new technical processes no longer involves any difficulty. An outstanding example of this fight to master and create new technical methods is furnished by the so-called Stakhanov Movement—a movement to increase the productivity of labour named after its initiator from the Donetz area, the hewer Alexis Stakhanov, who demonstrated that a correct organization of labour could be made to produce a considerable increase in output. Begun in the middle of the year 1935, the Stakhanov Movement had already spread to between 30 and 40% of the workers in all branches of industry by the end of 1936 and it is still spreading. The incalculable value of the Movement lies in the fact that it carries the seed of the future cultural and technical elevation of the working class and paves

[8] See N. Mikhaylov's article on the Soviet East, p. 30.

the way for a new standard of productivity such as can never be attained by labour under a capitalist régime. In 1936—the first year of the Stakhanov Movement—the productive efficiency of labour rose by 21% throughout the whole of large-scale industry, while that of heavy industry—in which the Stakhanov Movement started—went up by 26%.

This huge increase in the productivity of labour in Soviet industry is the direct result of the successful mastering of modern technical practice, which has not only made the labour of the worker more productive, but at the same time infinitely lighter. The realization of the policy of socialist industrialization and the increase in labour productivity due to the successful application of new methods of production have led to a marked improvement of the material welfare of the workers. Since 1931 there has been absolutely no unemployment, while the earnings of the workers rose by over 200% during the period of the First and Second Five Year Plans. There has, at the same time, been a huge increase in the state and trade union expenditure on social services for the workers.

The creation of a gigantic socialist industry has facilitated the task of reconstructing every branch of national economy.

The resources of the heavy industry enabled a complete re-equipment of the country's agriculture to be undertaken, thereby making it into the greatest agricultural industry in the world. The primitive wooden plough and harrows formerly used have been replaced by agricultural machinery of the latest type. On the 1st August, 1937, there were no fewer than 450,000 farm tractors with a total capacity of 8.3 million horse power, in use on the land, besides 121,000 combined harvesters and hundreds of thousands of other agricultural machines.

The agricultural machinery actually available is ample for the purpose of fully mechanizing all the essential branches of agriculture. There has been a large increase in the supply of chemical fertilizers for agricultural purposes. The social and technical reconstruction of agriculture and the creation of cadres of technically qualified experts made it possible to achieve a marked acceleration in the course of 1937 of the rate of increase of agricultural production.

Heavy industry has played an important part in the re-equipment and development of the railway transport system. In 1913 there were 418 new locomotives built in Russia, while in 1936 the Soviet engineering works built 1696 locomotives.

During the time of the Second Five Year Plan a number of powerful heavy locomotives of the "FD," "SO" and "TS" types were put into service. The construction of goods rolling stock in 1936 was more than five times that of 1913. The development of socialist agriculture and the re-equipment through the resources of heavy industry of every branch of the light industry and food industry have led to the expansion of production of consumption goods and to the development of Soviet trade. The heavy industry of the U.S.S.R. also enabled an extensive programme of housing and cultural construction to be undertaken.

During the period of the First and Second Five Year Plans heavy industry paid particular attention to the strengthening of the national defences by perfecting the technical equipment of the Red Army and thereby increasing its fighting power.

The years of strenuous labour on the part of the Government for the purpose of building up and developing a gigantic industry have not been wasted. Notwithstanding the nefarious activities of the enemies of the people, the industry of the U.S.S.R. is growing and expanding and it constitutes a firm foundation for the state and for the steady improvement of the material welfare of the working masses.

IV

AGRICULTURE

By Professor M. A. Krayev

If one wishes to understand the immense change that has taken place in agriculture under the Soviet régime and to appreciate the factors which caused the poverty-stricken, ignorant and illiterate village of Tsarist times to enter the path of technical and cultural progress, one must first of all remember that the Revolution gave the land to the peasants—both to those who possessed small holdings and to those who had none at all. The "Decree on the Land," which was passed by the Congress of Soviets on 8th November, 1917, i.e., literally the day after the victory of the armed rising organized by the Bolsheviks, proclaimed the abolition of private ownership of the land which passed into the hands of the state, and the state gave it to those who worked on it for their free use.

Article 6 of the Stalin Constitution runs as follows:—

"The land, mineral deposits, waters, forests, mills, factories, mines, railways, water and air transport, banks, means of communication, large state-organized agricultural enterprises such as state farms (sovkhozes), machine and tractor stations and the like, as well as municipal enterprises and the principal dwelling-house properties in the cities and industrial localities, are state property, that is, the property of the whole people."

There was a marked improvement in the condition of the peasantry even within the first few years after the Revolution. Before the Revolution, of the total number of peasants 65% were poor, 20% were moderately well-off (the "middle peasants"), and 15% were rich (the "kulaks" or "tight-fists"); in 1928 35% were poor, 60% were middle peasants, and 5% were kulaks.

Before the First Five Year Plan the agricultural economy of the Soviet Union was an ocean of over 20 million petty individual farms using the most backward technical methods of husbandry, and consequently incapable of ensuring the rapid development of industry and of the whole national economy. In the course of a speech on 27th December, 1929, J. Stalin said:

> "Can we develop our socialized industry at an accelerated rate with its agricultural basis consisting of a petty peasant economy which is incapable of increasing the extent of its reproduction and is moreover the predominating force in our national economy? No, we cannot. Can we base the Soviet régime and socialist construction for any length of time on two *different* foundations—on the foundation which consists of a large-scale and unified socialist industry and the foundation which consists of a scattered and backward petty commodity peasant economy? No, we cannot. It will be bound to end one day in a complete crash of the whole national economy. What are we to do, then? What we must do is to consolidate agriculture, to make it capable of accumulation, of extending reproduction, and thus to transform the agricultural basis of the national economy. But how are we to

consolidate it? We may choose one of two paths. There is the *capitalist* path, which consists of the consolidation of agriculture by means of implanting capitalism in it—a path which will lead to the impoverishment of the peasantry and to the rise of capitalist enterprises in agriculture. We reject this path as incompatible with Soviet economy. There is another path, the *socialist* path, which consists of the implantation of collective farms and state farms in agricultural economy, a path which leads to the union of petty peasant farms into large-scale collective farms equipped with technique and science, and to the ousting of capitalist elements out of agriculture. We have chosen the second path."[1]

During the period of the First Five Year Plan (1929-32) agriculture was completely reorganized. A mighty network of state farms, collective farms and machine and tractor stations was created and now preponderates in agricultural production. The Second Five Year Plan was the period of the growth and consolidation of socialist agriculture.

In accordance with the Constitution the state farms and machine and tractor stations "are state property, i.e., the property of the whole people." As regards the collective farms (kolkhozes), which are voluntary co-operative organizations with their own specific characteristics, the Constitution states:

"Public enterprises in collective farms and co-operative organizations, with their livestock and implements, products raised or manufactured by the collective

[1] J. Stalin, *Problems of Leninism*, 10th edn., (Russian), pp. 301-2.

farms and co-operative organizations, as well as their public structures, constitute the public, socialist property of the collective farms and co-operative organizations.

"Every collective farm household, in addition to its basic income from the public collective farm enterprise, has for its own use a plot of land attached to the house, and, as personal property, an auxiliary establishment on the plot, a house, produce, animals and poultry, and minor agricultural implements—in accordance with the statutes of the agricultural artel (association)."

The income of the collective farm is divided amongst the members in accordance with the quality and quantity of labour expended by each. This labour is measured in "labour days," which are paid for in kind and in the money earned by the sale of the produce of the collective farm. The distribution of the collective farm income has nothing in common with the wage-levelling system.

The statutes of the agricultural artel (association), which have been approved by all the collective farms, declare that the peasants unite voluntarily into an association in order to utilize their common means and labour for the purpose of building up a collective and public farm enterprise, of securing a complete victory over all exploiters and enemies of the workers, over want and ignorance, and over the backwardness of petty individual farming, of attaining a high level of labour productivity and hence of securing a better and happier life to the members of the collective farms.

Not all the peasants, however, enter the path of collectivization without further ado. Numbers of them observe the working of the new system for some time before relinquishing their old individualistic method of farming. This they are perfectly entitled to do, as we read in the Constitution:

"Side by side with the socialist system of economy, which is the predominant form of economy in the U.S.S.R., the law permits small private economy of individual peasants and handicraftsmen based on their personal labour and precluding the exploitation of the labour of others."

By 1937 there were 243,700 collective farms uniting 93% of all the peasant farms in the country and 99% of the peasants' sowing areas. The number of state farms (not including subsidiary agricultural enterprises), grew from 1407 in 1928 to 4137 in 1937. Machine and tractor stations, which were unknown before the First Five Year Plan and of which there were only 180 in 1930, numbered 5819 in 1937, and served 92% of the sowing areas of the collective farms.

The change in the structure of agricultural economy may be illustrated by the following table:—

THE PROPORTION OF THE VARIOUS CATEGORIES OF AGRICULTURAL ECONOMY IN THE TOTAL ACREAGE UNDER CROP

	1928.	1937.
State farms	1.5	9.0
Collective farms	1.2	89.4
Individual peasant farms	97.3	0.8
Small holdings of workers and employees for their own personal needs	—	0.8
Total	100.0	100.0

We thus see that nearly 90% of the acreage under crop belongs to the collective farms and 9% to the state farms. There have been corresponding changes in the distribution of the gross and commodity production of corn. The following table is illustrative of this:

	Gross production of corn.		Commodity production of corn.	
	1926-27.	1935-36.	1926-27.	1935-36.
State farms and collective farms - - -	1.7	95.0	6.0	96.3
Middle and poor peasants	85.3	5.0	74.0	3.7
Kulaks - - -	13.0	—	20.0	—

Modern Soviet agriculture is further characterized by an entire change in its technical basis. A complete technical revolution took place in agriculture during the period of the First and Second Five Year Plans. The wooden plough and harrow, the scythe and the sickle, which were the main agricultural implements of the peasants in Tsarist days, have been entirely replaced by up-to-date machinery.

Thanks to the machine and tractor stations, the peasantry has been enabled to employ the most advanced agricultural machinery. According to the agreement between the two parties, the machine and tractor station undertakes to execute all the tractor work in the collective farm in accordance with a definite plan, to supply the necessary fuel and lubricants, to give the collective farm all possible help in agricultural production, drawing up of production plans, training of agricultural experts and so on.

The collective farms, for their part, while retaining

their economic independence to the full, undertake to provide the requisite number of collective farm members for the work in the fields, including tractor-driving, in good time, to observe all the established agronomical rules, correct rotation of crops, &c. The work of the machine and tractor stations is paid for by the collective farms in kind, in conformance again with the signed agreement, the tariffs being fixed according to the quality of the harvest.

THE MACHINE AND TRACTOR PARK OF SOCIALIST AGRICULTURE IN THE U.S.S.R.

	1928.	1932.	1937 (incomplete figures).
Tractors (capacity in thousand h.p.) - -	278.1	2,225.0	8.200.0
Combined harvesters (in thousands) - - -	—	14.5	126.6
Motor lorries (in thousands) - - -	0.7	14.2	155.0
Agricultural machines and implements (in millions of roubles) -	279.2	1,503.8	2,439.2

We can see here the extraordinary rapid process of the introduction of mechanical motive power into agricultural production.

This process brought about a radical transformation of the power resources in agriculture. In 1928 the proportion of mechanical traction was equivalent to only 4% of the total, but by the end of the First Five Year Plan (1932) this figure had risen to 22.2%, while by the end of the Second Five Year Plan, according to the preliminary estimates, it had increased to 63.1%. Thus at the present time the principal form of power in agriculture is mechanical traction: the proportion of hand traction is equivalent to 36.9%.

These immense changes in the technical basis of agricultural production brought about the transition from manual labour to mechanical labour. The following table illustrates the growth of mechanization in the chief branches of agricultural work:—

THE MECHANIZATION OF THE CHIEF BRANCHES AS A PERCENTAGE OF THE WHOLE WORK IN EACH BRANCH

	1928.	1932.	1937.[2]
Ploughing for spring crops -	1.0	19.0	74.0
Spring sewing of grains - -	0.2	20.0	51.2
Harvesting of grains by combines - - - - -	—	4.0	36.7
Threshing of grains - - -	1.3	40.0	78.0[3]

The most important agricultural work is done at the present time by mechanically drawn machines. Agricultural labour, equipped with the most advanced machinery and based on large-scale socialist production, has become a form of industrial labour.

The state farms, machine and tractor stations, and collective farms required large numbers of trained workers. For this purpose the Government created a vast number of agricultural universities and technical schools, as well as other schools and courses for the training of various

[2] Preliminary figures.

[3] Figures for 1936.

agricultural experts. Before the Revolution there were only nine higher agricultural institutes in Russia: now there are 90. Hundreds of thousands of motor workers are trained in the different schools and courses created for the purpose. Thus, from 1934 to 1937 inclusive, the People's Commissariat of Agriculture and the People's Commissariat of State Grain and Livestock Farms trained 1,195,357 tractor operators, 139,402 combined-harvester operators, 84,502 chauffeurs, &c.

The cultural and technical progress of agricultural production and the example set by industry gave rise to the rapid development in 1935 of the Stakhanov movement in agriculture. The Stakhanovites displayed brilliant examples of highly effective machine utilization, crop cultivation, cattle-breeding and tendance, and so on. Together with Maria Demchenko, an Ukrainian collective farm member (and now a deputy to the Supreme Soviet) who was the pioneer in the campaign to gather 500 centals of sugar beet from each hectare, many others began to achieve record results; tractor Stakhanovites, Stakhanov pig-breeders, stablemen Stakhanovites, and so on.

Whereas the main line of development of agriculture during the period of the First Five Year Plan, when the socialist reorganization of agricultural economy was in progress, was the utmost extension of the acreage under crop, during the period of the Second Five Year Plan the chief consideration was the utmost improvement of cultivation and the endeavour to obtain good and steady harvests.

Gathering the cotton harvest in Uzbekistan—Growing wheat in the Pamirs

THE DYNAMICS OF SOWING AREAS IN MILLION HECTARES

	1913.	1929.	1933.	1937.
Total Sowing Area -	105.0	118.0	129.7	135.3
Including				
(*a*) grain crops - -	94.4	96.0	101.5	104.4
(*b*) technical crops -	4.5	8.8	11.98	11.15
(*c*) vegetables and gourds - -	3.8	7.6	8.7	9.0
(*d*) fodder crops - -	2.1	5.0	7.3	10.6
(*e*) other crops - -	0.2	0.6	0.22	0.15

This table illustrates the increase in the sowing areas, both as regards agriculture as a whole and as regards its different branches. Since the Revolution the sowing area has increased by 30.3 million hectares, an increase equivalent to 29%. This took place in the period before the Second Five Year Plan, and principally during that of the First Five Year Plan.

The proportion of grain crops was much lower in 1937 than in 1913, while there was a corresponding rise in the proportion of technical, vegetable and gourd and fodder crops. Everything points to the fact that Soviet agriculture has definitely entered the path of intensification.

Highly successful results were achieved during the Second Five Year Plan period in the struggle for good harvests. For grain crops the average yield for the five years 1909-13 was 7.5 centals per hectare, as it was, approximately, during the period of the First Five Year Plan (1928-32). There was a considerable increase in the yield during the period of the Second Five Year Plan. In 1933 it was 8.8 centals, in 1935 8.7 centals, in 1937 10.9 centals. In 1936, owing to exceptionally bad weather conditions, the yield averaged less than 8 centals per hectare.

At the same time the Stakhanovites achieved record results, gathering 40, 50 or 60 centals of grain per hectare. But besides these individual Stakhanovites, tens and hundreds of collective farms obtained a yield of 20, 25, 30 and more centals per hectare in 1937, in which year approximately 45% of all the collective farms in the land obtained a yield of over 11 centals of grain per hectare. As a result of all these achievements, the Second Five Year Plan of gross production was brilliantly carried out. The Second Five Year Plan set agricultural economy the task of attaining a gross output of 6300 million poods of grain in 1937. Actually the figure approximated 6800 million, and thus a big step forward was made towards the fulfilment of Stalin's directions regarding an annual output in the near future of 7000 to 8000 million poods.

There has been a marked improvement in the quality of the grain. The area under wheat increased from 31.6 million hectares in 1913 to 41.4 million hectares in 1937, and as the total area under grain increased by 10 million hectares during this period, it will be seen that practically the whole of this additional sowing area was utilized for the most valuable crop—wheat.

Much has been achieved in the cultivation of technical crops as well as in that of grain crops. Thus, for example, the area under cotton increased from 690,000 hectares in 1913 to 2,090,000 hectares in 1937. New regions of unirrigated cotton-sowing areas total over 500,000 hectares. The yield of cotton in the irrigated regions increased from 7.5 centals per hectare during the period of the First Five Year Plan to 15.3 centals in 1937.

The area under sugar beet in 1937 was 1,190,000 hectares, against 650,000 hectares in 1913. New beet-growing areas have been created. The output of sugar in 1937 was 26 million centals, against the 25 million laid down by the Second Five Year Plan.

Of incalculable significance is the extension far to the north of the wheat-growing regions, and special notice must be taken of this fact.

There has been a similar improvement in another branch of agricultural economy—cattle-breeding. The number of animals during the period of the Second Five Year Plan has increased as follows: oxen, from 38.3 million in 1932 to 50.9 million; sheep and goats, from 47.6 to 66.6 million; pigs, from 10.9 to 25.7 million. Particularly important achievements in cattle breeding were registered in 1937.

THE INCREASE IN THE NUMBER OF CATTLE IN 1937
including (in millions)

	Oxen.	Cows.	Sheep.	Pigs.	Horses.
By 1/1/37 -	47.5	20.9	53.8	20.0	15.9
By 1/1/38 -	50.9	22.7	66.6	25.7	16.2
Percentage increase -	7.2	2.3	23.8	28.3	2.1

There was a large increase in the number of every kind of cattle.

There was a particularly rapid increase in 1937 in the number of animals belonging to members of collective farms for their individual use; the number of oxen increased by 12.8%, cows by 10.8%, pigs by 48.5%, sheep by 33.7%, goats by 35.2%. The help proffered by the state to collective farm members who possessed no cattle contributed enormously to the increase in the number of animals belonging to collective farm members for their personal use. Thus from 1934 to 1937, 5·5 million calves, 15 million sucking-pigs, 4.4 million sheep and lambs were sold to members of collective farms on favourable terms. As a result of this help the collective farm members have become much richer in cattle and there are practically none who do not possess a cow. The following table illustrates the foregoing:

EACH HUNDRED COLLECTIVE FARM HOUSEHOLDS POSSESS

	Public and personal cattle.		Including personal cattle.	
Kinds of cattle.	1/1/34.	1/1/38	1/1/34	1/1/38
Oxen - - -	135	219	81	138
Pigs - - -	38	105	20	70
Sheep and goats -	141	293	76	169

Such, briefly, are some of the more important aspects of the development of agriculture within recent years.

But it is not only agriculture itself that has undergone such a great transformation under the Soviet régime: life in the rural districts has undergone a similar transformation.

The triumph of the collective farm system has been accompanied by a vast improvement in the life of the peasants. Poverty and misery have disappeared from the villages. During the period of the Second Five Year Plan the collective farms developed and strengthened economically.

The annual returns of 157,423 collective farms in 1937 showed, according to the preliminary estimates, an enor-

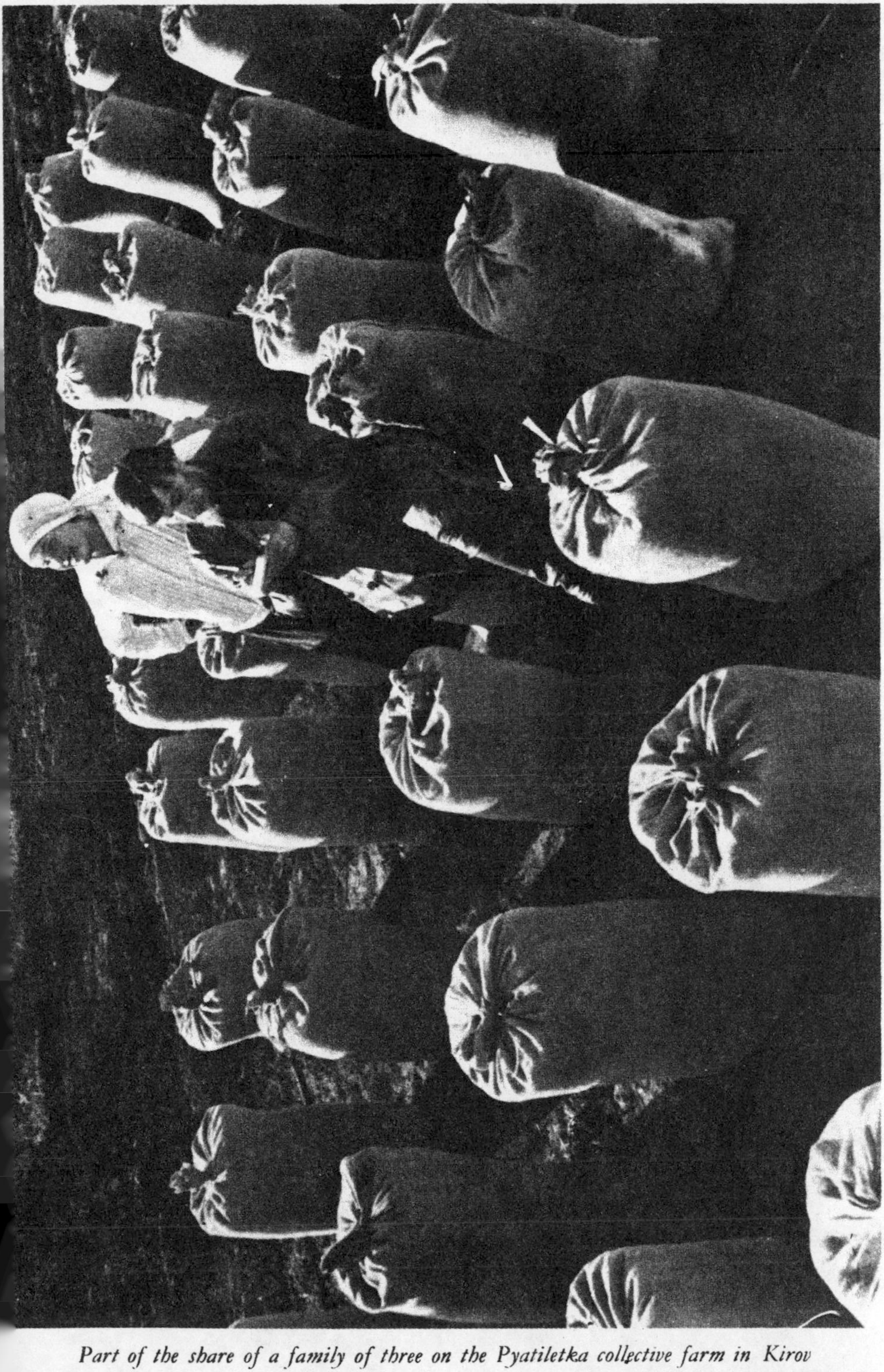

Part of the share of a family of three on the Pyatiletka collective farm in Kirov

mous increase in their incomes. Thus from 1935 to 1937 the income of each collective farm increased on the average by 61.5%. In the southern regions of the Union and in the Ukraine the average income increased by 100%. There are a large number of millionaire collective farms.

For example, the collective farms of the Berdiansk region in the Dniepropetrovsk area (the Ukraine), increased their income from 5.5 million roubles in 1933 to 20 million roubles in 1937. The collective farms of the Akimovsk region in the same area increased their income in the same period from 3.6 million roubles to 19 million roubles, and so on.

Side by side with these money incomes, there was a similar increase in the incomes in kind, which the collective farm members received for their labour-days. Thus the average increase in the produce received by collective farm members for one labour day was equivalent to 59% in the period from 1935-37. In the eastern and southern regions and in Siberia the average amount of grain given to one collective farm household in 1937 varied from 150 to 170 poods (48-56 centals). It must be remembered that these figures do not include the seed and insurance funds, the fodder supplies of the collective farms, nor the obligations regarding purveyance of grain to the state, as these funds and obligations are attended to, in accordance with the statutes of the agricultural association, before the distribution of incomes amongst the members of the collective farms.

The increase of the money and produce incomes of the collective farms and collective farm members has resulted in a vast improvement in the material and cultural conditions of the peasantry. The consumption of meat, milk, eggs, white bread, sugar, &c., is steadily increasing. The cultural requirements of the villages have grown to a colossal extent. Illiteracy in the rural districts has disappeared and newspapers, books, the wireless, cinemas and musical instruments are everyday necessities in the lives of the peasants.

Thousands of collective farms possess motor cars, and their number is increasing annually. Clubs and theatres are built in the collective farms. Hundreds of thousands of collective farm members graduate every year from the universities as agriculturists, doctors, engineers, organizers and managers of great socialist enterprises.

During the elections to the Supreme Soviet 320 of the best representatives of the collective farm villages were elected as deputies to this supreme organ of state authority in the U.S.S.R.

V

FINANCE AND MONEY

By PROFESSOR M. BOGOLEPOV
Member of the Economic Section of the U.S.S.R. Academy of Science

THE financial structure of the Soviet Union was built up on the ruins of the finances of the old pre-revolutionary Russia, whose participation in the World War exhausted her financial resources and brought the country to the verge of bankruptcy. The financial system of Russia, in so far as it was represented by the national budget, had practically broken down in the years 1916 and 1917, being replaced by a reckless policy of inflation with unlimited issues of paper money. The rapid devaluation of the currency and the destruction of the nation's economic life rendered the negligible remains of the usual sources of state revenue wholly illusory and at the same time the country's internal and external debts attained proportions devoid of any financial credit basis.

The Soviet Government were called upon to reorganize the finances of the new State under extremely unfavourable circumstances, with a depreciating currency, a ruined national economy and a civil war of exceptional fierceness, aggravated by foreign intervention. The difficulties connected with the first attempts to order Soviet finances were enhanced by the fact that there could be no question of reconstructing the financial organization of the Old

Russia, destroyed by the War and the Revolution; it was imperative to build up an entirely new system of finance on a totally different basis from that on which the whole fiscal structure of Old Russia was founded, since the entire social structure of the new state was the antithesis of that of the old.

Experience has proved that the Soviet Government's financial policy was successful, since it provided an adequate solution for the urgent and complicated questions bound up with the financing of the country's internal resources both as regards the restoration of the means of production and of the radical transformation of an agrarian country into one with highly developed heavy industries.

The basic principle of the Soviet régime is the socialist ownership of the machinery and means of production. Such ownership may be one of two kinds—of the state or of co-operative and collective farm. The revenues of all state-owned property accrue to the national exchequer and provide the main source of its income. The revenues of the co-operative and collective undertakings, on the other hand, belong solely and wholly to the latter after payment of the statutory taxes of the state exchequer. Taxation is in the form of income tax.

There are, therefore, two distinct categories of socialist ownership and each of these has its own relation to the national system of finance. The private ownership permitted by law is limited to individual peasants and handicraftsmen and must be based entirely on personal labour. At the present time it plays a negligible part in the life of the country and its sole relation to the national financial organization is represented by the payment of income tax to the state and agricultural tax to the local authorities. The fourth source of direct taxation is that provided by the private earnings of citizens which are subject to income tax on their salaries or wages from state-owned undertakings or co-operative undertakings, as well as on their share of profits as members of the latter. As the taxation of earned income is very light, the total yield from this source is trifling and is almost entirely retained by local financial authorities.

Of these four sources of national revenue, the first is by far the greatest, as the whole revenue of the state-owned property of the country goes to the national exchequer where it constitutes the actual basis of the fiscal system, whereas the other three sources of revenue merely serve to supplement the national income to a very limited extent.

The whole financial system is based on the presentation of a budget which is made up of that of the Union, the budgets of the various Union Republics and those of the Local Soviets. Three-quarters of the annual national income and expenditure relating to the country's economic life and essential public and social services figures in the National Budget. The remaining quarter is excluded from the latter and relates not only to revenues from co-operative and collective farm socialist property but likewise to certain items of those from state socialist property. The National Budget does not include the gross revenues of the latter, but only the net profits and even these are subject to certain deductions. These profits are defined as the difference between the cost of production in state-owned undertakings and the value—at wholesale prices—of their output, and they are of two separate categories. One of these is represented in the Budget by the yield of the tax on turnover, whereas the second remains at the disposal of the state-owned undertaking concerned and is regarded as its net profit. It is primarily devoted to the purpose of financing the undertaking and is, therefore, equivalent to a further investment of capital. Only such portions of these net profits as are surplus to the requirements of the undertakings are paid into the state exchequer and appear in the National Budget and such payments are always conditional on the money not being required by the undertakings for the purposes referred to above. State revenue in respect of such public income figures in the National Budget under the heading of "Deductions from profits of state-owned undertakings." The sum total of these deductions figuring in the Budget is variable and is now equivalent to between 40% and 45% of the total national revenue. The total revenue derived from both turnover tax and profits of state-owned property (about 100,000 million roubles in 1937) is made up in the approximate proportions of 80% and 20% respectively. About 85% of the 100,000 million roubles referred to above appears in the National Budget.

As the budgetary system is primarily based on the accretion of the revenues derived from the state-owned undertakings, the total sum of the national income from this source is infinitely greater than that which figures in the Budget under the headings of direct receipts from the population (taxes, subscriptions to loans and savings bank investments). The total amount of such receipts is, at the present time, only equivalent to 10% of the revenue appearing in the Budget.

In recent years approximately half the budgetary income has been applied to the financing of public undertakings, i.e., to subsidizing their capital and expenditure. Such budgetary subsidies are supplemented by the capital investments made by the undertakings themselves from the net profits remaining at their disposal. Co-operative enterprises and collective farms finance their capital expenditure from their own earnings. As this method of financing public undertakings increases the capital value and working capital of the latter, it will be appreciated that the whole structure of the financial system is far more elaborate than that of other countries. The national resources of the Soviet Union are not only represented by the accumulation of the capital invested in its property and figuring in the Budget, but also by the national income which does not figure under the various items of budgetary revenue but serves to supplement the internal financial resources of state-owned undertakings. Apart from the budgetary items of revenue and expenditure, the financial organization also includes those relating to the finances of all the state-owned undertakings administered by the various commissariats concerned with the national economy. The total amount involved is, in each branch of industry, immense, since the commissariats in question deal with the gross revenues of the establishments they administer, whereas the National Budget is only concerned with net profits. Furthermore and as already explained, the industrial enterprises receive state subsidies which may altogether amount to 50% of the total budgetary expenditure, apart from the credits granted to defray the needs of the various undertakings, by the State Bank.

The dual basis of the Soviet system of finance does not affect its homogeneity, as this system is subordinate to a financial plan which is based on the country's general economic planning programme. Under the new Constitution of the Union, the whole economic life of the country is regulated by this planning programme. The existence of a financial plan and the fact that the country's main financial resources have one source (socialist ownership) render the whole Soviet system of finance sufficiently cohesive to give it infinite flexibility and make it into the most reliable instrument for carrying on the economic policy of the country. This has been amply demonstrated by the experience of the past 20 years and, more especially, during the putting into effect of the two Five Year Plans of the development of the national economy. The Soviet financial system was called upon to mobilize immense sums for that purpose and thereby proved that it was not only highly efficacious and admirably adapted for such a purpose itself, but that the method of organized planning was of the utmost value. The work of the past 20 years has furnished a vast amount of financial experience and data for organization, which renders it possible for the Soviet Union to embark on a further extensive programme of economic and cultural development, with the full assurance that in the hour of danger which may soon threaten the world the financial system will be capable of meeting any demands made on it.

The whole of the credit system of the Soviet national economy is built up on the short-term credits of the State Bank.

There are a number of other banks for the express

purpose of financing industrial undertakings, but they are in effect merely centres of control for the payment of budgetary subsidies and the collection of funds from the state-owned enterprises for the purpose of adding to the capital investment of the latter. Credits on mortgage are non-existent in the Soviet economic system and although some of the special banks —such as the Bank of Agricultural Credit—grant long-term credits to economic organizations, the only difference between such credits and those granted by the State Bank is that, whereas the latter require repayment to be made in two or three months, the former relate to transactions of a nature in which repayment, owing to natural causes, cannot be made before one or two years.

The credit facilities offered to public undertakings by the State Bank are primarily intended for the purpose of enabling individual enterprises to finance current transactions in order to increase their turnover. Every socialist undertaking is adequately equipped with working capital for coping with its planned production and as the annual increase of the latter is accompanied by a proportionate increase of working capital, temporary loans from the State Bank are only provided to defray extraordinary seasonal expenditure such as might be involved by payments for periodic supplies of agricultural raw material.

The State Bank is not only the sole centre for credits to industrial undertakings, it fulfils another important function as a clearing-house for the whole of the socialist organizations of the country in their dealings with one another and with the exchequer authorities, who likewise use the State Bank for all financial transactions. The volume of business done by the latter may be judged from the number of branches established all over the country. At the present time there are over 3000 such branches. Each financially independent enterprise may open a banking account in the local branch of the State Bank for the purpose of collecting credits and settling debits. At the present time such individual accounts of state-owned or collective undertakings and institutions total 2,800,000 roubles, of which tens of thousands belong to factories and works, hundreds of thousands to commercial enterprises, 240,000 to collective farms, &c. The total turnover of the State Bank in 1936 was 2116 thousand million roubles, having increased 13 times during the period of the two Five Year Plans. The total credits granted by the State Bank to industrial and other undertakings in 1936 amounted to 7994 million roubles. The Bank provides the finance for its transactions from the temporarily surplus funds deposited with it by the state-owned enterprises and the budgetary organizations. As the State Bank is the general clearing-house for all financial transactions it is in daily receipt of immense sums in cash, while the daily increase of its clients' accounts provides ample temporarily surplus funds. The revenue proper of the State Bank is derived from the profits on its business. Half of these revenues are paid into the national exchequer, while the remaining half is utilized to strengthen the Bank's reserves of capital.

Obviously the important part played by the State Bank in the economic life of the Soviet Union and, more especially, the fact that the work of the Bank is closely bound up with that of the National Budget and the financing of the various branches of the country's industry, involves careful co-ordination of the Bank's policy with that guiding other financial plans and, above all, with the policy underlying the general economic programme of the U.S.S.R. For this reason the credit policy of the Bank is made to conform to the Government's general financial plan as well as to that of each branch of the national economy. In view of the inter-relation of these plans, the State Bank has now been made an independent state institution, its president being a member of the Council of People's Commissars of the U.S.S.R. At the same time the Bank constitutes the keystone of the whole unified system of Soviet finance. This unification of the plans of all the great organs of finance renders it easier to adhere to a definite financial policy and imparts a high degree of flexibility to the whole financial system.

It may, therefore, be seen that the Soviet State Bank, which is the largest banking institution in the world both in regard to size and to the scope of its activities, differs from the central banks of all other countries in that it is not first and foremost a banking institution for the country's banks. The status of all clients' accounts in the Soviet Bank is the same, irrespective of whether they belong to gigantic industries, rural collective farms or small trading enterprises owned by the state or a co-operative body. Consequently every aspect of the economic life of the country, the progress made with plans of production, of goods turnover, future National Budgets, plans of socialist accumulations, &c., &c., is something with which the Bank is intimately concerned. It is, in effect, a sort of economic observatory from which the whole economic activity of the country may be closely studied.

The fact that bills of exchange have no place in the

credit system of the Bank is of the utmost value to the latter. Bills of exchange cannot be used since the law prohibits the granting of credits of any kind by any one state-owned or co-operative undertaking to another. All credit business has to be transacted directly with the Bank, which deals with all financial transactions and can exercise the necessary control over their conduct. In case of any departure from the established plan, the Bank can take prompt and effective action to put things right.

Both the financial policy and the working of the financial organs of the country are vitally affected by the fact that the distribution of the national income due to finance is inseparable from that represented by its monetary form. The economic policy of the Soviet Union has, therefore, continually aimed at a correct representation of economic facts in terms of money. The authorities always endeavour to ensure that the national currency remains stable and fixed. Three important conditions ensure stability of currency. The first is that the value of the currency in circulation is always proportionate to a definite volume of trade, which increases from year to year and must always determine the total value of the currency issued. The second condition is that the actual sources of production for the country's trade are in the hands of the state itself as the owner of the various undertakings which constitute these sources of production. The third condition is the supremely important principle that commodities and goods are sold at fixed prices.

A policy of price-fixing is a factor of primary importance in the economic and financial policy of the country whose economy is a socialist economy conducted in all its essentials in accordance with a definite plan. The prices of all products of the nation's industries, whether wholesale or retail, are fixed by the Government and can only be altered by the latter. These prices depend on the cost of production and that of handling and selling the goods concerned and the margin of profit allowed for in the price is determined by the requirements of the current economic policy and the plan formulated to realize it. Cost of production is, therefore, not the governing factor of the selling price. For example, if some particular branch of industry is unsuccessful in carrying out the prescribed production plan in regard to reducing the cost of production and this last actually proves to be higher than the approved selling price, this circumstance cannot be used as a pretext for raising the selling price. The whole policy of price-fixing aims at stability of prices and their systematic reduction in the interests of the workers. This ensures stability of the currency and a constant rise in the purchasing power of the people. Production can be raised continuously without risking a slump, more especially as the output of every branch of industry is regulated by a definite plan.

The monetary system of a country whose economic life is constituted on socialist principles is readily controllable by planning and in actual practice, apart from the relatively small amount of currency changing hands in the rural communities—such as at fairs and bazaars—the amount of money in circulation in the Soviet Union is wholly dependent on the economic activity of the country. Most of the money comes into the hands of the people in the form of wages, or payment for agricultural produce and raw materials purchase by state-owned undertakings, or of premiums paid out on the drawings of bonds of state loans, or withdrawals from savings banks. The flow of money in the reverse direction is represented by retail trading and payments for services (communal feeding, transport, theatres, cinemas, &c.) which means that the whole of the currency disbursed by the people finds its way back to the one and only State Bank. The forces which set these centripetal and centrifugal processes of currency circulation in motion are wholly in the hands of the state and are governed by a definite economic plan.

The net result is that the U.S.S.R. possesses a really sound system of money circulation. Furthermore, the foreign trade of the country is a state monopoly and cannot disturb internal price levels even in times of international crisis. This fact makes the Soviet economic system into an infallible safeguard for the maintenance of monetary stability. Under these conditions gold in the Soviet Union is just a commodity like pig-iron or cotton and serves as a currency basis exclusively for economic relations between the U.S.S.R. and the outside world.

Soviet finance is part and parcel of the country's economic life and the expansion of the country's economic resources is accompanied by a corresponding growth of its financial wealth. There is no line of demarcation whatever between its economics and finances, a fact which constitutes one of the greatest benefits conferred by a socialist system of economy.

VI

SOVIET TRADE

By F. I. Belonozhko

Director of the Scientific Research Institute of Commerce and Public Feeding of the People's Commissariat for Trade of the U.S.S.R.

Soviet trade, in common with every other branch of national economy, is regulated and directed by a single national economic plan. Its function is to realize all the commodities produced by state enterprises, and also by co-operative organizations and collective farms. Private capital has neither part nor lot in Soviet trade, which is one of the most important branches of the socialist economy.

As it is regulated by a general plan for the whole country, trade is not subject to the influence of fluctuations in the market: it is carried on in such a way as to meet the needs of the population in accordance with its steadily improving material conditions, its cultural and national characteristics, tastes, and so on.

The plans for trade in the various republics, areas, territories, regions, &c., are drawn up in accordance with the requirements and characteristics of the peoples inhabiting them, and each of these plans is a part of the whole state plan for trade.

Every commercial enterprise has its own plan regarding turnover, the character of its trade, and the extent, put down in figures and facts, of its technical equipment, which is drawn up for a period of several years.

Trade is carried on in state shops (mainly in the towns and industrial districts) and in co-operative stores (in the rural districts). In addition to state and co-operative trade, there is that of the collective farms, collective farm members, and individual peasants (peasants who have not yet become members of collective farms), whose produce is sold direct to the population at the collective farm markets, as well as to the state and co-operatives.

Of the total trade turnover, the state and co-operatives are responsible for 85-90%, and the collective farms for 10-15%.

The State promotes collective farm trade and that of individual peasants in every possible way. Special buildings, known as collective farm markets, have been erected in the towns, workers' settlements, and other places where farm produce is brought for sale, and are provided with every convenience—refrigerators for perishables; store rooms for other goods; meat, milk, vegetable and other arcades or sections; cutting up and assortment of carcases; scales; bacteriological controlling stations under the management of sanitary officers. There are, in addition, special establishments in the markets erected for the convenience and to satisfy the cultural requirements of the collective farm members and individual peasants who have come up to town—reading-rooms, inquiry offices, dining-rooms, hairdressing saloons, clubs, cinemas and guest houses. The state and co-operative organizations have their own stalls in these markets where they sell many different kinds of manufactured goods for the convenience of the peasant market sellers.

One of the most important aims of the policy of prices is the raising of the real wages of the working-people. Consequently price-planning is organically connected with the planning of the whole national economy.

Prices as regards state and co-operative trade are fixed by the Government and are compulsory for every commercial establishment. Every arbitrary alteration of these prices is punishable by the law. Thus the policy of prices fixes and limits the amount of accumulation (profits) at every stage of the path taken by commodities from production to the consumer. Furthermore, the Government systematically improves and shortens this path by eliminating superfluous stages, and hence reduces the cost of commodity circulation and, consequently, the price of goods.

Prices in collective farm and peasant trade are not laid down by the Government, but are evolved at the collective farm markets. As, however, collective farm and peasant trade is a part of the whole of Soviet trade and is therefore influenced by it, prices in collective farm and peasant trade are influenced by those obtaining in state and co-operative trade. It stands to reason that the consumer will not pay more for articles at the collective farm markets than in the state and co-operative shops. Another factor making for the systematic reduction of prices in the markets is the constant improvement of the material well-being of the collective farm members, i.e., a continued increase of superfluous agricultural products in the hands of the collective farms, collective farm members and individual peasants. This growth of the wealth of the rural population is a result of the collectivization of farming (the creation of large collective farms), which enables those working on them to apply the most advanced technical methods and latest achievements of agricultural science to agricultural production.

Prices are continually being reduced by the Government. In 1935 alone the total reduction of prices in state and co-operative trade amounted to 5000 million roubles. Reductions in 1936 amounted to approximately the same sum. In 1937 they amounted to 1500 million roubles. These reductions naturally caused a similar movement in collective farm and peasant trade. It is estimated that within the period of the Second Five Year Plan alone prices of goods in the collective farm markets were reduced by 66.6%.

Quite obviously the systematic reduction of prices of manufactured goods and foodstuffs is equivalent to a systematic raising of the level of real wages. The purchasing power of the population is steadily rising and is being met by an ever-increasing flow of goods and trade turnover. In the period 1925-28 the turnover of state and co-operative trade increased by more than 100%—from 5100 million roubles to 11,800 million roubles. From 1928-32, i.e., by the end of the First Five Year Plan, trade turnover had increased by over 250% to 40,300 million roubles. In the period of the Second Five Year Plan, 1932-37, trade turnover increased by over 200%, as shown by the following table:—

Year.	State trade (million roubles).	Co-operative trade (million roubles).	Total (million roubles).
1932 - -	14,500	25,800	40,300
1933 - -	25,100	24,700	49,800
1934 - -	36,800	25,000	61,800

Year.	State trade (million roubles).	Co-operative trade (million roubles).	Total (million roubles).
1935 - -	62,800	18,600[1]	81,400
1936 - -	80,000	26,000	106,900
1937 - -	92,100	32,900	125,000

During the same period the turnover of collective farm and peasant trade increased from 7500 million roubles to 18,000 million roubles.

The above figures do not fully illustrate the level of consumption. The rural population buys agricultural products (bread, meat, milk, butter, vegetables and fruit) direct from the collective farms, or produces them itself: these operations are obviously not included in the above table. Secondly, the figures for retail trade do not include consumption by sick people, holiday makers, &c., in rest-homes, sanatoria and hospitals, and by children in crèches, kindergartens and children's homes. There is an immense number of these establishments in the country, and consumption in them constitutes a large item in the general figures for the whole Union.

One may judge of the steady increase of consumption by the increased sale of the most important foodstuffs and manufactured goods in the state and co-operative retail trade in the years 1933-37. Consumption of butter increased by 200%; cheese by 120%; eggs by 510%; sausages by 733%; sugar by 240%; linen fabrics by 1320%; cotton fabrics by 60%; ready-made clothes by 40%; knitted fabrics by 160%; leather footwear by

[1] The reduction in co-operative trade is due to the fact that in 1935 the co-operative establishments in the towns were transferred to state organizations. The co-operatives function solely in the rural districts.

140%; rubber footwear by 30%; and household soap by 210%.

It is estimated that consumption has increased by approximately 200% as compared with 1932—the last year of the First Five Year Plan—while that of certain commodities has increased a hundredfold.

Thanks to the vast improvement in the material prosperity of the population and to the rapid development of industry and agriculture, trade turnover is steadily increasing and the assortment of goods is becoming larger and more varied.

Nevertheless, in spite of this immense increase, the needs of the population are far from being satisfied as regards both various manufactured goods (high-grade woollen, silk and linen fabrics and good-quality smart footwear), and various household and cultural articles (bicycles, wireless sets, gramophone records). The earnings of the population and their purchasing power are still far ahead of the output of these commodities, in spite of the immense development of the different branches of light industry.

The commercial organizations exercise influence in every possible way upon those branches of industry which manufacture articles of common use in their endeavour to increase the variety and improve the quality of these articles. This is done by means of the many different forms of connexion between trade and industry, including the system of advance orders made by the commercial organizations and based on the known requirements of the consumers.

The industrial concerns receive orders to manufacture goods of a definite quality, colour and shape, in accordance with the tastes and requirements of the population. Conferences of commercial and industrial representatives and consumers are organized, as are clothing, household and food exhibitions. Only those goods are manufactured which win the approval of the consumers. Finally, very minute control of goods by the commercial organizations enables them to assort them carefully according to quality, shape and so on. Articles which do not come up to the required standard are labelled as wasters and are sold, if at all, at very reduced prices.

Much space in the press is devoted to questions connected with trade, such as the quality of goods, consumers' demands, &c. All this serves to link up trade with industry and the consumers, and makes for its improvement.

In Tsarist Russia delicacies and articles of luxury were imported from abroad for the benefit of the "upper ten," while the assortment of commodities for the great mass of the population was very poor. Soviet trade, aided by the light and food industries, is continually introducing large numbers of new kinds of goods into general use. Thus there has been an immense increase in the output, and a corresponding increase in the purchase, of the most varied kinds of culinary, fish and meat preparations, sausages, new kinds of canned goods, cheeses, sweetmeats, dairy produce, dessert waters, fruit drinks, wines, perfumery, &c.

While endeavouring to increase the output of new types of commodities, Soviet trade at the same time educates the taste of the consumer. In accordance with the plan for 1938 state and co-operative trade turnover must amount to 140,500 million roubles, which is 12.4% more than in 1937, or, in other words, the consumer will receive 15,500 million roubles worth of goods more than in the previous year. This increase alone is 250% higher than the total trade turnover of the state and co-operative organizations in 1925, while the retail trade turnover of 1938 will be 28 times that of 1925.

The increase of trade turnover is accompanied by a similar increase in the number of shops and in the improvement of their technical equipment.

By the end of 1924 there were 42,000 shops and stalls in the country; by the end of 1928 there were 155,000; by the end of 1932 (the beginning of the Second Five Year Plan) 284,000 and by October, 1937, there were 326,000. New shops furnished with all the latest technical equipment are continually being opened in every town, village and hamlet.

The small shop, with an insignificant turnover, was the typical commercial establishment of Tsarist Russia. Since the Revolution, and particularly during the period of the First and Second Five Year Plans, there has not only been an immense increase in the number of shops (as shown by the above figures), but the whole system has been largely reconstructed. Many new shops have been built, including large universal stores (in Moscow, the Donbas, the Urals, Transcaucasus, Magnitogorsk) whose annual trade turnovers attain hundreds of millions of roubles. Some of these universal stores have a daily turnover of four or five millions. There has been a great change in technical equipment and commercial culture; the shops are provided with refrigerators, cutting, packing, and measuring machines, automatic scales, goods lifts, &c.

There are also separate shops for meat products, dairy produce, confectionery, groceries, provisions, haberdashery, footwear, knitted fabrics and clothes, ready-made clothes, perfumery, tobacco, &c. Certain shops only deal in ready-weighed goods. There is a great demand for prepared but uncooked foodstuffs, which greatly ease the housewife's burden. In 1938 340 million roubles will be spent on the construction of new shops, which is nearly double the sum spent on the same purpose in 1937.

The object of Soviet advertising is the encouragement of the production of new kinds of goods, and their popularization; the promotion of speed in the path taken by goods from production to the consumer; and the description of the use and taste of various new foodstuffs and preparations. Soviet advertising is quite free of that feverish clamour characteristic of private trade advertisements, which only serve the interests of competition. The technical and artistic quality of advertising is steadily improving, and advertising exhibitions are arranged from time to time.

The rapid growth of trade was accompanied by an equally rapid development of the public feeding service, which is an essential constituent of Soviet trade. There is a steady increase in the number of dining-rooms, restaurants, cafés, refreshment bars, and the like.

The following figures are illustrative of the development of the public feeding service:—

On 1st January, 1929, 750,000 persons utilized this service: by the beginning of 1934 this number had risen to over 18 millions. The turnover was 550 million roubles in 1929; by 1936 this sum had increased to 7,233,000 million roubles, which refers only to the urban population and industrial workers.

The public feeding service has attained good results in the manufacture of concentrated foodstuffs and the preparations of ready-to-cook foods for private households.

Commercial culture and conscientiousness depend mainly on the personal qualities, cultural standard, and knowledge of the work of those engaged in trade. The People's Commissariat for Trade directs a large number of universities and technical schools which prepare highly skilled specialists for every branch of trade. In Moscow alone over 4000 students attend the three higher commercial institutes; many thousands of those employed in trade and the public feeding service attend the technical schools; while hundreds of thousands take various commercial courses. Of these last two categories 308,100 persons passed the state technical examination within the past few months (end of 1937 and beginning of 1938).

Trade in the Soviet Union is directed by the People's Commissariat for Trade of the U.S.S.R. through the People's Commissariats for Trade of the Union Republics. The People's Commissariat for Trade of the U.S.S.R. draws up the plan of development of the wholesale and retail trade, and of that of commercial establishments, dining-rooms, restaurants and of commodity circulation in general, and supervises the execution of these plans after they have been approved by the Government. It also fixes retail prices and commercial discounts and imposts, subject to the approval of the Government, and sees that they are observed, taking strong measures against any departure from these fixed prices. It elaborates questions of commercial legislation, lays down the rules for every trading organization and establishment and exercises control over the latter in respect to their observance of all the laws and rules of trade laid down by the Government.

It works out and establishes the system and procedure of financing these commercial organizations. It gives orders to industrial enterprises to manufacture the requisite assortment of articles of common consumption and to produce new types and varieties of goods; takes extensive measures to enlarge the market for all these commodities; and exercises control over the execution of plans relating to the unloading of merchandise and over the quality of this merchandise.

It elaborates and carries out measures for improving and extending collective farm trade; directs the construction and improvement of commercial establishments, and provides them with the most up-to-date equipment and stock in trade; and, finally, watches the situation of the market and keeps a statistical account of trade.

In the autonomous republics, areas, territories and regions the Soviets of Workers' Deputies have trade departments which control and direct the work of the trading organizations in their districts.

The People's Commissariat for Trade has a special Scientific Research Institute of Commerce and Public Feeding and a number of scientific research laboratories. As in every branch of the national economy the Stakhanov movement, the highest form of socialist competition, is very widespread among those engaged in trade.

VII

FOREIGN TRADE

By Professor D. Mishustin

Director of the Scientific Research Institute of Foreign Trade

The foreign trade of the U.S.S.R. is an essential part of the national economy of the country and its primary object is to assist the work of building up and consolidating the socialist structure of the Republic.

Foreign trade has played an immensely important part in the transformation, during the last ten years, of the Soviet Union from a backward agrarian state into an industrial country. In order to hasten the process of industrialization and for the purpose of establishing large-scale home industries of metallurgical and engineering products as quickly as possible, it was imperative to expand Soviet trade with other countries. By means of imports the technical resources of the leading capitalist countries were used for the purpose of accelerating the process of national industrialization, while exports served to build up the reserves of foreign currency required to pay for imports.

At the same time foreign trade was, and still is, of great value as a factor in the peace policy of the Soviet Union.

Commercial contact between the U.S.S.R. and other countries is maintained by means of a *foreign trade monopoly,* under which the exclusive right to engage in commercial operations abroad is vested in the Soviet state. The latter conducts its business through a special department established for the purpose—the People's Commissariat of Foreign Trade, which controls and co-ordinates the work of the various exporting and importing bodies under it. In accordance with a decree signed in 1918 by Lenin and Stalin and still in force at the present time, no other organizations or persons are entitled to engage in foreign trade activities of any description.

The principle of the state monopoly of foreign trade is a vital part of the *economic plan* adopted for the country. The details of the various trading operations, i.e., the nature and quantities of the commodities and goods to be exported from the country and to be imported in lieu, are determined in advance in conformity with that part of the Economic Plan applicable to the space of time in question. The planning system is itself dependent on a monopoly of the country's foreign trade, as such a monopoly protects the U.S.S.R. against any competition by goods produced abroad and prevents foreign capital from buying Soviet goods in the open market.

The actual volume of the foreign trade of the Soviet Union between the years 1918 and 1937 may be judged from the following table:—

(in millions of roubles.)

Year.	Exports.	Imports.	Turnover.	Trade balance.
1918	6596.4	6022.5	12618.9	+ 573.9
1928	3518.9	4174.6	7693.5	+ 655.7
1929	4045.8	3857.0	7902.8	+ 188.8
1930	4539.3	4637.5	9176.8	− 98.2
1931	3553.1	4839.9	8393.0	− 1286.8

Year.	(in millions of roubles.) Exports.	Imports.	Turnover.	Total balance.
1932	2518.2	3083.5	5601.7	− 565.8
1933	2167.5	1525.1	3692.6	+ 642.4
1934	1832.4	1018.0	2850.4	+ 814.4
1935	1609.3	1057.2	2666.5	+ 552.1
1936	1359.1	1352.5	2711.6	+ 6.6
1937	1728.6	1341.3	3069.9	+ 387.3

Note.—For the years 1928-37 the figures given are based on current prices. The rate of exchange for the rouble has in all cases been calculated in accordance with the rate laid down for foreign trade on 1st April, 1936.

The *imports* of the Soviet Union were particularly heavy during the years of the First Five Year Plan, which had, as one of its primary objects, an expansion of heavy industry at home, for which reason fully 90% of the volume of imports consisted of machinery and productive equipment. Approximately 45% of the total imports during the time of the First Five Year Plan consisted of machinery and plant of all kinds for the purpose of equipping the newly established industrial undertakings and making the country more self-supporting and less dependent on foreign imports.

The effects of this objective policy were quickly felt and already in 1932 there was a reduction of 36% in imports as compared with the previous year, while during the period of the Second Five Year Plan the fall in imports was even more marked (which may be seen from the figures given in the table).

A few further examples may be quoted.

In Tsarist Russia fully 80% of the *lathes* in use were of foreign make. Before the First Five Year Plan scarcely any lathes were built in the Soviet Union and practically all the country's requirements in this respect had to be met by means of imports. Already during the period of the Second Five Year Plan Soviet factories were beginning to produce numerous types of lathes and whereas the proportion of imported lathes in the U.S.S.R. in 1928 was equivalent to 59% of the total number in the country, this figure had dropped to 14% by 1935.

As regards *agricultural machinery* Tsarist Russia used to import 40% of her annual requirements from abroad and such imports were for the most part made up of the simplest agricultural implements and equipment. In the years 1929-31 the wholesale conversion of the peasant proprietors' holdings to collective farms and the increasing number and size of the state farms created a huge demand for tractors and accessories, and it became necessary to import a large proportion of these from abroad. But at the same time a number of great establishments, such as the Stalingrad, the Kharkov and the Cheliabinsk Tractor Works and the Rostov Agricultural Machinery Works, were being built, and beginning with 1932, the output of these factories enabled further imports of agricultural machinery from abroad to be dispensed with entirely.

At about the same time *motor-car works* were built in Gorky and in Moscow. The importation of foreign-made motor cars on which the equivalent of 355 million roubles in foreign currency was spent during the years 1929-31, was drastically curtailed in 1932 and subsequently entirely suspended.

No less than 2500 million roubles were spent during the period of the First Five Year Plan on the importation of *ferrous metals*. But at the same time vast metallurgical establishments were being built at Magnitogorsk, Kouznetsk and elsewhere and these, when brought into production, made it unnecessary to import anything like the same quantity of ferrous metals during the period of the Second Five Year Plan.

The achievement of technical and economic self-sufficiency by the Soviet Union did not, by any means, lead to a total cessation of imports; on the contrary, since 1935 there has been some increase in the import trade of the country (see foregoing table). However, the object of these imports is somewhat different as there is no longer the same urgent need for foreign-made goods, the home industry being able to produce all that is required for the needs of the country. The foreign imports largely consist of machinery and equipment of the latest type for the purpose of enabling the engineering industry of the Soviet Union to keep up to date. In addition to this, the imports include a certain amount of essential raw materials and semi-manufactured goods and also a quantity of foodstuffs, such as cocoa, coffee, &c., the importation of which is enabling the work of building up the socialist structure of the country to be accelerated.

The volume of the *export trade* in relation to the country's economic development has in general corresponded to its import trade, since the sole purpose of exports under Soviet conditions is to secure sufficient foreign currency to pay for imports. In order to pay for the increased imports during the time of the First Five Year Plan, it became necessary to export more, while the reduction of imports during the Second Five Year Plan enabled exports to be reduced.

The actual nature of the exports underwent a radical change in consequence of the industrialization of the country. Whereas Tsarist Russia's exports were mainly agricultural products (which accounted, on an average, for 71% of the total exports in the years 1909 to 1913), the exports of the Union have since 1927-28, to an increasing extent, been made up of manufactured goods. During the last few years the total weight of the latter has accounted for between 70 and 85% of the total weight of the country's exports. The following table gives particulars of these exports, their value being quoted in millions of roubles:—

	1930.	1933.	1936.	1937.
Total value of exports -	4539.3	2167.5	1359.1	1728.6
Timber products - -	743.5	336.1	359.5	437.8
Oil products - -	687.9	331.4	160.8	150.1
Furs and skins - -	336.6	168.9	155.1	153.6
Flax, yarns and linens -	155.0	97.1	80.6	54.8
Coal - - - - -	73.5	45.5	42.8	31.0
Ores - - - - -	78.8	31.6	41.9	60.1
Metals and metal products, - - -	40.2	30.6	42.7	48.9
Machinery and transport equipment -	10.1	20.1	25.5	49.0
Grain - - - - -	882.4	176.9	35.9	257.6

It is particularly interesting to note that amongst the goods exported are a whole series of categories which could not, under any circumstances, have been exported by Tsarist Russia. The importation of coal was discontinued in 1927-28 and since that time a considerable quantity has actually been exported by the Soviet Union. As a sequel to the commercial exploitation of the apatite deposits in the Kola Peninsula, the export of phosphates was begun in 1930 and in 1933 the completion of the potash factory for utilizing the Solikamsk feldspar deposits, not only enabled Soviet agriculture to use home-produced chemical fertilizers, but also allowed large quantities of these to be exported. Beginning with the year 1934, the great industrial establishments constructed during the time of the First Five Year Plan made it possible to export products like tractors, motor cars, electrical equipment, pig iron, sewing machines for the textile industry, sulphate of ammonia, &c.

From 1930 to 1932 the U.S.S.R. had an adverse *trade balance*. A large part of the payments for the increased imports of those years was made by means of short-term bills and the indebtedness of the Soviet Union to the foreign importers during the period of the First Five Year Plan rose to a considerable figure, more especially towards the end of 1932, when it reached something like 6100 million roubles.[1] In 1933, the first year of the Second Five Year Plan, there was a favourable trade balance and this was maintained during the following years, being especially large from 1933 to 1935. The Soviet Union utilized it to repay the indebtedness incurred during the time of the First Five Year Plan.

Throughout the period of the Second Five Year Plan there was a *steady drop* in the foreign indebtedness of the Union and by the end of 1935 it only amounted to the relatively small sum of 500 million roubles. This was paid off that year, which ended with a *favourable trade balance* and this, as already stated, has been maintained ever since.

[1] Calculated at the new standard rate of exchange for the rouble.

The radical improvement brought about in the currency situation has since made it unnecessary to have recourse to the forms of credits used during the earlier years. The Soviet Union no longer required credit from suppliers of the goods it imported, neither did it need any short-term export credits from brokers and banks. Imports, previously financed to a large extent by bills, have, since 1935, been paid for in cash, except in a few isolated cases in which long-term credits have been arranged. However, the total amount of these is very small and in 1936 it only represented 18% of the total cash payments made for imports.

While taking care to meet its financial obligations abroad with the utmost punctuality, the Soviet Union has at the same time accumulated substantial reserves of gold and foreign currency. Both in 1935 and 1936 the favourable trade balance enabled considerable reserves of foreign currency to be built up abroad.

The Soviet Union's trade with Great Britain is greater than that with any other country, its volume amounting to 21% of the total foreign trade of the Republic in 1936 and to 25% in 1937.

The following figures illustrate the growth of Anglo-Soviet trade in millions of roubles according to the Soviet Customs returns:—

	Exports from U.S.S.R. to U.K.	Imports to U.S.S.R. from U.K.
1934 - -	303.0	202.6
1935 - -	337.8	190.0
1936 - -	361.7	204.3
1937 - -	566.1	192.0

(£1 = 26.3 roubles.)

As may be seen from the foregoing figures, the balance of trade is against the United Kingdom, the difference being, in accordance with the terms of the Anglo-Soviet Trade Agreement, represented by the expenditure incurred by the U.S.S.R. in chartering British vessels.

The main imports of the U.K. from the Soviet Union consist of timber and account for about a third of the total imports. According to the trade returns for 1937, the remaining Soviet exports to the U.K. are: wheat, furs, oil products, veneers, butter and flax. British exports to the U.S.S.R. consist of non-ferrous metals, machinery, iron and steel, wool and other goods. By far the most important re-exports from the U.K. to the Soviet Union consist of non-ferrous metals, rubber and tea.

In July, 1936, the Export Credits Guarantee Department granted the Soviet Union a credit of £10,000,000 for five years, and on the occasion of the completion of the negotiations for the arrangement of this credit, the British press paid a special tribute to the exceptional scrupulousness invariably displayed by the Soviet Government in meeting their obligations in contrast to the conduct of certain other governments in these matters. This credit was used to finance a number of orders placed with British firms in 1936 and 1937.

The British consumers of timber (and of other commodities) have frequently emphasized the fact that they are in need of Soviet products, while the British manufacturers have repeatedly declared their interest in the U.S.S.R. as a market for their products. Because of this, Anglo-Soviet trade has continued to prosper notwithstanding all the obstacles put in its way in the shape of various campaigns to boycott Soviet goods, embargoes and other artificial difficulties. It may be anticipated that Anglo-Soviet trade will continue to prosper in the future.

The Soviet Union will have nothing to do with the idea of autarchy so sedulously preached in the Fascist countries. The technical and economic self-sufficiency achieved within the past decade does not in any sense imply isolation from the outside world. That may be judged by the growth of the trade between the Soviet Union and other countries in recent years and it should be remembered that Soviet foreign trade is closely bound up with the policy of peace. In the words of Stalin: ". . . the foreign policy of the Soviet Union is the maintenance of peace and the development of trade with all countries."[2]

[2] Stalin, *Problems of Leninism*, 10th edn., p. 552.

VIII

THE RAILWAYS, MERCANTILE FLEET AND INLAND WATERWAYS

By V. Volkov

Member of the State Planning Commission of the U.S.S.R.

The generally backward condition of the national economy of Tsarist Russia included that of its transport services. The old Russia possessed inadequate means of communication and at the outbreak of the World War the total railway mileage of that territory of the Russian Empire, which now lies within the borders of the Soviet Union, was only just over 36,000 miles. The total length of the navigable inland waterways was not more than 37,000 miles, notwithstanding the natural facilities afforded by the numerous great rivers of the country. The mercantile fleet was out of date; it was the customary practice to have its ships built abroad and 90% of the country's imports and exports were carried in foreign vessels. The technical equipment of the railways and inland waterways was extremely primitive and nearly all the railways were worked by low-power locomotives of a great variety of types and of very low speed. The rolling-stock for the carriage of goods was wholly composed of four-wheeled trucks of small dimensions and an average carrying capacity of 15.2 tons, about 70% of the number

MAP OF THE USSR WATERWAYS IN 1938

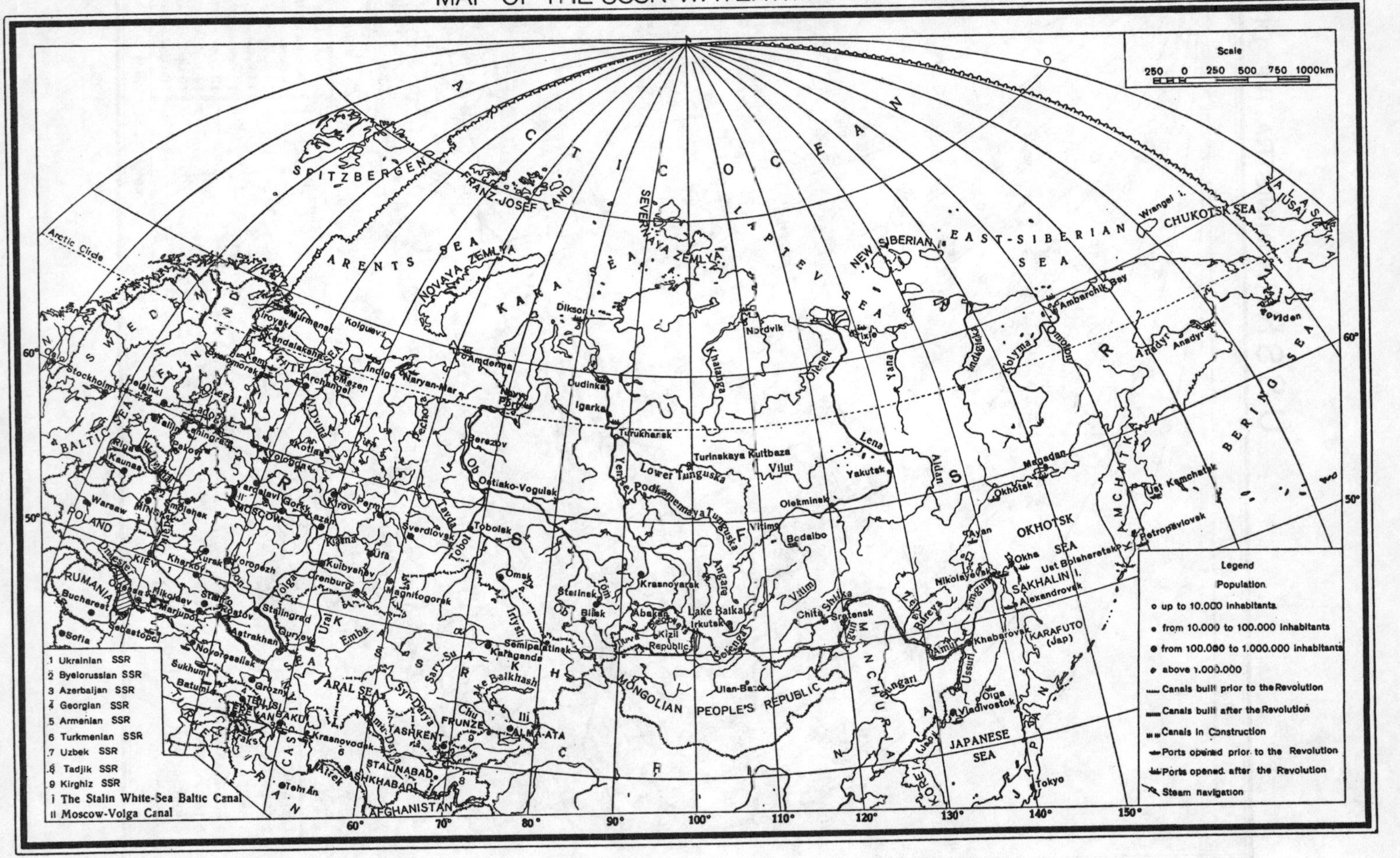

USSR (ADMINISTRATIVE DIVISI

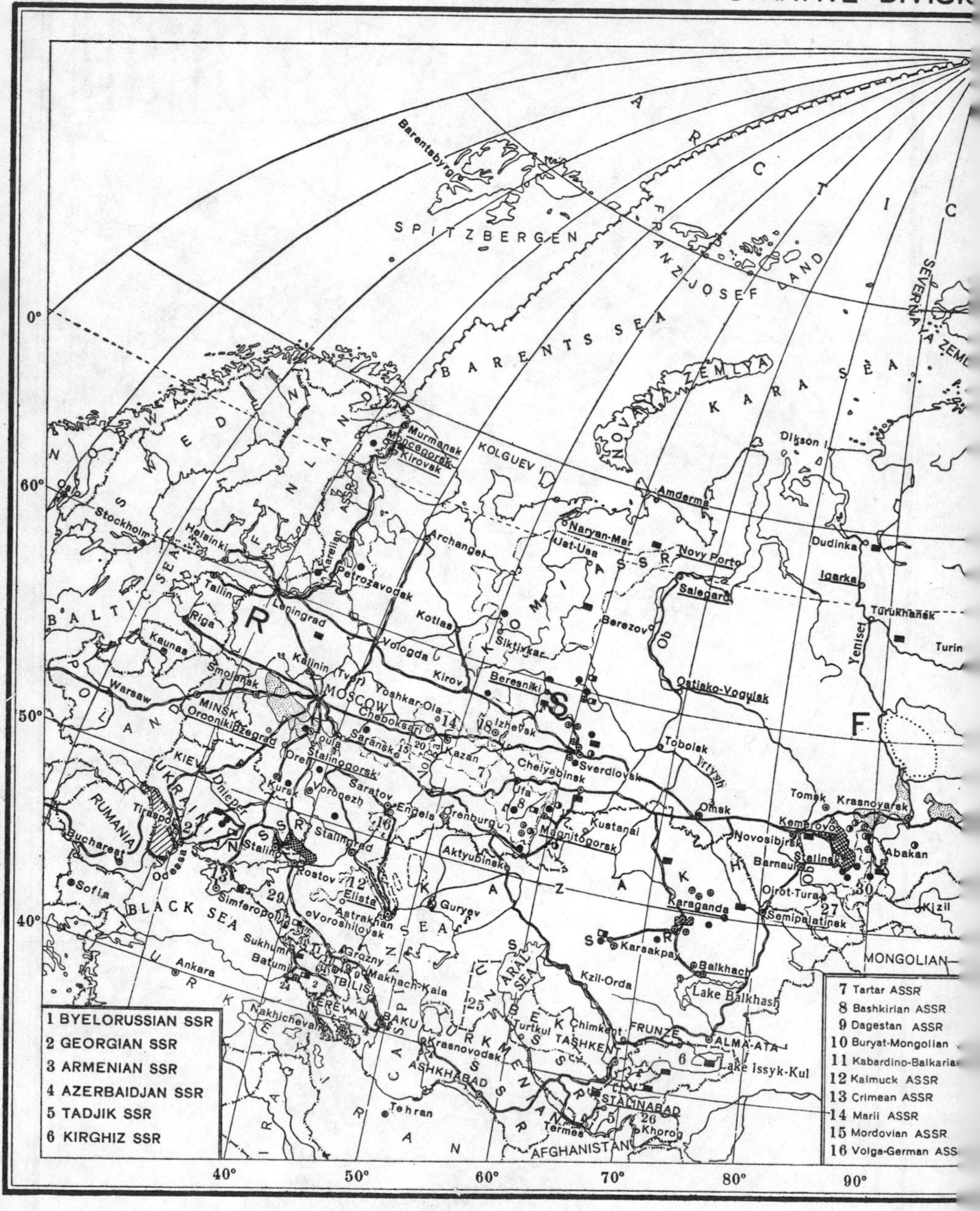

MINERAL RESOURCES, NEW TOWNS).

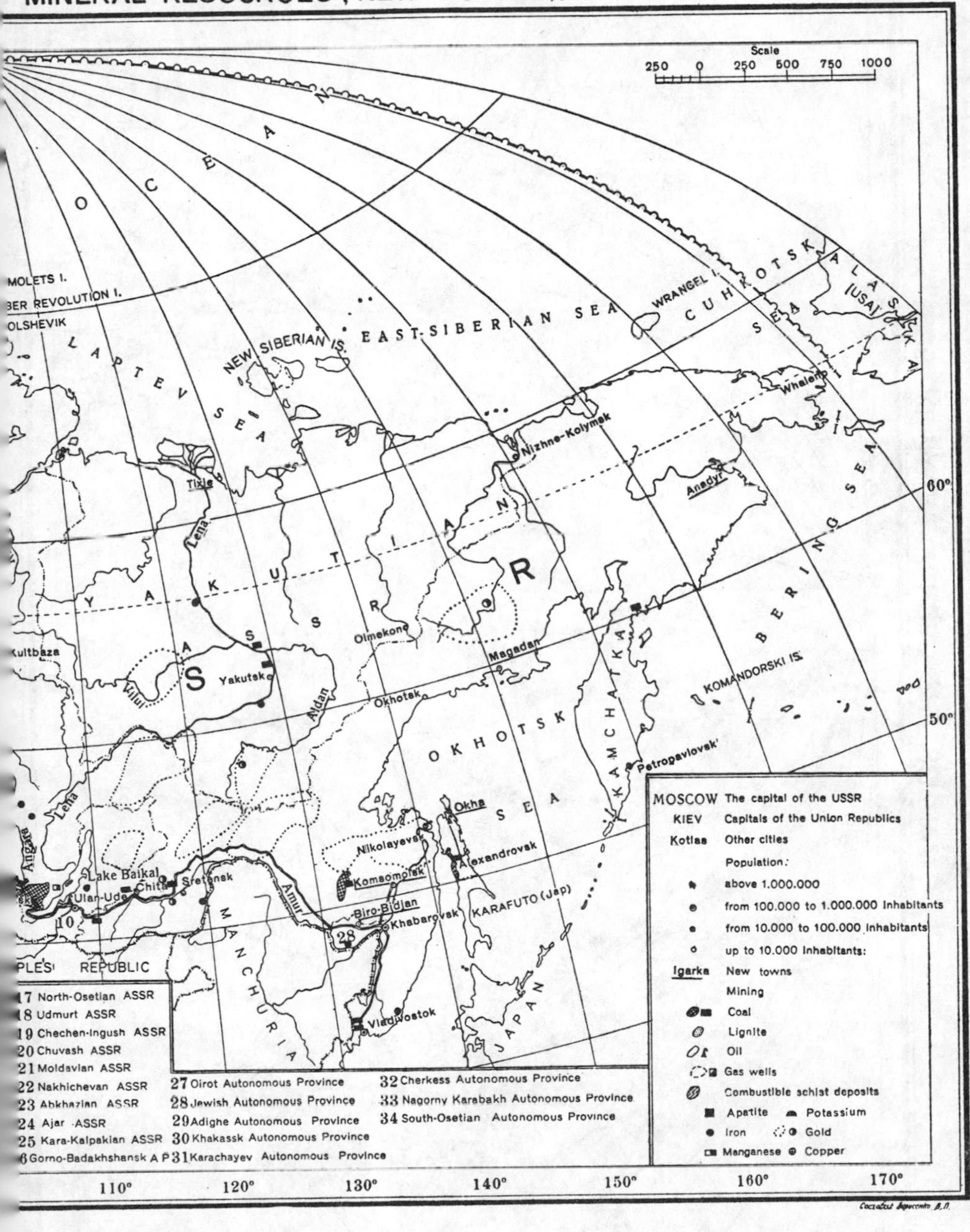

MAP OF THE USSR AIRWAYS IN 1938

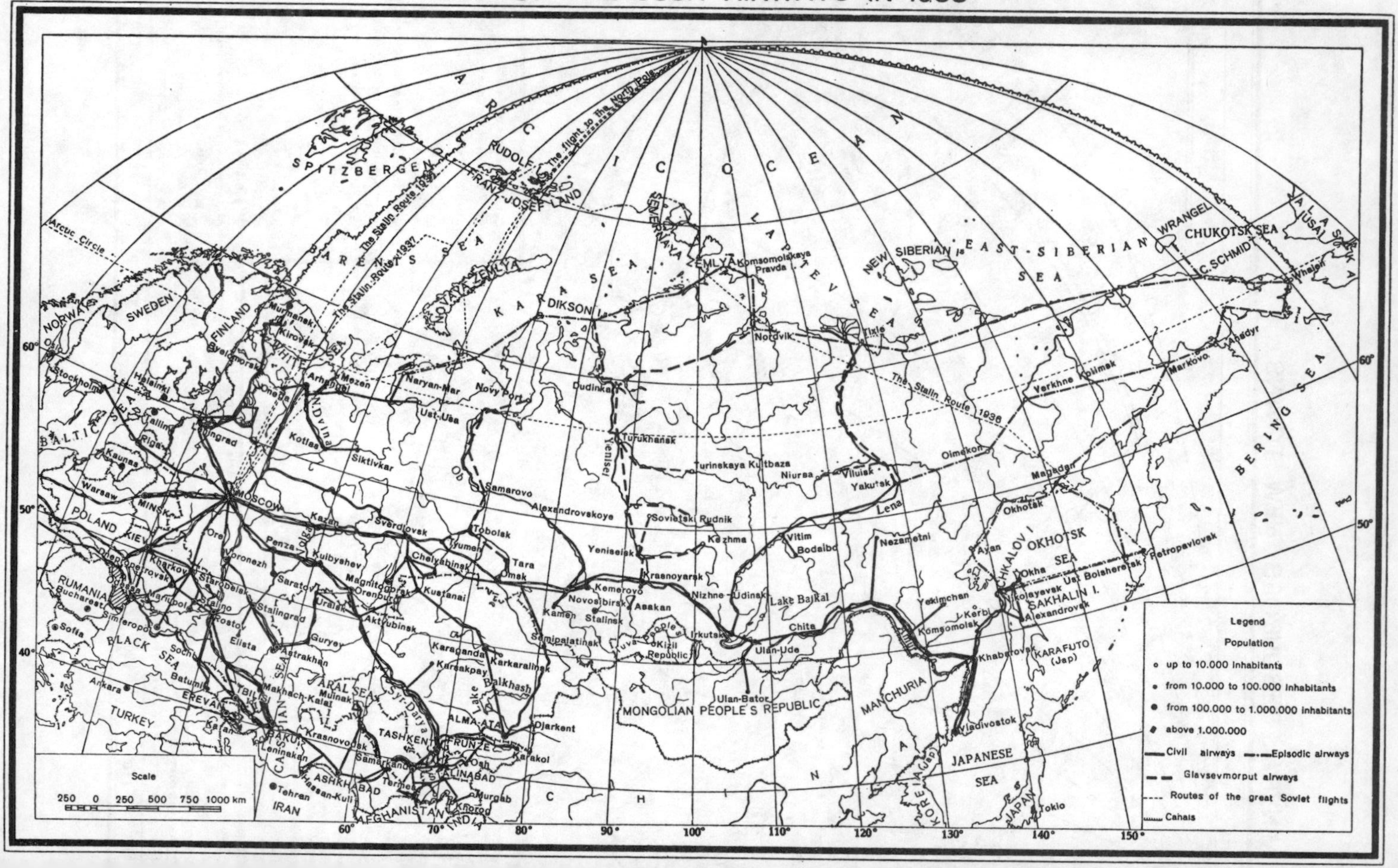

consisting of four-wheeled box-cars. The average speed of the trains was 75 miles per 24 hours.

The river flotillas, owned by numerous independent companies, were totally lacking in uniformity and the equipment of the inland waterways in general was lamentably inadequate, only 25,000 miles out of the total mileage of 37,000 being provided with primitive marks as aids to navigation. The total length of the canals did not exceed 1200 miles and cargo-handling plant was entirely lacking at the wharves, so that all loading and unloading had to be done by manual labour. The backwardness of the inland water transport of pre-revolutionary Russia is vividly depicted in the painting of the famous Russian artist Repin entitled *Volga Boatmen,* which shows a number of men exhausted by the prodigious labour of towing a heavily laden barge along the bank of a river.

The World War inflicted untold damage on the transport services and the Civil War completed their ruin. At the end of the Civil War fully 60% of the locomotives had become unserviceable. The best of the river flotillas —that on the Kama—had been burned by Kolchak, while that on the Dnieper had been burned and sunk by Wrangel. Over 200 sea-going vessels had been seized by the Whites and taken to foreign ports. The remaining river and sea-going tonnage left in the hands of the Soviet was in a deplorable condition.

On the termination of the Civil War the Soviet Government embarked on a policy of systematic reconstruction and expansion of the nation's economic resources, in the course of which special attention was paid to the transport services. Owing to the devotion and care of the authorities, a rapid and general improvement of those services was effected.

The tempestuous rate at which the economic development of the country took place during the period of the Stalin Five Year Plans raised a whole series of fresh problems of an urgent nature in regard to the transport services. A system of railways and inland waterways capable of meeting the minimum requirements of a backward agricultural state, was totally inadequate for the needs of a country undergoing an ultra-rapid process of industrialization and general improvement of its economic and cultural standards. The transport services were faced with problems not only of quantitative expansion, but of a radical reconstruction and rationalization of their entire work.

The railway system of the Soviet Union made especially great progress in the years 1935-36 when the national railway services were under the immediate control of L. M. Kaganovich. During this time these services were brought thoroughly up to date in respect of the rapid general growth of the national economic resources of the U.S.S.R. and recovered the ground lost during the early years of the First and Second Five Year Plans. Important changes in the location of the railway system and the structure and distribution of its goods-carrying organization have been effected together with substantial improvements in the provision of new locomotives and rolling-stock, adequate engineering workshops for repairs and new construction. Much has also been done to mechanize the routine work on the railways.

During the last 10 years over 6100 miles of new railways have been built and put into service. A large improvement in the number and quality of the locomotives working the more important lines has taken place and over 6000 miles of track have been converted from single to double track. Many new railways have been built in the various national republics, thereby assisting their people to achieve the economic and cultural progress formerly denied them. Among the most important of the newly built lines put into service is one of 900 miles connecting the fertile wheat-growing and richly timbered districts of Siberia with the republics of Central Asia. The construction of the Leninsk-Novosibirsk railway furnishes the Kuznetsk coalfields with a reliable outlet to the Ural and that of the new trunk line of Borovoye-Karaghanda-Balkhash, with a length of over 600 miles, connects the rich Karaghandine coalfields and the important metallurgical industries of Kazakhstan with the main railway system of Siberia. Over 600 miles of new railways have been built in the Ural and the European regions of the U.S.S.R.; a new trunk line of 700 miles from Moscow to the Don Valley has been completed.

The number of locomotives has been increased by 150% as compared with the pre-War figure, and in 1936 Soviet industry turned out four times as many locomotives as pre-revolutionary Russia in 1913.

Moreover, the new locomotives of the railways include an ever-increasing number of improved and high-power engines and there are already about 3000 new goods locomotives of the "FD" and "SO" types in service. Improved types of passenger engines are also coming into service and over 100 great passenger locomotives of the "IS" type, with a speed of 80 miles an hour, are now in service, while in November, 1937, deliveries of a new and greatly improved type of passenger locomotive were commenced.

The freight-carrying capacity of the rolling-stock has been doubled in the last 10 years and the increase on the pre-War figure is something of the order of 150%.

The whole of the rolling-stock is equipped with automatic brakes and over 100,000 vehicles are fitted with automatic coupling gear. Railway signalling equipment has been largely mechanized and some 6000 miles of railway are worked on the block signal system.

A good start has been made in the direction of electrification. Before the beginning of the First Five Year Plan in 1928 none of the railways of the U.S.S.R. was electrified, but by 1937 some 950 miles had been converted to electric traction.

An immense amount of work has been done in improving the permanent way equipment and mechanization of upkeep, and these improvements, in conjunction with those made in the quality and quantity of the rolling-stock and locomotives and—above all—the greatly improved standard of technical training achieved by the railway personnel, have contributed in a large measure to the successful exploitation of the country's railway communications. The average speed of travel of goods trains has been raised by 50% in the last five years, while the standard loads carried have simultaneously been increased by 25%. The improved standard of railway engineering attained through the growth of the productive capacity of the personnel is reflected in the immense increase of the transportation work performed by the railways of the U.S.S.R. in recent years.

The following statistics illustrate this increase:—

	1913.	1928.	1936.
Average number of trucks loaded per 24 hours, in thousands, - - - -	27.4	32.3	86.2
Total load transported in millions of tons, - -	132.4	156.2	483.2
Number of ton-miles worked, in thousands of millions, - - - -	41	58	207

Whereas the load represented by the proportion of the whole country's industrial output at the eve of the Great War was equivalent to 75.5% of the total load carried on the railways in 12 months, it had risen to 84.0% in 1932 and had reached 87.7% in 1936.

The general rise in the standard of living and education of the people has led to a sharp increase in the volume of the passenger and goods traffic carried by the railways. In 1913 the total number of passengers carried by the Russian railways was 184.4 millions, in 1928 the Soviet railways carried 291.1 million passengers and in 1937, 1145 millions.

The improved performance of the U.S.S.R. railways is due to the success of the policy of rationalization, the overcoming of running defects in the locomotives and rolling-stock and the greater productiveness of the railway personnel. Much credit is also due to the system of "shock workers" initiated by a young engine-driver of the Donetz railway, Peter Krivonoss, who is now a member of the Supreme Council of the U.S.S.R. He was primarily responsible for increasing the working speed of goods trains to 31 miles an hour and more.

The Krivonoss movement made an immediate appeal to the rank and file of the railwaymen and under the direction of L. M. Kaganovich it quickly spread over the entire railway system. The successful growth of the movement led to the adoption of improved technical practice and a better organization of the railwaymen's work and resulted in the adoption of higher standards for the maintenance and exploitation of the railways themselves.

Great improvements have, in the last 10 years, been observed in the performance of the inland waterway transport services. The mileage of navigable waterways has increased by nearly 16,000 miles and that equipped with proper marks and aids to navigation has been doubled as compared to the pre-revolutionary era. Over 37,000 miles of waterways are now illuminated at night as against 15,000 miles in 1928. Systematic dredging is carried out along stretches totalling over 18,000 miles, whereas in 1929 only 5500 miles were regularly dredged. The total length of the canal system of the Soviet Union is now greater than that of Germany and the U.S.A. During the First Five Year Plan J. V. Stalin initiated the construction of the White Sea and Baltic Canal with a length of 140 miles. This immense work was completed in 20 months and provides excellent means of communication between the White Sea and the Baltic and also with the Volga through which it gives access to the Caspian Sea and, in the near future via the Volga-Don Canal, to the Sea of Azov and the Black Sea. The construction of the White Sea and Baltic Canal ushers in great possibilities for the economic and cultural development of Soviet Karelia and the entire north of the Soviet Union.

During the Second Five Year Plan another great canal from Moscow to the Volga, a distance of 80 miles, was completed. The Moscow-Volga Canal provides a satisfactory solution to the problem of the water supply of the metropolis, besides giving Moscow direct access by water to the Volga and through the latter to the Baltic, White and Caspian Seas. The completion, in the near future, of the Volga-Don Canal will also connect Moscow with the Sea of Azov and the Black Sea. Within the next few years the port of Moscow will be accessible from five different seas.

Successful surveys of numerous navigable rivers in Siberia, Central Asia and the Far East are in the course of completion. These cover the Kolyma, Indigirka, Lower Tunguzska, Bira, Boureya, Tli, Syr-Daria, Issyk-Kul, Lake Balkhash and others. The survey work done in the Arctic Ocean for the purpose of rendering it navigable and opening up the North Route, has yielded first-rate results. In 1935 and for the first time in the history of navigation, the ocean-going cargo steamers "Anadyr" and "Stalingrad" made voyages from Vladivostok to Murmansk and the "Iskra" and "Vanzetti" from Murmansk to Vladivostok.

The Soviet Union is now in possession of an efficient salvage service, which is responsible for the salvage of scores of vessels every year, in the rivers and off the sea coasts of the country. In former days there was no salvage organization whatever.

The two Five Year Plans have likewise been marked by an expansion of shipbuilding resources. Ocean-going tonnage has, in the last five years, increased by 75%, while the river flotilla has, during the same period, received an addition of over 1370 self-propelled vessels.

A vast amount of work has been done in regard to the provision of new and improved wharves and equipment. Up-to-date cargo-handling plant has replaced manual labour to the extent of over 40%.

The rapid expansion of the national economic resources of the U.S.S.R. has laid a heavy burden on the country's waterways and, notwithstanding the immense strides made in the technical equipment of the latter, there is still an acute shortage in the necessary facilities for coping with the ever-growing volume of passenger and cargo traffic.

The following figures speak for themselves:—

Total Cargo carried in Sea-going and River Vessels in Millions of Tons

	On Inland Waterways.	In Sea-going Vessels.
1928 - - -	18.4	7.9
1932 - - -	47.0	14.8
1937 - - -	66.2	29.2

There has also been a considerable increase in the volume of passenger traffic. In 1928 the number of persons carried on the inland waterways was 19.6 millions, while in 1937 it was 61 millions.

The general development and growth of the economic and transport resources of the U.S.S.R. has been accompanied by a correspondingly great improvement in the material well-being and cultural situation of the transport workers. Ever since the First Five Year Plan unemployment has completely disappeared. The majority of

Moscow-Volga canal: (a) one of the sluices, (b) Khimki Station, Moscow

the transport workers work a seven-hour day. The earnings of the railwaymen have, during the past 10 years, increased by over 400%, and those of the water transport workers by 120% in the last five years alone. Greatly improved health services are now provided. Whereas there were in 1913 only 160 hospitals, in 1936 there were 280 hospitals, 442 infirmaries, 658 surgeries, 559 medical stations, &c.

The improvement of the cultural and material welfare of the transport workers is a natural sequel to the general expansion of the transport industry as an essential feature of the general development of the country.

IX

COMMUNICATIONS

By A. Fortoushenke

Director of the Scientific Research Institute of Communications

In pre-revolutionary Russia one of the most backward branches of the national economy was that of communications. A simple postal and telegraph service was all that the vast country possessed: wireless telegraphy was still in its infancy. The Tsarist Government made no effort to develop the system of communications: in their fear of the propagation of revolutionary ideas they endeavoured to keep the people in a condition of political and cultural backwardness, even taking special measures to prevent extensive communications between the different parts of the immense territory of Russia, so that there should be no connexion between the numerous peoples inhabiting the Empire.

The rural districts especially were cut off from all cultural life in those days. Even the postal service was very primitive. The whole system of communications in former Russia was notorious for its red tape, blind worship of tradition and the stupidity of those employed in it. The types of postmaster and telegraphist in the works of Gogol and Chekhov and other Russian writers are vividly expressive of the miserable life of the inferior functionaries and the fustiness of provincial life characteristic of that era.

The rise in the standard of culture, the desire to draw the inhabitants of even the most remote districts into active public and political life, the creation of new political, cultural and industrial centres, all called for a vast extension of the system of communications. The rapid technical progress which accompanied socialist construction in the Soviet Union made the technical perfection of the means of communication possible, while new methods, unknown in pre-revolutionary Russia, were brought into use.

The present technical equipment of communications cannot be compared with that in Tsarist Russia. Let us first of all consider the oldest and most widespread form of communication—the post. As a result of the cultural growth of the masses of the population, postal correspondence increased by more than 600% during the last 20 years. It is a highly significant fact that the number of newspapers sent by post increased from 358 million in 1913 to 5720 million in 1927. The number of letter boxes and post offices increased correspondingly: there were seven times as many letter boxes in 1937 as in 1913, and the number of post offices increased from 12,787 to 40,515. The postal service is provided with new technical equipment: the length of air mail lines will total 91,250 miles. The mechanization of postal processes is now coming into use and automatic post offices, the invention of Soviet engineers, have recently been exhibited.

The postal employees themselves are quite unlike the postmasters of former days; they are now perfectly cultured people who understand and like their work.

Electrical communications have developed at an even

more remarkable rate. The telegraph and telephone are of paramount importance in a vast country like the Soviet Union. In former days the telephone existed mainly in the towns, and consisted of petty systems belonging to foreign companies, while it was used almost entirely by the privileged classes. The "Zemstvo" telephone, which was intended for the rural districts, was the monopoly of the police and landowners.

The Tsarist Government were quite indifferent to such a question as the reconstruction of the telephone system, whose technical equipment was exceedingly poor. The telephone exchanges were all manual, and there were no prospects of improvement—no such thing as a technical policy was dreamed of. All the technical experts in charge were representatives of foreign firms. There was no industry, for the existing foreign enterprises were nothing more than repair and installation shops. There was not a single school of electrical communications in Russia. Suburban and subordinate telephones were unknown. Postal employees had never heard of automatic telephones, although the automatic system was already widespread in the more advanced countries. The telephone service in the towns was mainly built up on the system of overhead wires, and in spite of the many different kinds of equipment, no effort was made to standardize the apparatus. The telephone lines in the towns were constructed without any plan and there was never any question raised of bringing them all into one system. Such was the telephone in former Russia.

The Soviet state inherited a poor system and obsolete technical equipment. Since the October Revolution 21 years ago the telephone system has changed beyond recognition. During the period of the Stalin Five Year Plans it underwent a process of reconstruction in the shape of automatic re-equipment and division into districts. The construction and working of automatic telephone exchanges have been fully mastered, and Soviet technical experts, who are themselves doing much to improve the telephone service, have replaced the former foreign specialists. The whole system is radically different from what it was before. It is developed in accordance with general plans and definite aims. The lines are grouped into districts and intersect. The telephone is not only intended for the use of the national economic and defence departments; it is also at the service of the great masses of the population and has become an everyday necessity in their lives.

In even the most remote rural districts, as well as in the towns, an extensive telephone network connects the different villages and collective farms by whose members it is being utilized to an ever-increasing extent. By the beginning of 1937, 727 village Soviets were in telephonic communication with the regional centres. In 1913 the total length of telegraph and telephone wires was 313,750 miles, while by 1936 it had risen to 1,365,652 miles.

There was not a single automatic telephone exchange before the Revolution, whereas now there are nearly 100. In Leningrad, Kiev, Kharkov, Baku, Tbilissi (formerly Tiflis), Tashkent, Minsk and other towns, the telephone has been reconstructed (or constructed, where no telephone had existed) on the automatic system, and suburban, office and subordinate lines have been installed. Soviet engineers and technical workers are striving to perfect the automatic telephone system and to improve the whole service in the interests of the population. The widespread introduction of the automatic telephone and of innovations, such as the automatic talking clock in Moscow, is a striking example of the way in which the U.S.S.R., from being last as regards technical equipment, has become as up-to-date in this respect as any other country.

In former Russia the principal form of long-distance communication was telegraphy, for trunk-line telephones were practically non-existent. During the years of socialist construction there has been a vast extension of the telegraph and telephone systems.

The use of apparatus for multiple communications by wire is very widespread. All the most important towns are connected by telephone as well as by telegraph. A direct result of the intensive political, cultural and economic life of the country is the extraordinary increase in the number of telegrams sent: from 36 millions in 1913 to 103 millions in 1937. In this respect the Soviet Union occupies first place in Europe.

Within recent years photo-telegraphy has become a more and more popular form of communication. The first photo-telegraphic line was set up in 1930; now, in 1938, there are 31 such lines, and the number of telegrams transmitted is 200,000. The photo-telegraphic system is equipped entirely with Soviet-made apparatus.

Wireless telegraphy and telephony are a particularly important form of communication in an immense country such as the U.S.S.R. Russia was the cradle of wireless telegraphy, for, as is well known, the Russian scientist Popov invented wireless telegraphy before Marconi, though the inertia of the Tsarist bureaucrats gave it no scope for development. It was only under the Soviet régime that the rapid development of wireless telegraphy began and at the present time the country possesses an extensive short-wave system. The capital of the Union —Moscow—is in wireless communication with the remotest corners of the earth, while wireless stations are scattered all over the vast country, including the Far North, at Dickson Island, Novaya Zemlya, and so on. Everyone remembers the flights of the Soviet airmen over the North Pole to America. The success of these flights was due, not only to the perfection of Soviet aviation and the heroism of the airmen, but in large measure to a good system of wireless telegraphy.

By 1937 the Soviet Union was first in the world in regard to the number of wireless telegrams sent.

In the Soviet Union broadcasting is considered to be one of the most important forms of cultural dissemination. The country possesses a large number of broadcasting stations, and, here again, the U.S.S.R. has been first in Europe since 1932 as regards the total capacity of its broadcasting stations.

In 1938 there were in the U.S.S.R. 73 radio broadcasting stations and 7000 relay stations, each one of these in reality being a radio station of its own with its own listeners-in. The number of radios registered by January 1, 1938, amounted to 5,000,000. This, however, does not give a real picture of the number of listeners-in, since not less than 15 to 20% of the radios are placed at the service of clubs, reading-rooms, Red Army barracks, parks, stadiums, &c., where collective listening-in takes place. To this must also be added the collective listening-in of students of correspondence courses, the number of such gathering places exceeding 6000. Thus the number of permanent listeners-in may safely be given as 25-30 million people.

The programmes are usually drawn up as follows: political information, lectures and reports on social-political and historical subjects, music which makes up about 70% of the programme, a literary section, broadcasts from the country's best dramatic theatres, special programmes for individual groups, as, for instance, for the Red Army, for students, for housewives, for the young and special children's programmes.

Lately television has been introduced into the broadcasting service. For several years television programmes of sight definition (30 lines) have been transmitted regularly. At the present time television is perfectly up to date in technical equipment and television programmes have become a regular feature of the Moscow wireless programmes. They are transmitted on ultra-short waves at a definition of 343 lines. Regular television programmes are now being transmitted in Leningrad, and very soon a fairly extensive television system will be introduced into the capitals of all the republics of the Soviet Union.

Much is being done in the country to perfect the technical equipment of communications and the result of this work will be a rapid development of the whole system as regards both its technical quality and the volume of communications with which it will be called upon to deal.

X

CIVIL AVIATION

By N. Islentiev
Managing Editor of "The Journal of Aviation" of Moscow

In order to appreciate the immense importance of civil aviation in the economic life of the U.S.S.R., it is necessary to remember two figures: that the country has an area of 8,241,673 square miles and a population of 170 millions. The main air routes of the Soviet Union are the longest in the world, that from Moscow to Vladivostok having a length of over 5000 miles and the remainder averaging 1800 miles each.

The relatively small number of railways in the eastern and Asiatic parts of the country invests air communications in these remote districts with a special value for every phase of their economic life, particularly in the Soviet republics of Central Asia, in Western and Eastern Siberia and in the Far East. In these districts air transport is used for the conveyance of mails, passengers, goods of all kinds, cotton and even livestock, besides foodstuffs and—in the desert of Central Asia—fresh water.

Before 1923 civil aviation was practically non-existent in the U.S.S.R. The first commercial air route, opened to traffic 15 years ago, was between Moscow and the city of Nijni Novgorod (now Gorky). The rapid industrialization of the U.S.S.R., in accordance with the programme of the Stalin Five Year Plans, enabled an extensive development of civil aviation to be realized.

The earliest Soviet air services utilized foreign-made aircraft (Junkers and Fokker machines) but from 1925 onwards an increasing number of commercial aeroplanes of home manufacture were brought into service. These comprised machines of the "K-1," "K-3," "K-4," "PS-3," and "PS-4" types. Some of them were of all-metal construction and were used for long-distance flights to Western and Eastern Europe and to the U.S.A., thereby demonstrating the success achieved in constructing aircraft and engines of native design and in the training of a corps of experienced and efficient pilots.

However, it was only after the establishment of a regular aircraft industry in the country during the First Five Year Plan that commercial aircraft of the type of the all-metal twin-engined "PS-9" carrying 10 persons, the single-engined eight-seater "K-5," the mail 'plane "P-5" and the 2/3 seater "U-2" with its 100 h.p. engine, were produced. All these machines were equipped with engines of Soviet manufacture. Since 1925 all the civil aircraft used in the Union have been built in the country.

The extension of the air routes and the great increase in the loads carried rendered it necessary to have aircraft with a cruising speed of over 130 miles an hour, and so machines with a considerably higher speed began to come into service after the beginning of 1935.

The first of these was the single-engined "HAI-I" which carried six passengers at a cruising speed of over 190 miles an hour. It was the first commercial machine to be equipped with a retractable undercarriage.

Then came the all-metal twin-engined air liner "PS-35" carrying nine passengers and fitted with air-cooled engines of the "M-85" type. During one of its regular flights from Moscow to Leningrad and back, this particular air liner averaged over 218 miles an hour over the entire distance of 770 miles, flying at a height of 14,000 feet.

The Soviet Union inherited a legacy from the Tsarist régime in the shape of several minute factories, resembling village workshops, in which foreign-built aeroplane engines were copied. In addition to developing aircraft construction, Soviet industry had also to create means for the design and construction of mass-produced aeroplane engines of various sizes. The success achieved in this direction has been brilliantly demonstrated by the powerful engines of the "AM-34" which enabled a whole series of record long-distance flights to be carried out, including a flight to the North Pole and two flights over the North Pole from the U.S.S.R. to the U.S.A.

Finally, in describing the technical progress made by Soviet aviation, it is essential to remember the importance played by the high-precision aircraft instruments, the excellent working of which is largely responsible for the successful flights carried out by modern air liners. The achievement of the Soviet Union in this direction is one of which it may justly feel proud. Its factories are, at the present time, capable of constructing *any* aeronautical instruments or accessories in existence and many new types of such instruments have actually been evolved and produced in the U.S.S.R., including the auto-pilot, radio-compass and solar course-indicator, all of which worked admirably during the important flights recently carried out in the Arctic Circle.

The successful reconstruction of the technical resources of the Union enabled a great commercial air force to be created, capable of affording substantial assistance in the work of building up the political, economic and cultural life of the country. The immense distances and the inadequate means of overland communications called for a rapid development of air transport. The need for it was accentuated by the phenomenal rate at which the country was expanding its industry. Huge factories and works were springing up in remote districts which had formerly been looked upon as a wilderness, and these had to possess direct and rapid means of communication with Moscow and other administrative and economic centres.

The first experimental air line between Moscow and Gorky, opened in 1923, had a length of just over 260 miles. The next air services to be established were in the roadless deserts of Central Asia. By 1927 the total length of the commercial air routes of the U.S.S.R. had risen to 3750 miles. Air services in the Northern Caucasus, Transcaucasia and Eastern Siberia were instituted and in the same year two foreign air routes were established—from Ulan-Ude to Ulan-Bator, the capital of the National Republic of Mongolia, and from Tashkent to Kabul, the capital of Afghanistan.

Whereas during the First Five Year Plan (1929-32) the growth of commercial aviation was mainly characterized by the increase in the length of the air routes, the Second Five Year Plan was marked by an intensive development of the ground equipment required for these services. The work involved was no less formidable than the actual establishment of the air services, as in many of the airports aerodromes, hangars, staff quarters, fuel storage and repair shops had to be constructed. In order to ensure a maximum measure of safety and efficiency for the air lines, most of the airports had to be equipped with suitable beacons for night flying, together with the directional wireless transmitters which were required for the guidance of aircraft flying in bad weather.

"The great air route" from Moscow to Vladivostok is of special value to the economic and cultural life of the people of the country. It serves to connect numerous administrative and economic centres in the European part of the Union with Western and Eastern Siberia and the distant coast of the Pacific Ocean. As this service is linked up in the capital with the western air lines, it therefore connects the Atlantic and Pacific across the entire continent of Europe. Furthermore, the eastern portion of this line is of special importance on account of the subsidiary air services with which it is linked up for the purpose of ensuring communication with important industrial centres or over roadless tracts of country. A case in point is the journey from Irkutsk to Yakutsk which in the summer takes 18 days by river steamer and in the winter involves a laborious 30-day trip by sleigh. Aeroplanes make the journey in two or three days.

Each of the main air lines between Moscow and Tiflis, Moscow and Simferopol or Moscow and Tashkent, works in conjunction with numerous branch services, thereby providing a comprehensive network of air communications.

In order to illustrate the important part played by civil

aviation in the life of the remote border republics, the example of Tadjikistan, situated on the slopes of the Pamir Range, may be cited. The number of passengers carried by air liners on this route already exceeds 15,000 per annum, in addition to which they transport thousands of tons of freight of various kinds over the Pamir, including salt, sugar, corn, kerosene, textile fabrics and books, &c. The advantages gained by using air travel in the case of Tadjikistan may be judged from the fact that the overland journey from Stalinabad to Khorog (at the centre of the Pamir) takes no less than seven days in summer and anything up to 30 days in the winter, whereas passengers and freight are conveyed from Stalinabad to Khorog by air in two hours.

The air communications of the other republics and remote districts of the Union are being developed and exploited no less intensively. Two Soviet air services to the west connect Moscow with Prague (Czechoslovakia) and Stockholm (Sweden).

The network of air lines is by no means limited to services of national or republican importance. During the Second Five Year Plan a whole series of air lines of purely local importance were established. Their function is to ensure rapid communication between regional, provincial and remote centres and between workers' settlements, state and collective farms. In 1937 the total length of the local air lines was no less than 18,500 miles.

The growth of the network of air services and the improvement of aerial transport has been accompanied by a corresponding increase in the use made of transport aviation, as may be clearly seen from the following table giving particulars of the work done in the carriage of passengers, mails and freight.

	Year.	No. of passengers carried by			No. of tons transported.	
		Main Air Services.	Local Air Services.	Arctic Services.	Mails.	Freight.
	1923	200			1.8	.1
First Five Year Plan	1929	9,300.	—	—	72.5	123.0
	1930	12,000.	—	—	116.6	134.3
	1931	19,000.	—	—	324.2	228.3
	1932	27;200.	—	—	429.7	447.2
Second Five Year Plan.	1933	41,600.	1,100.	400.	2,034.4	1,508.2.
	1934	68,500.	4,200.	600.	3,866.9	6,787.0.
	1935	96,300.	7,700.	2,800.	5,972.7	10,187.4.
	1936	163,400.	13,800.	6,300.	7,930.8	35,104.1.
	1937	180,000.	15,150.	—	8,500.0	36,000.0.

The above figures do not include the returns of the international air lines or the transport work done by the Maxim Gorky propaganda squadron.

The functions performed by civil aviation are by no means confined to air transport. It likewise plays a conspicuous part in the national economic life of the country in agriculture, forestry, health service, aerial survey, scientific research and many other spheres, all of which duties come under the heading of "special air service."

Aircraft are carrying out extremely valuable work in combating locusts, whose depradations formerly caused the loss of hundreds of thousands of tons of corn, and the parasites injuring the cotton fields. Civil aircraft are also extensively used to destroy the swarms of moths which constitute one of the greatest menaces to the vast forest tracts of the Soviet Union, as in this instance the only way to deal with the pests is by attack from the air. The aeroplane has likewise proved victorious in the fight against the malarial or anopheles mosquito and in 1937 alone the larvæ of the latter were completely destroyed over an area of 11,570 square miles. The use of aircraft for the destruction of the anopheles mosquito has freed many regions of the Union from the scourge of malaria.

In agriculture, aeroplanes have been extensively used for "feeding-up" rice and flax during the period of flowering and ripening, when the plants suffer from a shortage of nitrogen. The rice growing in the paddy fields is only accessible from the air, as neither rice nor flax can be reached on the ground without injuring the growing plants.

The huge forests of the Soviet Union are patrolled by air not only for the purpose of locating and combating forest pests. Within the last few years aerial surveys of nearly half a million square miles of forest have been completed, by means of aerial photography, where necessary.

In certain forest regions air patrols are maintained to locate forest fires. When a small fire is observed by an aeroplane, a fireman with the necessary equipment is dropped by parachute to deal with it, but in the case of large fires a complete fire brigade with chemical fire-extinguishers and accessories is dropped by parachute from a number of aeroplanes. The fighting of forest fires by air action has proved so successful that the State Forestry Department has now organized parachute fire brigades with a special training school for the personnel.

Soviet aircraft have proved equally successful in dealing with fires in the steppes by flying over the edges of the conflagration and spraying the adjacent ground with a fireproof chemical solution which prevents the fire from spreading.

In suitable districts aircraft are used for afforestation purposes by means of pollination from the air, and in 1937 an area of over 7000 acres near Moscow was successfully treated in this manner.

Aeroplanes are used for the systematic patrolling of the high tension overhead cables from the electric power-stations, in which they can quickly locate external defects and serve to transport repair parties and tools to the scene. Amongst the numerous other miscellaneous functions discharged by Soviet aircraft are many duties connected with scientific research work, including experiments with various devices for dissipating fog.

There are, in the Soviet Union, special organizations for utilizing aircraft for specific purposes, among them being the "Red Cross and Red Crescent Air Service." There are 40 medical air stations in the country and in cases of emergency, ambulance 'planes, carrying doctors, are sent out from these to attend patients. The arrival of a "flying doctor" has frequently been the means of saving life.

The work carried out in the Arctic air services under the direction of the Northern Sea Route Department is of a particularly valuable and responsible nature, including, as it does, ice surveys and the piloting of Soviet and foreign shipping to the northern ports. These aircraft are also used for locating seals, walruses and shoals of fish for the benefit of the hunters and fishermen working from the industrial bases in these regions. The fur stations scattered all over the Far North keep in touch with each other by air and the carriage of passengers and freight by air transport is an important function of the Arctic air services, which work three main routes—following the rivers Ob, Lena and Enissei—with a total length of 7500 miles.

As an example of the valuable work done by civil aviation in the Arctic, that of the Tchoukhotsk division might be cited. Tchoukhotsk is a naturally wealthy region and apart from its forests, valuable wild fauna and fish, it possesses great mineral riches, but the climatic conditions normally prevailing in this mountainous region are extremely severe. The frequency of fogs and blizzards makes flying arduous and dangerous, owing to the poor visibility which is usually experienced there, and in the summer the central regions of Tchoukhotsk are inaccessible even for amphibious aircraft.

In the summer of 1937 a number of aircraft were employed on prospecting work for gold, tin and precious metals in the Tchoukhotsk Peninsula and the skill displayed by their pilots enabled three valuable deposits of precious metals to be located. At the present time they are already being worked and commercially exploited. The special value of the service rendered by aircraft in this instance was the communication which they afforded between the bases of the prospecting expedition at Cape Schmidt and in Cross Bay. They covered the distance in two to three flying hours, whereas the journey formerly took over a month.

The Arctic air services of the Soviet Union have provided the flying training of many world-famous pilots of the present day, as e.g., Vodopianov, Molokov, Alexeiev, Golovin and a host of others.

The remarkable achievements of Soviet aviation have

enabled the Union to capture dozens of international and world records. The altitude records of the Soviet pilot Kokinaki are well known and in recent years the flights of Soviet air aces have won the admiration of the entire world and constitute a milestone in the history of Soviet aviation. Among these achievements are the Polar flights of the national heroes Chkalov and Gromov, who carried out non-stop flights in a Soviet-built machine from Moscow to the United States over the North Pole, across the most inaccessible regions of the earth. In the course of a second flight from Moscow to San Diego (California), the crew of Gromov's machine broke the world records both for straight and indirect long-distance flights.

Much of the success achieved in the above flights was due to the experience gained through the Polar flight carried out in May and June, 1937, by the four amphibians "N-169," "N-170," "N-171" and "N-172" equipped with Soviet-made engines of the "AM-34" type, when they landed on the ice near the North Pole. It was the first time in the history of aviation that heavy machines of 25 tons' weight had flown over uncharted seas and icefields where navigation is rendered peculiarly difficult owing to the unreliable behaviour of the aeronautical navigating instruments normally used. Practically the entire flight from Rudolf Island to the North Pole had to be made with the aid of a new device—the solar course-indicator designed and constructed by Soviet engineers.

As is well known, this expedition landed four scientists at the North Pole—Messrs. I. D. Papanin, P. P. Shirshov, E. T. Krenkel, and E. K. Fedorov—who spent nine months on a drifting icefloe and carried out an immense amount of valuable research work.

The results of the services rendered by civil aviation indicate the vast possibilities and incredible prospects existing for it in the U.S.S.R. Everything possible is being done to foster its development and the utmost importance is attached to it not only by the authorities and the ruling Bolshevik Party, but by the entire nation. Flying is popular and is encouraged in every way. It might be mentioned that the pilots of the civil air service constitute the most highly paid group of workers in the country. They also enjoy two months' holiday with full pay annually, and facilities for spending it at a sanatorium free of charge. The well-organized and powerful aircraft industry provides the necessary basis for further development and technical progress not only in the construction of aircraft, but in providing the best possible ground equipment.

XI

SCIENCE

By V. L. Komarov

President of the U.S.S.R. Academy of Science, Member of the Supreme Soviet of the U.S.S.R.

The Russian Academy of Science, which was founded as far back as the eighteenth century in what was then St. Petersburg, was linked up with similar institutions in Western Europe, but completely isolated from the people of its native country. Eminent Russians, like the embryologist Behr, the mathematician Chebyshev and others who revolutionized science, worked in close co-operation with the scientists of Western Europe, but had no contact whatever with Russia herself. The Academy of Science was like a tiny island in the vast Russian ocean of actuality.

This position of the Academy of Science was typical of that of science generally in Russia. Its development was extremely slow and characterized by a ridiculously small number of scientific workers and the excessively primitive nature of the laboratory equipment, more especially for research purposes.

A very different state of things obtains nowadays. Soviet science has a broad social basis and is deeply rooted in the country. From being the realm of a chosen few, science has now become accessible to every worker or collective farmer who may be interested in it. Both research work and the study of popular science are conducted in various types of institutions from academies to the so-called "hut-laboratories" in the rural districts and a thirst for scientific knowledge is displayed all over the country. The work of the U.S.S.R. Academy of Science is known and not infrequently debated in collective farms and the most remote districts of the Soviet Union. There is not a single spot in its widespread territory in which scientific questions generally and technical knowledge in particular are not discussed.

Instead of the 96 scientific workers of 1913, there are now 3000 such workers, exclusive of the staff of scientific and technical assistants. Even this is not all—the total number of people actively engaged in or connected with scientific work is actually 41,000.

Science is no longer an island. It might appropriately be likened to a pyramid with an extremely wide social base and with the U.S.S.R. Academy of Science as its apex. There are at the present time 2292 scientific research establishments in the Union, 211 of them dating from before 1918 and 1002 from the years 1923 to 1932. Among these establishments are 603 technical research institutes, 456 for natural science and mathematics, 385 for social science, 393 for agricultural science, and 455 for medical research work of various kinds.

Mere numbers are, of course, not evidence of quality. In some cases there is actually a movement on foot to reduce the number of scientific establishments in order to concentrate and co-ordinate their work and to extend its scope. Nevertheless, the total number of scientific institutions is not growing less, because while some of the smaller ones are being absorbed to form larger establishments, new ones are continually being created to serve new requirements arising from the general growth of the country.

It is obviously impossible to deal in a single article with all the research work done in recent years on the atomic theory, on energetics, chemical equilibration, the geological structure of mountain ranges, philology and stymology. An immense amount of work has been in the direction of transforming science from being merely a number of individual interesting and instructive items of knowledge into a single comprehensive system of Marxian-Leninist philosophy.

During the last few years we have had a number of international conferences which have enabled the work done by our scientists to be reviewed and summed up. In 1935 we had the International Conference of Physiologists presided over by the academician Pavlov. In 1937 we had the International Conference of Geologists which also proved very successful and constituted a stimulus for the further investigation of the geological conditions prevailing in our country. Besides these, there was a whole series of conferences on various branches of science, which proved the importance to science of the results of our work.

A complete summary of the work done in every branch of science cannot, of course, be set out here and it will suffice to mention our most important achievements.

Professor I. P. Pavlov, whom we lost in 1936, created an entire epoch in the realm of physiology. His teachings on conditional reflexes and on the processes of irritation and inhibition are widely known. This teaching is dialectic as it concerns two opposite processes and deals with their interactions and transitions. A logical and passionate scientist, Professor Pavlov devoted himself to paving the way for his new teaching on the behaviour of the organism of the higher animals under the action of the cerebrum. He created his own school which embraced an army of young workers imbued with the spirit of Pavlov's methods of work and ambition to make further discoveries in the field of psychophysiological processes. The expression "school" in this instance denotes a very large group of scientific thinkers. There was a conference of physiologists in the autumn of 1937 in Tbilissi (Tiflis), the capital of Georgia, which proved remarkably successful and yielded important results. Formerly it would have been extremely difficult to find a sufficient number of scientists capable of organizing a conference solely for the purpose of dealing with such a specialized branch of science.

The work of the academician I. J. Marr in regard to the study of philology should be mentioned, as he has presented it in a completely novel light; the fact that Professor Marr has brought a detached branch of science like comparative philology into intimate contact with the life, history and labour of mankind is highly noteworthy. This aspect of comparative philology is being closely studied and developed in the Institute of Languages and Thought attached to the Academy of Science. The revolutionary effect of Professor Marr's work in regard to the study of languages is conferring an immense benefit on humanity by establishing a close relation between this specialized subject and the practical aspect of our lives and our history.

Another special branch of science in which outstanding

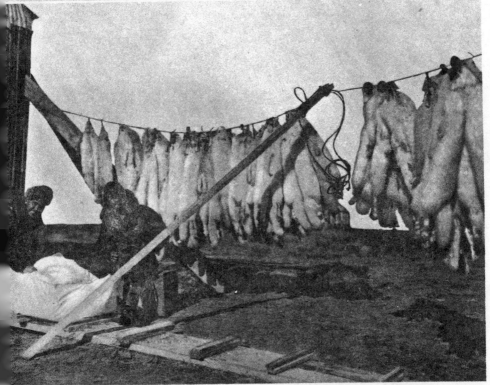

The living tent of the Papanin Polar Expedition on the drifting ice flow—
A hunting station in the Arctic

progress has been made is that of mathematics. The work done in this field by our Mathematical Institute, the Tbilissi (Tiflis) Group and other bodies, constitutes one of the foremost achievements in the world of science. The academicians I. M. Vinogradov and Bernstein, Professor Delaunay and a number of young Soviet scientists are every year presenting us with solutions of various theorems and new methods of calculation which can be applied to problems of construction. For this reason we give them every encouragement.

However, this is not all. We cannot be reproached for concentrating on questions relating to the present only, as our work in the sphere of pure mathematics has proved to be very extensive.

The strength of Soviet science lies in the fact that we base our theoretical reasoning on applied science.

Early in 1918 when the young Republic was passing through a difficult time of economic chaos and counter-revolutionary sabotage, V. I. Lenin looked far ahead when he indicated the broad nature of the lines on which science should be applied to the service of mankind. In his *Draft Scheme for Scientific and Technical Work* Lenin enumerated a series of problems for the Academy of Science relating to the reconstitution and reconstruction of the nation's economy.

A solution of the most important questions connected with the national economy is the basis of the exploratory, research and theoretical work of the Academy of Science. Examples of this work include the expeditions organized by the Council for the Investigation of the Productive Resources of the U.S.S.R. for research work dealing with the geological structure, the extent of the local resources of power and raw materials, the economics and the population of various parts of the Soviet Union. During the seven years of its existence the Council has organized over 150 expeditions. A thorough survey of the Kola Peninsula was undertaken as early as 1920 and the industries established there to exploit the deposits of apatite and nepheline are a direct result of this survey. Similar survey expeditions have served both to raise and solve a number of important theoretical problems.

Exploratory surveys in the Urals, in the republics of Central Asia and, quite recently, in Altai (V. A. Obrouchev) have established the existence of natural mineral wealth of an extent hitherto undreamed of, since it had almost been taken for granted that the mountains of Central Asia held nothing of industrial value. Recent surveys have proved that they actually contain deposits of nearly every element of the Mendeleev System.

The geological surveys of the Soviet Union were carried out on the basis of the classic work of the founder of Soviet geology, the academician A. P. Karpinsky. The research work envisaged by his plan could never have been fully carried out under any system of government other than that of the Soviet régime. The research and survey work undertaken in the realm of mineral combustibles is an example of the new approach to the problem of natural sources of power and raw material. The Soviet Union leads the world in this respect.

The activities of the recently established Institute of Physical Problems working under the direction of Professor Kapitza is worthy of special notice, as it is the only one of its kind in the world. There is nothing comparable to it as regards the scope of its laboratory research work and the significance of the problems dealt with.

The nature and extent of the chemical and technological questions presented by the growth of Soviet industry have necessitated a close study and application of relatively remote aspects of science. The views propounded by the greatest Russian chemist of the nineteenth century, D. I. Mendeleev, directly inspired the ideas of chemical analysis evolved by the academician Kurnakov. These ideas are closely bound up with the investigation and utilization of the chemical resources of Kara-Boghaz-Gol, the Kulundin Lakes, &c., and various mineral deposits of the U.S.S.R.

Bio-chemistry is represented by the academician A. N. Bach, one of our most eminent scientists. There was a time when bio-chemistry was regarded as a subsidiary subject of certain medical and physiological professorships, but now we possess a great institute devoted solely to the investigation of theoretical structures in bio-chemistry and to practical work of great importance. For instance, we now bake our bread by mass-production processes in huge bakeries. The quantity of bread required for consumption is represented by almost astronomical figures, so every improvement that can be introduced in the process of baking is of the utmost value. Professor Bach and his colleagues, in investigating the indications of fermentation, are therefore rendering a great service to humanity.

The year 1935 saw the establishment of the Institute of the Academician Severtsov, the founder of the evolutionary school of morphology. Darwin's Theory, so well known to the people of the Soviet Union and so closely concerning many problems of biology, cannot be allowed to remain stagnant and must be developed in all its branches. The school of Professor Severtsov presents us with brilliant examples of what can be done in the way of further developing an apparently completely covered realm of science. Comparisons of the processes of embryology and of those of individual development with the processes of development of the organism, species and type, provide a great quantity of valuable data for furthering the teachings of Darwin. The philo-embryo-genesis of Professor Severtsov constitutes a new current of scientific thought which permits a solution of the problems of Darwinism and establishes the whole teaching of Darwin on even more substantial foundations than those hitherto recognized.

The Institutes of Botany and Zoology are conducting a vast amount of statistical research work into the flora and fauna of our country and provide scientific instruction regarding the correct methods of exploiting them to the best advantage, for preserving them in special reserved areas and for combating the vegetable and animal elements which are inimical to agriculture and other productive processes.

The academicians Vernadsky and A. E. Fersman were the pioneers of the study of geo-chemical processes in our country. The mineral masses which constitute the geological base of the earth in this country may be investigated from various angles, e.g., historically, petrographically, &c. Our research workers are approaching geology from the aspect of the chemical processes which cause the formation of the earth's solidity. The latter thereby presents itself to us as a living organism. We see its history, accumulations of definite mineral elements, ores and other deposits. Thus we can develop a perfect theory concerning the life of the earth as one of the celestial bodies of the universe and the rôle of its separate components, the part played by life in geological structures and the migration of chemical elements in the earth's crust. Furthermore, we are furnished with an admirable medium for research, as the combination of geology and chemistry into a single study produces wholly unexpected results.

We must name the academician Favorsky who is building up a new theory of organic synthesis and whose work has led to the introduction of a whole series of new industrial processes founded on organic matter, in addition to giving us new compounds.

The academician Zelinsky is doing valuable work in regard to the use of synthetic fuel—a subject of the utmost importance, as the main fuel of the future will, quite possibly, be wholly synthetic.

The Physical Institute of S. I. Vavilov is quite a new scientific establishment. We formerly possessed a physical laboratory of sorts, but it was far too small to be efficient and produced nothing in the way of results. The present Institute compares favourably in size and equipment with its counterparts in Western Europe and allows us to develop physical research independently. The work now in progress there includes elaborations of the theory of photographic reproduction, the dielectric properties of compressed gases, the rate of change of velocity of electric waves, the luminescent quantitive method of analysis, the interaction of neutrons and protons, &c. All these subjects are very comprehensive and involve much time and intensive study for their effective development.

In the U.S.S.R. Darwin's Theory was daily verified and extended by the application of productive practice. Even before the Revolution, Russia produced the brilliant genesist, I. V. Mitchurin, but he was unable to substantiate his ideas at that time. It is only under the Soviet régime that Mitchurin successfully developed hybridization. He established the existence of new laws governing vegetable growth, successfully limited it in certain cases, produced dozens of novel forms of plants, greatly improved the quality of many fruit-bearing plants and enabled them to be cultivated much farther north.

The conditions governing the large-scale and advanced form of socialist agriculture practised in the Soviet Union have resulted in progress in agricultural science to an extent unheard of in any other country or age. The part played by science in collective agricultural farming may be illustrated by the example of the great work done by the academician T. D. Lysenko in connexion with the conversion of winter wheat into spring wheat, a work which he began in 1925. When the leading collective farm workers first heard of the spring sowings of winter wheat advocated by Professor Lysenko in 1929-30, they displayed a remarkable degree of initiative and enabled his theory to be fully confirmed in practice.

The work of the academician N. I. Vavilov on the history of cultured plants, their selection and genesis, is widely known and enables our scientific institutes to produce many valuable additions to the scientific literature of the world.

Finally, we must refer to our geographic work. The

hundred and fifty expeditions sent out since the Revolution have done much to fill in former "blanks" in our maps. Much of the success achieved by these expeditions is due to the participation in our work of the academician O. Y. Schmidt. One of the heroes of the Soviet Union, a brilliant mathematician, an intrepid Polar explorer and a scientist of encyclopædic knowledge, Professor Schmidt is a man who is a credit to his country. The Polar expeditions of the Soviet Union have surveyed the northern territories of our country and of many remote islands in the Arctic, besides making it possible to establish a scientific station at the North Pole and to deal with problems in Polar regions hitherto regarded as absolutely inaccessible. The winter spent at the Pole by the Papanin Expedition proved of immense value to the cause of science. They determined the depth of the Arctic Ocean at the Pole, thereby finally exploding the theory of land at this point. The tests of the water made by Shirshov determined the direction of flow of the warm Atlantic currents over the Pole. The observations made by the members of Papanin's party proved that the assertions concerning the absence of life in the Central Arctic were false.

There can be no doubt that we are progressing in every realm of science. Special stress has been laid on those branches with which the writer has been personally concerned, in so far as they form part of the work of the Department of Natural Science. However, other scientific establishments and scientists working under the Department of Social Sciences of the U.S.S.R. Academy of Science have achieved much. The full extent of their labours has not yet been reviewed, but their exploits in the reconstruction of methodology and thematics in this Department demonstrate that all that has been said above regarding the work of Soviet scientists applies equally to this section of our collaborators.

Historical research work has proved exceptionally difficult. The observations of Stalin concerning the need for a history of the peoples inhabiting the U.S.S.R. in place of a history of the Russian Empire are in complete accord with the views and requirements propounded by modern scientific thought. We are, at the present time, doing all we can to utilize the resources at our disposal for this purpose both in the central regions and in the border districts, the resources in the form of the actual people to be studied.

Our great socialist country is being steadily enriched by scientific study, which it has come to appreciate at its true value. In 1937 over 142,000 persons graduated from our higher educational establishments and their number continues to rise. The idea of providing higher education for *the whole* of the population is surely more than an idle dream, and will be realized in due course.

Soviet science, supported by the affection of the people and the attention of their leader, moves forward from victory to victory. The breadth of our scientific thought, its untrammelled liberty, the possibility of propounding and solving novel and daring theories—all this is very different to pre-revolutionary conditions and the time when eminent scientists were frequently compelled to waste their genius in wretchedly equipped laboratories, cramped by bureaucratic restrictions and cut off from practical work and their own people. It seems as if centuries had elapsed since that time.

XII

EXPLORATION AND SURVEYS OF THE ARCTIC REGIONS AND EXPEDITIONS TO THE NORTH POLE

By Professor V. Y. Wiese

Assistant Director of the Soviet Union Arctic Institute in Leningrad

The brilliant success achieved by the Polar expedition of the heroic Papanin and his companions in 1937-38 on a drifting ice-floe evoked the admiration of the entire world, but it was only rendered possible by the vast amount of preliminary survey work carried out in the Arctic by the Soviet authorities.

The immense natural resources of the Arctic—in the shape of its fauna and valuable mineral deposits—have been more or less known for many years owing to the activities of individual Polar explorers, but such information as was available on this subject was wholly inadequate for the purpose of enabling anything like a complete appraisement of the possibilities of these resources to be made. As early as 1918 the Soviet Government established a special institute for dealing with the exploration of the Far North and this is now known as the Soviet Union Arctic Institute. This is an important scientific establishment in which more than 280 scientists are permanently employed and which sends out annual expeditions to all parts of the Arctic regions, mainly for geological and oceanographic survey work. In 1937 the Arctic Institute sent out 38 Polar expeditions.

In the western part of the Soviet Arctic the explorers have paid particular attention to surveys of the Barents Sea, where survey vessels of special construction have taken 6500 deep-sea soundings. Since 1921 a systematic survey along the meridian between the Kola Peninsula and latitude 75° N. has been carried out with the object of determining the seasonal and secular variations of temperature of the water of the Barents Sea. As is well known, this sea is fed from the west by a great warm current from the Atlantic—the so-called North Cape Current—which is the cause of the relatively mild climate of the extreme north-west territories of the U.S.S.R. Scientists have for many years studied the variations of temperature of the Atlantic Current (frequently termed the "Gulf Stream") and its branches and have noted the connexion of these variations with those of meteorological conditions, the amount of ice and the catches of fish made, &c. A complete study of the variations of the Atlantic Current should yield extremely valuable data for long-term weather prognostications which are of such importance for the economy of the country.

Parallel with the intensive programme of scientific survey work, a detailed study of the fish resources of the Barents Sea has been undertaken. These are largely made up of cod, the quantity of which is so great that with a rationalized method of cod fishing, it may be regarded as inexhaustible. Prior to the Revolution there were practically no Russian trawlers engaged in the cod fisheries of the Barents Sea, but at the present time the Soviet Union possesses a fleet of trawlers based on Mur-

A Soviet ice-breaker

mansk—an Arctic port which does not freeze and which, from being a settlement with a few hundred inhabitants at the time of the Revolution, now has a population of 120,000. The catches of cod made by these trawlers in the Barents Sea are rapidly increasing and in 1937 totalled 100,000 tons. Within the last few years a herring-fishing industry has also been established in the Barents Sea.

There are, of course, a number of other fishing grounds in the Soviet Arctic and the waters around the estuaries of the great rivers—the Ob, Enissei, Khatanga, Lena, Indigirka, Kolyma, &c.—abound with fish of the highest grades. There is every reason to believe that a huge scope exists for the development of the fishing industry in those waters.

In addition to the fisheries of the Barents Sea, the western sector of the Soviet Arctic was of special interest to the Soviet Government on account of the sea route to the Ob and Enissei.

A whole series of Soviet scientific expeditions have already been sent to carry out surveys of the waters around the estuaries of the Western Siberian rivers in the Kara Sea. Navigational marks have been erected at various points on the shore of the mainland and the islands, lighthouses have been built, aerial surveys of ice have been instituted, a meteorological service has been established and a number of powerful ice-breakers and special ice-clearing vessels have been stationed there to keep the sea route open for shipping. These measures have enabled a regular service of steamers between the Barents Sea and the estuaries of the Western Siberian rivers to be maintained for a period of two months per annum, but it is hoped that technical improvements will soon enable this period to be extended.

Most of the steamers go to the Enissei—not the Ob—for timber. The absence of any appreciable bar at the mouth of the Enissei allows ocean-going steamers to proceed right up the river—as far as the port of Igarka, 450 miles from its mouth. The construction of this port, which is just outside the limits of the Arctic zone (normally defined as being bounded by the July isotherm of 50° F.) was begun in 1928, when the first party of 45 workers arrived there. In 1935 the population of Igarka was already 12,000 persons and it is still rapidly increasing. There are now several sawmills at Igarka and this sub-polar city is well equipped with hospitals, schools, theatres, &c. An interesting series of large-scale experiments in Arctic vegetable growing have been proceeding in Igarka, both in the open air and in hothouses. The latter have proved extremely successful even in the Arctic regions and at Dixon Island (74° N.) hothouse cucumbers, tomatoes and other vegetables are grown, in sufficient quantities to meet the vitamin requirements in the food of the local inhabitants.

The fuel burned by vessels on voyages between European ports and Igarka is now chiefly Spitzbergen coal. The mining of coal in Spitzbergen was begun by Soviet undertakings in 1932 in the Barentsburg collieries acquired from Dutch interests. Very shortly vessels engaged in "the Kara trade" will be burning not only coal from Spitzbergen, but from Norilsk as well. A great programme of construction is now in process of development at Norilsk—recently linked up by a new railway with the settlement of Dudinki on the Enissei—in connexion with the rich deposits of valuable metal ores discovered there.

Not long after the opening up of the western area of the Soviet Arctic, similar developments were undertaken in the eastern area, where regular sea communication with the estuary of the Kolyma via the Bering Strait, was established. The first steamer under the Soviet flag sailed from Vladivostok to the mouth of the Kolyma in 1923, and since 1932 the exploitation of the immensely valuable gold mines in the Kolyma district has led to the inauguration of a regular steamship service between Vladivostok and the estuary of the Kolyma. This formerly desolate river now possesses its own flotilla of steamers and a port is being built in Ambarchik Bay at its mouth.

The successes achieved by Soviet navigators in the western and eastern sections of the Soviet Arctic have served to revive public interest in the old problem of the "North-East Passage." As is well known, this passage was made three times—by Nordenskiold, Vilkitzky and Amundsen—prior to 1920, but the vessels of each of these three expeditions had been compelled to winter in the Arctic. For this reason the "Northern Sea Route"—as it is termed in the U.S.S.R.—was not regarded as of any practical importance, and it was only in 1932, when the whole of the Northern Sea Route (from Archangel to the Bering Strait) was traversed in a single voyage by the expedition in the "Sibiriakov," that this view of it was altered. The "Sibiriakov's" voyage was followed in 1934 by that of the icebreaker "Lütke," sailing in the reverse direction.

In 1935 the regular navigation of the Northern Sea

Route was undertaken and in the following year 14 vessels made the whole voyage and 21 sailed round the northernmost point of Asia, Cape Chelyuskin.

The solution of the problem of the North-East Passage was largely due to the establishment along the shores of the Arctic Ocean of a continuous chain of meteorological radio stations and to the efficacy of the scientific survey work carried out there. There are, at the present time, over 50 Polar meteorological stations in the Soviet Arctic, whereas only four existed in the days of Russian Tsardom. The northernmost shore station is on Rudolf Island (Franz-Josef Land) in a latitude of 81° 48′ N.

The extensive surveys carried out have enabled complete sets of charts for the whole of the Northern Sea Route to be made. Immense areas of sea formerly left blank are now marked with innumerable soundings and a large number of new islands have been discovered. In particular, a great number of geographical discoveries have been made, and extensive cartographic work has been done in the northern part of the Kara Sea.

Much attention has been devoted by Soviet scientists to the hydrology and marine zoology of the Polar seas, as well as to the geological structure of the Arctic. The exploratory work carried out in this connexion naturally includes searches for mineral deposits. In 1930 the exploitation of the lead and zinc deposits on the island of Vaigatch was begun and in 1933 the mining of fluorspar at Anderm on the southern shore of the Kara Sea was commenced, the deposit of fluorspar being one of the richest in the world. The region of Nordvik Bay in the Gulf of Khatangha is certain of great industrial importance in the near future as oil has been found there and the commercial exploitation of the enormous deposits of rock salt has already begun. A few hundred tons were exported from Nordvik to Kamchatka in 1936. The region is also rich in bituminous coal.

Aviation has played an extremely important part in the opening up of the Northern Sea Route and the exploration of the Far North of the Soviet Union. It was in 1936 that the airman V. S. Molokov made the first complete flight from Moscow to Yakutsk and the Bering Strait, returning via Cape Chelyuskin and Archangel. In the same year M. Vodopianov flew from Moscow to Franz-Josef Land and V. Tchkalov made a non-stop flight from Moscow to the mouth of the Amur via Franz-Josef Land, Novaya Zemlia, the mouth of the Lena and Kamchatka.

As the southern regions of the Soviet Arctic came to be explored and surveyed, the Polar explorers went farther north. Ever since 1935 the ice-breaker "Sadko" has made annual survey voyages. In that year the "Sadko" reached a point north of Novaya Zemlia 82° 41′ N., thereby creating a record for a ship navigating the open sea (i.e., not drifting with the ice). Prior to that, the record was held by the American s.s. "Roosevelt," which reached a point 82° 30′ N. in the Lincoln Sea in 1908.

The exploration of the northernmost latitudes of the Arctic was inspired both by scientific and practical considerations. These last arise from the fact that there is a close relation between the conditions prevailing in the shallow Arctic waters traversed by the Northern Sea Route and those of the deep-sea area of the Polar region. The importance of the bearing of the atmospheric conditions of the Central Arctic on weather report services in northern and temperate latitudes, has long been recognized by meteorologists. There was also the question of trans-Arctic aerial communication, for which surveys of the Central Arctic zone were essential. More than 10 years ago Dr. Fridtjof Nansen propounded a scheme for the establishment of a scientific station on the ice of the Polar Zone, which he proposed to do by means of a dirigible airship. Notwithstanding the great scientific prestige of Nansen, his scheme found little support in the countries of Western Europe and America and did not materialize. This scheme for establishing a station on the drift-ice of the Central Arctic was first considered by Soviet scientists in 1930, and the success achieved by Soviet Polar aviation proved a decisive factor in its realization.

Preparations for carrying the project into effect began in 1936 and involved a vast amount of work dealing with every aspect and minute detail of the proposed expedition. In March, 1937, five aeroplanes under the general command of Professor O. Y. Schmidt started from Moscow and on the 21st May the first aeroplane landed on an icefield near the North Pole, being quickly followed by the remainder. The total weight of the equipment brought by all the machines was over nine tons. On the 22nd May the first meteorological radiogram was sent out from the North Pole. The aeroplanes flew back to Moscow, leaving four men on the ice—I. Papanin, leader of the party; E. Fedorov, astronomer and magnetologist; P. Shirshov, hydrologist and biologist, and E. Krenkel, wireless operator. They spent nine months doing invaluable scientific work under quite exceptional conditions at the North Pole station on drift-

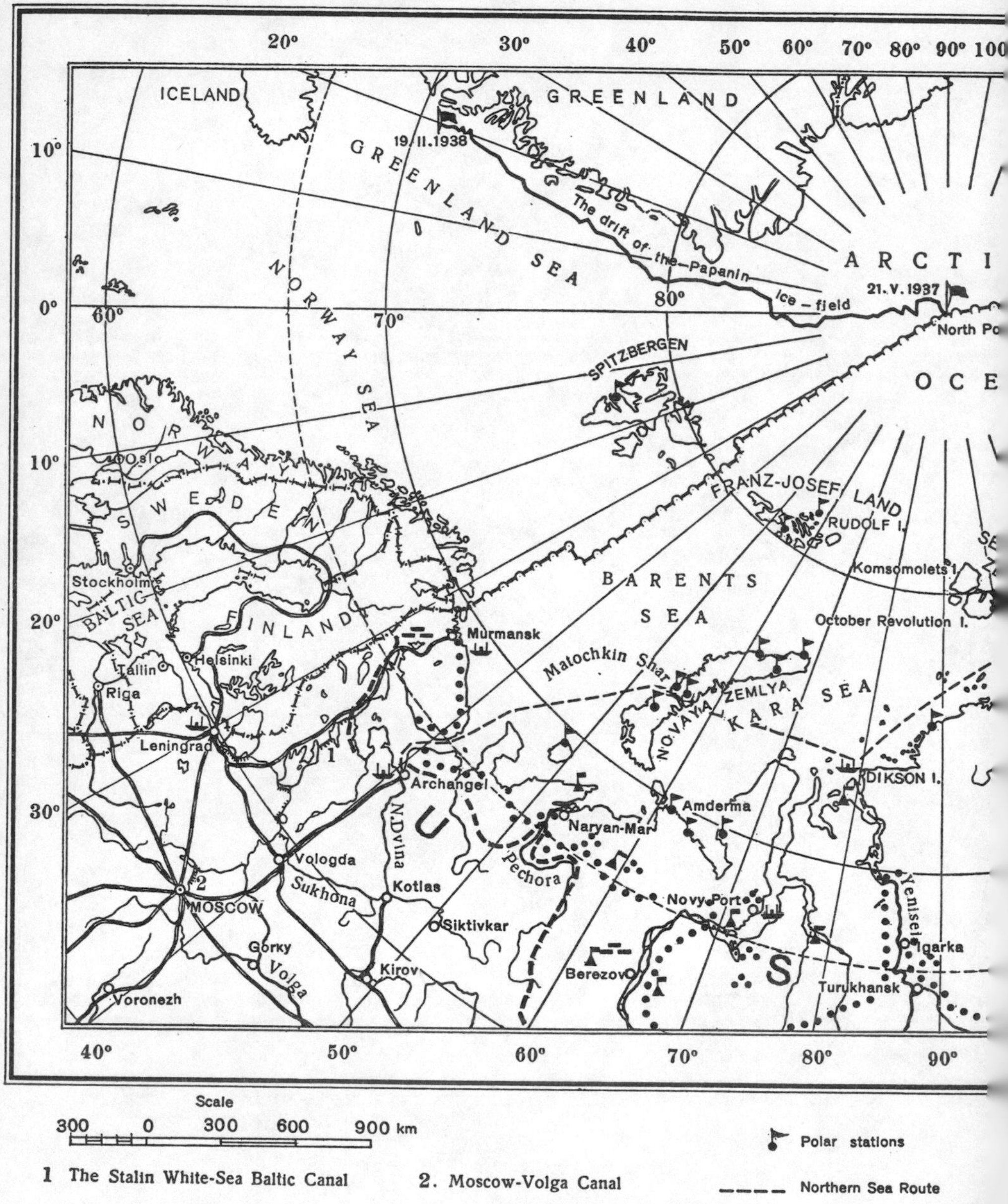

1 The Stalin White-Sea Baltic Canal

2. Moscow-Volga Canal

MAP OF THE SOVIET ARCTIC

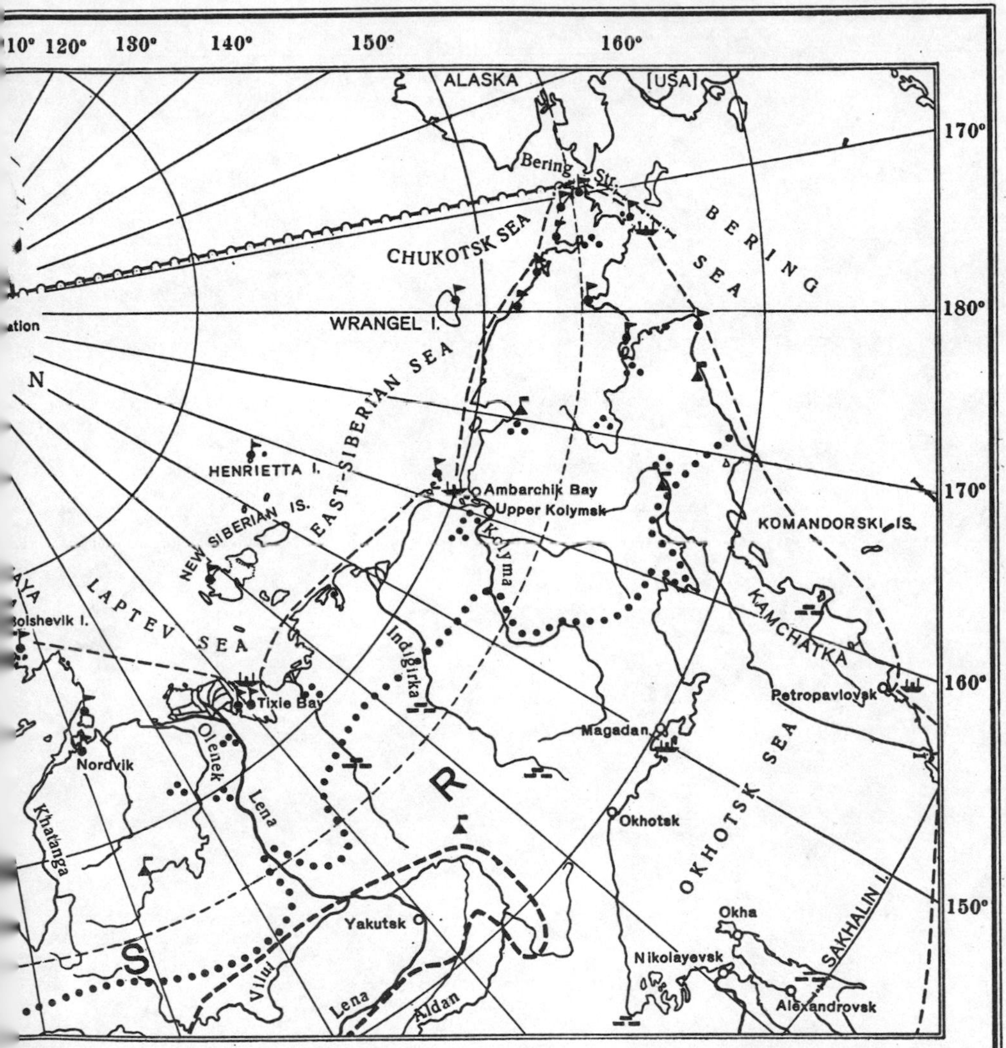

LEGEND

Kultbaza	• • • • • •	Northern Borderline of Agriculture in 1935	Separate agricultural regions in 1935
Port	— — — —	Northern Borderline of Agriculture in 1916	Separate agricultural regions in 1916

ice. The heroism and endurance of these four intrepid scientists won the admiration of the entire world.

During the winter the ice-floe drifted to the Greenland Sea and southwards along the east coast of Greenland. On the 19th February, 1937, when the ice-floe was in latitude 70° 54′ the party were brought off by the ice-breaking steamers "Taimyr" and "Murman" dispatched for that purpose.

During their sojourn on the ice-floe which drifted about 1600 miles, the scientists of the post established on it carried out an immense amount of valuable research work in meteorology, terrestrial magnetism, gravitation, hydrology and hydrobiology. There can be no doubt that the use of drifting posts, similar to Papanin's station, should enable the Central Arctic Zone to be thoroughly surveyed.

XIII

THE JUDICIAL SYSTEM

By A. Beloroussov

Chief of the Codification Section of the U.S.S.R. Legislature and of the Legal Advisory Service of the People's Commissariat for Justice of the U.S.S.R.

The judicial system and procedure of the Soviet Union, the investigation of crime and the conduct of criminal prosecutions are all regulated by law.

The Stalin Constitution is now the keynote of the entire legal system, since it deals with every aspect of present-day socialist jurisprudence and with the administration of all branches of socialist law—constitutional law, administrative law, criminal law, civil law, the judicial system and court procedure and international law.

By ensuring the stability of Soviet laws, the Stalin Constitution emphasizes the character and significance of the Soviet socialist legal code. The Constitution of the U.S.S.R. defines the special functions of the courts and the procurator's office as organs for the execution of socialist laws, for combating all breaches of the latter and for the inculcation of respect for the rules of socialist society among the citizens.

The Constitution defines the structure and the duties of the courts and procurator's office in their capacity as guardians of the Soviet legal system, watching over the maintenance of the social and state organization of the country as well as over the political and civic rights of each individual citizen.

The judicial system of the U.S.S.R. was defined by a special law relating to the judicial systems of the U.S.S.R. and of the Union and Autonomous Republics passed by the Second Session of the Supreme Soviet of the U.S.S.R.

In accordance with this law (Article 2), the aim of the judicial system is to defend from all encroachments:

(*a*) the social and state organization of the U.S.S.R., as laid down by the Constitution of the U.S.S.R. and by the constitutions of the Union and Autonomous Republics; the socialist system of economy, and socialist property;

(*b*) the political, labour, housing, and other personal and property rights and interests of the citizens, which are guaranteed by the above-named Constitutions;

(*c*) the rights and legally protected interests of state establishments and enterprises, collective farms, co-operative and other public organizations.

The aim of the judicial system is to ensure that the Soviet laws are carried out to the letter by every establishment, organization, official and private citizen.

The aim of the various penal measures applied by the courts is not only to punish criminals, but to reform and re-educate them. The court, in every possible way, educates the citizens in a spirit of devotion to their country and to the cause of socialism, in a spirit of exact and unwavering fulfilment of Soviet laws, in a spirit of respect for socialist property, of labour discipline, of honesty in the discharge of their state and public duties and of respect for the rules of socialist society.

The judicial system is based on the following principles:

(*a*) a single and equal court for all citizens, irrespective of their social position and property and of their race or nationality;

(*b*) a single criminal, civil, and court procedure code which is compulsory for every court.

The Stalin Constitution has laid down that judges in the U.S.S.R. are independent and subject only to the law (Article 112).

Judges may be dismissed from office and people's assessors relieved of their duties only on the demand of their electors or by sentence of a court of law. The institution of criminal proceedings against a judge, involving dismissal from office and trial in court, lies exclusively within the competence of the procurator of the Union republic concerned with the sanction of the Presidium of the Supreme Soviet of that republic; while, as regards members of the Supreme Court of the U.S.S.R. and special courts, this right belongs only to the procurator of the U.S.S.R. with the sanction of the Presidium of the Supreme Soviet of the U.S.S.R.

True to the Stalinist national policy, the law on the judicial system states, in accordance with Article 110 of the Constitution, that court proceedings are conducted in the language of the Union republic or autonomous region, while persons not knowing that language are ensured every opportunity of fully acquainting themselves with the material relating to the case through a translator and the right to speak in court in their own language.

In conformity with Article 111 of the Constitution, in all courts cases are heard in public, unless otherwise provided for by the law, and the accused is guaranteed the right of defence. For example, cases relating to state secrets, sexual crimes, &c., may be heard *in camera*.

In all courts cases are tried with the assistance of people's assessors (one member of the court and two people's assessors), except in cases specially provided for by the law.

The backbone of the juridical system is the people's court in which a people's judge sits with two people's assessors. Under Article 109 of the Constitution of the Soviet Union the people's judges are appointed for three years by a direct ballot of local citizens, this ballot being universal, equal and secret.

All local citizens, irrespective of their race, nationality, religion, education, residence, social origin, proprietary status and past activities, are entitled to vote at elections for people's judges. The only persons debarred from voting are those certified as insane or deprived of electoral rights by sentence of a court of law.

The Constitution also lays down that people's assessors shall be appointed by election to sit with the judge for a period of not more than ten days in each year. The people's assessors sitting with the judge have the same powers as the latter in regard to the interpretation of court procedure, the delivery of verdicts and the pronouncement of sentence.

People's judges are elected from among citizens enjoying confidence and authority in the district and possessing the necessary qualifications (experience, carefulness, judgment, experience of social work) for the high office of a people's judge. No standard of any kind in respect of education, personal property or other status is prescribed for candidates.

On 1st February, 1938, the people's judges throughout the whole of the Soviet Union were drawn from the following classes of society:

Manual workers, - - - -	43.0%
Peasants - - - - -	23.0%
Officials and employees - -	34.0%

The number of women among the people's judges was 18%. Of the total number of people's judges 61.9% have received special legal training, being graduates in law of some higher educational establishment.

The people's courts, which are the courts of first instance, deal with the most varied cases of a civil or criminal nature. The people's court deals with:

(*a*) criminal cases relating to crimes against the life, health, liberty and dignity of citizens: murder, infliction of bodily injury, performance of illegal abortions, illegal imprisonment, violation, malicious non-payment of alimony, outrage, ruffianism and libel;

(*b*) relating to property crimes: brigandage, robbery, theft, swindling and blackmail;

(*c*) relating to breach of trust by persons in official positions: abuse of power, excess of power, inaction of power, embezzlement, mismanagement, forgery, giving of short weight and short measure and illegal raising of prices;

(*d*) relating to crimes against the established administrative system, infringement of the election law, malicious non-payment of the taxes and levies established by the law, refusal to fulfil state contracts for supplies and other obligations, evasion of military service and infringement of decrees passed by authoritative organs;

(*e*) civil cases relating to property suits, to infringement of the statutes on labour, to alimony suits, to inheritance suits;

and other criminal and civil cases brought within the competence of the people's court.

It can thus be seen that the powers of the people's courts are very extensive and being closely associated with the inhabitants of the local district they are readily accessible to all citizens. The people's courts handle most of the local law cases.

In order to relieve the people's courts of unnecessary work, so-called comradely courts are organized in each large house or group of smaller houses. They deal with various cases such as quarrels between tenants, troubles connected with apartments and so on. These courts are elected by a general meeting of tenants and are legally empowered to inflict penalties comprising reprimands, public censure and monetary fines of up to 50 roubles.

The comradely courts of industrial undertakings and other establishments deal with cases connected with work and the employees.

If the case is of a criminal nature, the comradely court transfers it to the people's court for examination, the cognizance of the latter being established by the criminal and civil judicial codes.

The next stage in the judicial system consists of the territorial or regional courts and the supreme courts of the autonomous republics which serve both as courts of appeal for the people's courts of the autonomous republic, territory or region concerned, and as the local judicative authority for trying the more important criminal and civil cases of the character laid down by the Soviet criminal and civil codes. When hearing appeals from the lower courts, the territorial and regional courts and supreme courts of the autonomous republics may either confirm the judgment of the people's courts, reduce the sentence, quash the proceedings, or refer the case back for retrial by a people's court composed of judges who did not try the case in the first instance.

The judges of the supreme courts of the autonomous republics and of the territorial and regional courts are elected by the Supreme Soviet of the autonomous republic, by the territorial or regional soviets of workers for a period of five years. On 1st February, 1938, the judges of the territorial and regional courts throughout the Soviet Union included 39.7% members of the working-class and there were also 14.1% women among them.

When dealing with first hearings of cases, supreme courts of autonomous republics and territorial and regional courts include people's assessors who sit with the judges.

Each of the 11 Union republics belonging to the Soviet Union has its own supreme court which exercises supreme judicial supervision over all the courts in the republic concerned. It examines the work of the people's courts, territorial and regional courts and of the supreme courts of autonomous republics in regard to all cases tried by these bodies and has power to alter or annul their judgments if these are not in accordance with the law.

The supreme courts of the Union republics hear appeals from the territorial and regional courts and from the supreme courts of the autonomous republics within the boundaries of the Union republics concerned, when all these courts have functioned as courts of first instance.

The supreme court of a Union republic can also deal with the first hearing of any case of special importance to the republic concerned.

The supreme court judges are elected by the Supreme Soviet of the republic concerned for a period of five years.

On 1st February, 1938, the judicature of the supreme courts of the 11 Union republics included 26.1% members of the working-class, and 14% women.

The highest tribunal of the Soviet Union is the Supreme Court of the U.S.S.R. Under Article 104 of the Constitution it is entrusted with the supervision of the administration of justice in all the courts of the U.S.S.R. and Union republics. Apart from exercising supervision over their work in regard to verdicts and sentences, the Supreme Court may, if deemed necessary, itself try cases of exceptional importance as a court of first instance, if these are of a criminal or civil nature which affects the interests of the whole Soviet Union or of several Union republics.

In addition to the general judicial system, the Constitution provides for special courts, such as military tribunals, railway courts, and water transport courts, all of which are an integral part of the whole judicial system and deal with offences against the strength or power of the Red Army or the normal working of railway and water transport. Such cases are reserved for hearing by special courts as their proper trial renders it essential for the court to possess specialized knowledge and practice. Only judges who are thoroughly acquainted with the specific conditions relating to the case in the army, railway or water transport service concerned are in a position to conduct a complete investigation of it for the purpose of arriving at a finding and sentence in accordance with the penal and criminal procedure code applicable.

In pronouncing sentence, judges are guided by the criminal code and the necessity for protecting the socialist state from acts of a character injurious to the community.

The Soviet penal code prescribes as penalties for these offences: proclamation as an enemy of the workers with exile from the territories of the Soviet Union; detention for a period of up to 19 years; reformatory labour without loss of liberty for a period of up to one year; forfeiture of political and various civil rights (such as parental rights in cases of ill-treatment of children); temporary exile from the Soviet Union or from one of the Union republics; dismissal from employment with or without prohibition to engage in some particular occupation during a prescribed period (e.g., a cashier convicted of embezzlement being debarred from accepting a post connected with valuables of any description); prohibition from continuing some particular calling or trade (e.g., a doctor performing an abortion in contravention of the decree on the "Prohibition of Abortions" of 27th June, 1936, being debarred from engaging in medical work). Further penalties are total or partial confiscation of property, monetary fines, order for reparation of the damage done and cautions.

As a temporary and exceptional measure in cases of high treason, grave offences against the state and military offences, the penalty of death by shooting may be inflicted.

In order to combat espionage, sabotage, conspiracies to bring about explosions, disasters, arson with loss of life and similar criminal acts, a law of 2nd October, 1937, empowers the court not only to impose the extreme penalty (shooting), but also detention for periods of more than 10 years (not exceeding 25 years). These penalties are imposed in cases of very grave offences against the Soviet states.

The death sentence cannot be pronounced on a person under 18 years of age or on a pregnant woman. The Soviet criminal code does not apply the extreme penalty of death by shooting to cases of murder.

Soviet courts are not bound down by any rigid regulations in regard to procedure for framing criminal charges against persons connected with cases they may be dealing with. A court cannot arraign such a person for an act not specifically defined as an offence by the criminal code and at the same time a court may, at its discretion, refrain from imposing a penalty for an act which constituted an offence at the time it was committed, but which, owing to changes in the law or altered social and political circumstances, might not be considered dangerous to the community at the actual time of the trial, or which might not be regarded as a crime in the absence of serious consequences.

Should the court be of the opinion that a convicted person is not deserving of punishment to the extent of the minimum penalty prescribed by law, it may inflict a lesser penalty and, in pronouncing sentence, explain precisely why the minimum penalty laid down by the relevant article of the criminal code is not applied to the case in question.

In cases in which the convicted person's character does not necessitate his isolation from the community, the court may impose a conditional penalty and put the offender on probation for any period between twelve months and five years.

In considering penalties and their application to convicted persons, Soviet courts are invariably actuated by motives of socialist humanism. The law states that the object of punishment is neither vengeance nor chastisement and that it may never be inflicted for the purpose of imposing physical suffering or human degradation. Persons undergoing punishment in places of detention or camps are required to work. As they work the prisoners undergo a process of reformation, study and learn a trade in which they can engage on their release. When the White Sea and Moscow-Volga canals, which were constructed by convict labour, were completed, many of the prisoners employed on that work rendered excellent service for which they were duly rewarded by the Government and granted remissions of their sentences, while those who performed work of special merit were even awarded decorations.

Legal inquiries are conducted mainly by the organs of the procurator's office. The duty of the latter, as laid down by the law, is the direction and supervision of all the organs' conducted inquiries into criminal cases. The bodies comprise the militia, the criminal investigation department, and the examining magistracy. When the inquiry has been completed, they send the whole dossier to the procurator's office, which will either stop the case, if there are sufficient legal grounds for doing so, or will send it to the proper quarters for further investigation, or will transfer the case to court for trial.

Other organs of the legal system include bailiffs, the Colleges of Public Defenders, and notaries. The bailiffs are attached to the people's courts for the purpose of collecting the payments involved by judgments in civil suits and for enforcing penalties involving the confiscation of property in criminal cases.

The members of the Colleges of Public Defenders are available to the community for the purpose of giving legal advice and their duties in court include the defence of accused persons in criminal cases and the representation of litigants in civil suits. Each College of Public Defenders is administered by its own council, elected by secret ballot. Every citizen is entitled to be defended in a court of law. Public defenders are remunerated in accordance with a statutory scale; indigent persons are entitled to their services free of charge.

Apart from the court judicature, the Constitution of the U.S.S.R. provides for the procurator's office which is charged with the duty of seeing that the law is kept not only by individual citizens and state employees, but also by the People's Commissariats and their subordinate departments. The procurator's office is independent of all local authorities and only responsible to the procurator of the U.S.S.R. appointed by the Supreme Soviet of the Soviet Union for a term of seven years. His department supervises the conduct of judicial investigations by all the services and officials appointed for this purpose (the militia, the People's Commissariat of Internal Affairs, and the prosecuting magistracy).

The Soviet courts of justice and procurator's office are organs of the Socialist State of Workers and Peasants acting solely under the authority of the Stalin Constitution and other laws of the Soviet Union and Union Republics as the guardians of the socialist order and the established rights of the citizens of the land of Socialism.

XIV

LABOUR

By L. Falin

Responsible Editor of "The Trade Unions of the U.S.S.R."

Work in the U.S.S.R. is the honourable duty of every able-bodied citizen in the land. The right to work is secured in the Constitution and guaranteed by the socialist organization of national economy, the steady growth of the productive powers of society and the absence of economic crises and unemployment.

The conditions of work in the Soviet Union are the decisive factor in the attitude of the people towards work and production. They all know that in whatever branch of socialist construction they are participating, whatever work they are engaged in, they themselves are the masters there, and therefore they endeavour to do the work as well as possible and to achieve a higher level of labour productivity.

This socialist attitude towards labour and production is expressed in the organization of socialist competition between individual workers, groups of workers, different shops and departments and whole factories.

The socialist agreements entered upon by the working-people enumerate their self-imposed obligations, which are undertaken with the purpose of fulfilling the tasks facing the enterprise in question, and of giving comradely help to each other in such matters as the mastering of new methods of work and of new technical appliances and the acquirement of higher qualifications.

The highest form of socialist competition is the Stakhanov movement, whose origin lay in the vast improvement of the material, cultural and technical standard of the working-people. The Stakhanovites are workers who have completely mastered new technical methods of production, who organize labour on entirely new lines and who beat world records of labour productivity under normal working conditions. The strength of this movement lies in its widespread mass character. The Stakhanovites in every factory are not isolated persons, but comprise at least 35-40% of all the workers employed there. This mass of Stakhanovites exceeds the established output capacity of its machines, to the not infrequent amazement of the engineers in charge, who are forced to admit that the Stakhanovites have studied technical processes so thoroughly that they have succeeded in upsetting all established theoretical calculations and in achieving in practice a higher output capacity for their lathes, machines, &c. The Stakhanovite enjoys the respect and admiration of all the working-people, for his fight to attain a higher productivity of labour not only improves his own standard of living, but also that of the whole of society. The people's affection for the heroes and heroines of labour, and their trust in them, were vividly demonstrated during the elections to the Supreme Soviets of the U.S.S.R. and the Union and Autonomous Republics. The initiators of the Stakhanov movement—the miner Alexis Stakhanov, the Vinogradovas, both weavers, the smith Boussigin, the engine-driver Peter

Krivonoss, and many others, were elected deputies to the highest organs of the Soviet state.

Of great importance in the training of a socialist attitude towards work and production are the production conferences organized in every enterprise. Through these conferences the workers and employees participate in the running of the enterprise, combat various defects, suggest different methods of rationalization, discuss their experiences in production and acquaint the whole mass of workers with the achievements of individuals. The decisions of the production conferences made in conjunction with the management are compulsory for all.

The active participation of the working masses in the building up of socialist society resulted in the steady growth of the national economy. The growth of the national income, as shown by the following figures, illustrates this movement. The national income in 1937 was 4.6 times as great as in 1913, rising from 21,000 million roubles to 96,300 million roubles (in terms of 1926-27 prices). During the years of the First and Second Five Year Plans the average annual increase in the national income was equivalent to 29 per cent.

One of the results of the socialist system of economy and the accompanying continuous growth of productive power is the steady increase in the number of working-people. The introduction into industry of new scientific and technical methods does not cause the formation of an army of unemployed: the planned regulation of the whole of national economy in the U.S.S.R., the rate and extension of construction, unprecedented in history, and the continual increase in the number of factories and other industrial establishments preclude the very idea of unemployment, indeed, they ensure the true and full realization of the right to work.

Certain branches of the national economy actually suffer from a lack of hands. This lack became particularly acute after the triumph of the collective farm (kolkhoz) system in the rural districts.

The collective farm system altered the whole social aspect of the village and changed the character of production relations. The collective labour of the kolkhoz peasantry, based as it is on the most advanced technical methods, expelled poverty from the village. As a result the village ceased to be the natural supplier of superfluous hands for the towns and industrial centres, whither formerly poverty and hunger drove hundreds of thousands of villagers in search of work. The Soviet peasantry leads a cultured and prosperous life. The recruitment of villagers for work in industry is achieved by means of voluntary agreements entered into by the industrial organizations and the collective farm members.

Human beings are considered the most valuable capital in the Soviet Union. The aim of the whole policy of the Government and of the work of every public organization is to make work a genuine manifestation of human activity and life itself happy and joyful.

The safeguarding of the labour, life and health of working people is the everyday care both of the Government and of all the public organizations, including the trade unions. The function of state control over the observance of labour legislation is fulfilled by the trade unions through the special labour inspectors appointed by them and the great mass of voluntary inspectors elected at meetings of workers and employees. Thus control

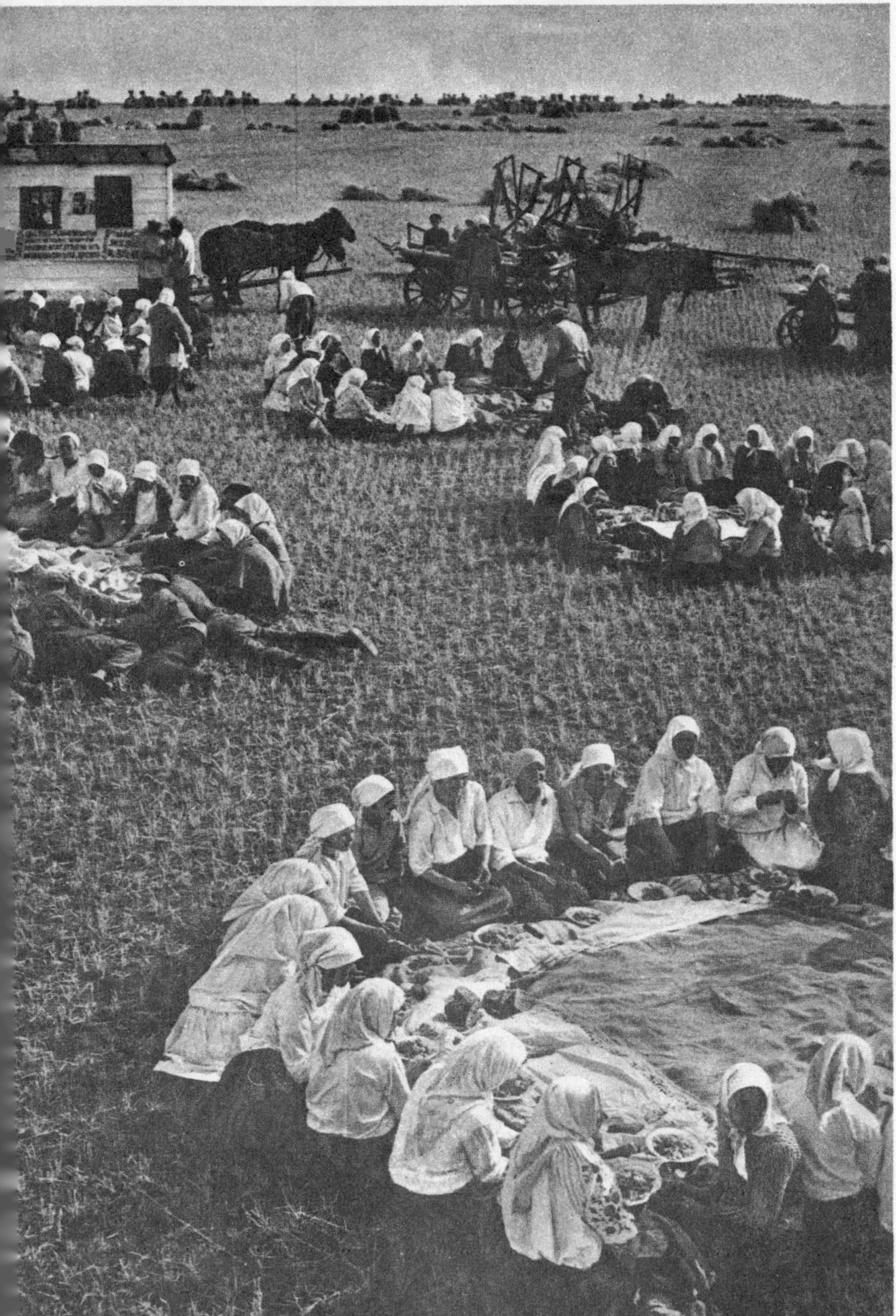

Lunch time on a collective farm

over the observance of labour legislation is in fact effected by the workers and employees themselves. Draft labour laws are also drawn up by the trade unions in conjunction with the workers and employees, and when they have been confirmed by the Government, they acquire the status of compulsory laws.

In order to achieve the utmost safety in industry and to eliminate unhealthy fumes, &c., the Government spends immense sums every year on the construction of barriers and ventilators, and on the planting of trees and flowers round the factories and separate departments. The trade unions possess a network of scientific research institutes which study questions connected with the safeguarding of labour and work out methods of improving working conditions for every branch of the national economy.

On the character of the work and its degree of harmfulness depend the length of the working day, the length of the annual holiday, the provision of special prophylactics, such as free milk, fats, &c. The overwhelming majority of the workers work seven hours a day. Those who work underground work six hours a day. Everyone who works has the right and the means to rest. The length of holidays varies from a fortnight to one month, according to the character of their employment, and the working-people receive full pay during their holidays, which they usually spend in homes, sanatoria and health resorts.

The trade unions alone, not counting the People's Commissariat for Health and other bodies, are in possession of 621 rest-homes and 216 sanatoria, where trade union members spend their holidays. Within the last

10 years nearly 12 million persons have been sent to rest-homes, sanatoria and health resorts by the trade unions at the expense of the state social insurance and the funds of the trade unions.

The workers and employees spend their free day, which generally occurs every sixth day, in the palaces of culture, clubs, parks of culture and rest, stadiums, swimming-pools, boating-stations, &c., placed specially at their disposal. The trade unions alone, apart from other organizations, possess 5824 clubs and palaces of culture, 174 sports stadiums, 151 boating- and swimming-stations, 145 skiing-stations and 667 sports grounds.

In cases of illness the worker and employee are granted full pay during the whole course of their illness at the expense of the state social insurance, whose funds consist of the contributions paid in by the industrial enterprises and other establishments. No contributions whatever towards social insurance are made by the workers and employees.

The trade unions are the largest organization of the workers and employees. Of the 25,400,000 workers and employees in the country, over 22,000,000 are members of trade unions, which number 165. The Soviet trade unions are built up on the production principle (one enterprise—one union), so that all the workers, engineers, technical experts and employees in one enterprise belong to one union.

In addition to the work already described, the trade unions do a vast amount of cultural and educational work through the medium of their clubs, palaces of culture, "Red corners" (political club rooms), &c., and over a million persons participate in the amateur literary, music, general educational and art circles organized by them. There are, in addition, 13,000 trade union libraries with 42 million books.

The purpose of the trade unions is to satisfy the cultural and everyday requirements of their members to the fullest extent. They spend millions of roubles on this purpose, the money coming both from special state grants and from the funds of the trade unions themselves, which consist of the monthly contributions of their members who contribute 1 per cent. of their earnings for this purpose.

In the U.S.S.R. work is paid for according to the socialist principle: "From each according to his ability, to each according to the work performed."

This principle of payment aims at securing for each worker the remuneration he has earned in accordance with the quality and quantity of work he has expended, that is to say, in accordance with his active participation in the creation of the material wealth of socialist society. This principle of remuneration not only stimulates the worker to produce more and to improve the quality of what he produces but also to raise his qualifications, for the difference between the remuneration of skilled labour and unskilled labour holds good even in socialist society.

The wages of the workers are increasing annually, as may be seen by a comparison of the total wages fund for a number of years. In 1933 it was 34,000 million roubles; in 1935, 36,200 million roubles; in 1937, 82,000 million roubles, and in 1938 it will be no less than 95,000 million roubles.

During the last 10 years the real wages of the working-people have increased by 300 per cent. This increase is a result of the state regulation of Soviet and co-operative trade and the accompanying steady reduction in prices, which saved the working-people a sum of 10,000 million roubles during the past five years.

Women have exactly the same rights as men. They receive equal pay for equal work and every road is open to them. They display their gifts and are very active in every branch of national economy and public life. They work as mechanics, chauffeurs, doctors, scientists and professors, and occupy high posts in People's Commissariats and professional organizations. They are active participants in the construction of socialist society, and thousands of them have attained positions of prominence. The state has created every condition to enable women to work peacefully and fruitfully and their labour is safeguarded by the law.

The labour of young people is likewise safeguarded by special legislation. According to these laws only citizens of 18 years of age and over are allowed to work in industry. Boys and girls under 18 are only allowed, when they have received the required minimum of elementary education, to enter factory apprentice schools, where apprentices from 14-16 work for four hours a day, and from 16-18 six hours a day. During their work as factory apprentices they are trained as skilled workers and receive monthly wages which enable them to complete the whole course of apprenticeship. Their wages, as those of grown-up workers, increase every year.

The whole aim of Soviet society is to attain such a standard of labour productivity, of technical development, and of subjugation of the forces of nature, as will permit labour in a minimum length of time to produce the quantity of goods necessary to satisfy all the requirements of the whole of society. Then the principle of remuneration: "From each according to his ability, to each according to the work done," will be replaced by another principle: "From each according to his ability, to each according to his needs."

XV

THE POSITION OF WOMEN

By Olga Leonova

Member of the Supreme Soviet of the U.S.S.R.

The Supreme Soviet of the U.S.S.R., the highest legislative organ of the Soviet Union, includes 189 women deputies among its members. This figure is many times greater than that for any other parliamentary body in the world. Moreover, the composition of this group of deputies is of unusual interest, as in addition to a number of women who achieved prominence in the course of the Revolution, it includes newcomers to public life drawn from the ranks of working women, collective farmer members, tractor drivers, school teachers, &c.

The women deputies of the Supreme Council are a minute fraction of the immense army of Soviet women in the cities and countryside employed in every kind of work under the state, on economic bodies, and in connexion with the social services, science, art, &c.

In the very first few months of its coming to power, the Soviet authority, representing as it did the workers of the country, inaugurated a series of drastic reforms affecting the legal status of women. Every vestige of the old laws relegating women to a subordinate position has been swept away.

Already in 1917 Lenin wrote: "There can be no talk of any sound and complete democracy, let alone of any

Socialism, until women take their rightful and permanent place both in the political life of the country and in the public life of the community in general."[1]

Throughout all the years of Soviet rule, the principle laid down by Lenin has been adhered to consistently and continuously in every sphere of the life of the country.

The Stalin Constitution, which has sealed the conquests won by the people, defines the position of women in the U.S.S.R., in Article 122, which reads as follows:—

> "The women of the U.S.S.R. enjoy exactly the same rights as the men in all spheres of the economic, public, cultural and political life of the community.
>
> These rights are secured to women by the fact that they are entitled to equal rights with men to labour, payment for work, rest, social insurance and education, state protection of the interests of mothers and children, leave on full pay for women during pregnancy and to the benefit of an extensive system of maternity homes, crèches and nurseries."

The authorities have not only given women equal rights with men in the eyes of the law; they have also succeeded in giving them the same status in actual fact by ensuring that both legislation and the whole organization of society enable women to lead their own life as free and independent workers.

Ever since the Soviet Union achieved victory in the Civil War and made good the havoc wrought by it and the Great War in the economic structure of the country, the number of women workers and employees in the national economy has increased year by year. The final

[1] *Lenin*, vol. xx, p. 121.

settlement of the problem of unemployment in 1930 gave a great impetus to the demand for female labour by the rapidly expanding industries of the country. Many of the women who were formerly content to be housewives became workers in factories and industrial establishments, regarding productive labour not only as a means of material existence, but as an opening to a fuller and more interesting life.

With the sole exception of a very few professions involving heavy physical labour, there is not a single branch of industry in which women are not employed. In 1937 approximately 35.5% (nearly 9½ millions) of all persons employed in the various public institutions and industrial establishments were women. Of these 3,298,000 were employed in industry, 1,252,000 in educational establishments, 725,000 in the health services, 477,000 in the transport services, &c.

At the same time there has been a marked increase in the proportion of female labour employed in the more productive branches of industry and the individual efficiency of the women workers in general is continually rising.

Notwithstanding the usual practice of paying female workers less than male labour, the authorities have from the very first insisted on equal rates of pay for women and men. Many millions of roubles were expended on overcoming illiteracy among women, on their technical training for industry and on the provision of cadres of women experts in all branches of industry. There has been a huge increase in the percentage of women among the students attending courses at higher educational establishments, technical colleges, universities and similar institutions. In 1937 no less than 41% of the total number of students in the workers' faculties were women. Women have entered many professions formerly closed to them. There were, in 1937, nearly 100,000 women engineers and technicians employed in industry. There were also about 50,000 women doctors. There is nothing unusual in seeing women working as engineers, agricultural experts, ships' captains, mechanical harvester and tractor drivers. Over 57,000 women are employed in driving tractors on the land. The extensive automatization and mechanization of laborious industrial processes has done much to facilitate the introduction of female labour into industry.

In every sphere of industrial and communal life the women have amply demonstrated their capacity to carry out the duties entrusted to them in an efficient and conscientious manner, even where these are of a nature which are comparatively new to them. There are just as many "Distinctionists" and "Stakhanovites" among female workers as among the men employed in industry. Although the movement for increasing individual output in production and an improved organization of the work bears the name of the Donetz collier, Alexis Stakhanov, the names of the "Stakhanovite" textile workers, Doussia and Maroussia Vinogradova, or the Ukrainian farm worker, Maria Demchenko, who was the first to harvest 20 tons of sugar-beet per acre, or the tractor driver, Pasha Angelina, are only a few of the many modern heroines of labour who have distinguished themselves as such in the work of building up the socialist structure.

In order that women should be able to give of their

best in labour, study and the social work of the community, it is essential that their functions as mothers should be adequately safeguarded and provided for. The authorities have never attempted to minimize the importance of these functions and there is not a single profession or calling from which married women are debarred. The authorities make a special point of assisting women to bring up and educate their children in order to ensure a healthy younger generation, and for this reason the state has from the earliest days of the Revolution devoted special care and attention to mothers and their children. Women employed in industry and public undertakings are granted four months' leave on full pay, two months before, and two months after, confinement. Immense sums are paid out from the state social insurance funds in the form of maternity benefits, and there is an extensive system of child welfare centres throughout the entire country, with nurseries, crèches and milk kitchens for infants, kindergartens and playgrounds for young children, and schools, stadiums, pioneers' palaces, summer camps, sanatoria and homes of rest for school children.

In Tsarist Russia there were, in 1914, only 550 beds in the permanent crèches and nine consulting rooms. In 1937 there were no fewer than 627,817 beds in crèches and 4175 consulting rooms. Milk kitchens for infants and children were unknown in Tsarist Russia, whereas there are now over 1500.

Hundreds of millions of roubles were spent in 1937 on building and equipping crèches, maternity centres, kindergartens and schools. Crèches are extremely popular, and although there is, of course, no compulsion whatever for a working mother to place her child in a crèche, she is invariably only too ready to do so, as she knows that the physical and spiritual welfare of her child will be the object of the utmost care and attention in the crèche.

Mothers with several children are entitled to special allowances from the state. A mother of six children receives at the birth of each additional child an annual grant of 2000 roubles for five years, while a mother of 10 children gets 5000 roubles at the birth of each additional child, plus an annual grant of 3000 roubles for four years.

The state expenditure on these grants totals thousands of millions of roubles, as in the first nine months of 1937 there were 3,300,000 infants born in the Soviet Union—a figure equal to the total population of Finland.

Notwithstanding the generous and extensive assistance afforded to mothers by the Government, neither the father nor the mother of a child is thereby relieved of parental responsibilities. Parents are obliged to educate and care for their children and this obligation devolves equally on both the father and the mother. Contrary to what obtains in certain other countries, the authorities not only refrain from any prohibition of "paternity suits," but actually facilitate and encourage them by every lawful means, deliberate non-payment of amounts due under affiliation orders being punishable under the criminal code.

If a mother should abandon her children—as, e.g., in the case of a divorce or separation—the law may in certain circumstances, and if she is earning an independent income, order her to pay alimony to her former husband.

In cases of marital disputes the law is unable to intervene unless the interests of the children are involved; except for this, the law cannot be invoked and the relations between the partners (their wish to continue their married life or to put an end to it) are solely matters for their own concern. There is complete equality of rights for the husband and wife and the Soviet woman knows nothing of the humiliating lack of civic rights in the family so common in many other countries and which, together with various social causes, leads, on the one hand, to prostitution and, on the other, to the problem of the "old maid."

While the gospel of Fascism is proclaiming that woman should revert to her original status of domestic drudge and regards her as an inferior being, materially and morally dependent on the man, the Soviet woman is absolutely free to develop her own individuality and work out her own destiny. Socialism has inspired and encouraged hosts of women to master culture, science, the arts, public administration and industrial production. The ranks of the masses have consequently produced a whole series of remarkable women who have made their mark as organizers and administrators, as actresses and artists, as bold aviatresses and parachutists and as distinguished scientists whose names are known far beyond the borders of the U.S.S.R.

The emancipation of women and their assumption of the full rights of citizenship involved the overcoming of many difficulties—more especially where it was necessary to break down traditions, hallowed by centuries, in regard to the attitude towards women. The prevailing attitude in the villages of Russia was expressed in the popular proverb "a hen is not a bird, neither is a woman a human being." The drastic change effected in the status of the peasant woman is largely due to the establishment of the system of collective farming. In the words of Stalin:

> "The work of the collective farm has emancipated the woman and has made her independent. She is no longer labouring for her father as a girl or for her husband as a wife, but primarily for herself. It is this which constitutes the liberation of the peasant woman and it is this which is the essence of the principle of collective farming by making the working woman equal to the working man."

The collective farms in the Soviet countryside have enabled the peasant women to stand on their own feet. The labour of the women on a collective farm is assessed in labour-days, just like that of the men and the number of labour-days to the credit of a young woman collective farm member is the best "dowry" she could have, since it remains at her exclusive disposal and her parents cannot touch it.

Social legislation and the establishment of a wide organization of child welfare centres in rural districts in the shape of crèches, &c., have helped the peasant women to assert their independence. When a woman collective farm member is working on the land, her child is close to her in a transportable field crèche. She gets exactly the same leave during pregnancy as the woman worker in the city and she enjoys the same benefits in respect of maternity homes, hospitals, schools, training courses and clubs of all kinds.

Material independence, opportunities for study and for

rising in the social scale, an awakening sense of self-confidence and, above all, a realization of the support given her by the laws of the country and by public opinion—all these considerations have served to arouse the latent ambition and ability of the peasant woman and of the Soviet woman in general. The women of the collective farms frequently occupy important posts and more than 18% of the members of the administrations of collective farms are women.

The progress made by the women of the Eastern races of the Soviet Union is particularly remarkable. Under Tsarism the women of the East possessed even fewer rights than those of Central Russia. They were not allowed to earn their own living by working on the land or in industrial undertakings. The articles which they made in their own homes (carpets, embroidery, &c.) were purchased from them for negligible amounts and in accordance with the generally prevailing custom, women were immured in harems and not allowed to go out without their husbands' permission. Even then they were obliged to conceal their faces by special veils.

In order to induce the women of the East to adopt the Soviet mode of life, it was necessary to break down old family customs and to educate them accordingly—a formidable undertaking. Equal rights for the women and men of the East were proclaimed by law and stringent legislation was introduced to suppress the kidnapping of girls and polygamy. Valuable work was done by the numerous women's clubs and schools in raising the standard of culture among the women of the East. The latter were impelled to take an active part in the new life of the community by the growing industrialization of the country and the introduction of collective farming. The woman of the Soviet East discarded her veil and went to work on the collective farm lands and in the newly built factories. At the present time the women of the Soviet East hold all kinds of responsible posts in the administrative and social services, enjoying exactly the same facilities for education and training and performing the same kind of work as the men. The young Turkoman and Uzbek women have taken up sport, and among these Eastern women there are now quite a number of aeroplane pilots, scientific workers, artists, actresses, &c. Fully one-third of the state employees in the national republics and regions are women.

During the years of the Soviet régime, not only has a radical change been brought about in the position of women, but the whole attitude of public opinion on the matter has undergone a complete transformation. Nobody would ever think of suggesting that a woman is incapable of carrying out this or that duty because of her sex. Women who have made their mark in industry or in the social services are treated with the utmost honour by everybody. Girls are no longer brought up for marriage, but are trained for some definite profession or calling on exactly the same footing as boys. A young man does not choose a wife for the sake of her dowry—which is now regarded as an archaic idea—but in accordance with the real dictates of his heart, while a young girl no longer thinks of marriage as her sole means of livelihood and as an inevitable destiny.

There are, of course, plenty of women in the Soviet Union who are only housewives and frequently women workers give up their occupation in a factory or other establishment on getting married, in order to devote their whole time to domestic and family duties.

However, a housewife in the U.S.S.R. need not by any means consider her life to be bounded by the four walls of her kitchen and her nursery. She is afforded every facility for co-ordinating her domestic life with a variety of communal activities. During the last two years there has been a widespread movement in the country termed the "Woman Social Workers' Movement," which aims at enrolling the wives of engineers, technicians, schoolmasters, doctors and artists for the purpose of carrying on social service within the sphere of their husbands' activity. Scores and hundreds of thousands of these housewives devote their energies, their abilities and their services to the work of improving the cultural standard and mode of life of the people. They pay special attention to all the institutions for children, communal feeding centres, amateur theatrical and artistic organizations, &c., and not infrequently they discharge important functions as public and voluntary inspectors, calling attention to irregularities and shortcomings. For these reasons the movement is meeting with sympathy and encouragement throughout the Soviet Union, being regarded as both useful and necessary. It is significant that among the hundreds of women decorated for their services to their country are a number of housewives engaged on social service work.

XVI

HOUSING CONSTRUCTION

By Professor D. Arkin

The past 10 or 12 years of the Soviet régime may be justifiably regarded as an epoch of great works. During these years new cities have sprung up all over the huge country, such as Magnitogorsk, Zaporojie, Stalinogorsk, Komsomolsk, Khibinogorsk and others. The old cities, existing for 1000 years, have grown and undergone complete reconstruction, canals have altered the flow of rivers, while factories and great generating stations have given a new aspect to the whole country.

Building in the Soviet Union is regulated by the state plans which relate both to industrial constructions and to general schemes of construction for the civil population, such as residential buildings, public institutes, schools, hospitals, clubs, palaces of culture, sanatoria and sports grounds. Town-planning is based on the fact that the municipal economy in the U.S.S.R. is the sole property of the city or town and does not belong to various private interests. The unification of municipal building plans and extensions of the urban district enable the best possible distributions and arrangement of industrial undertakings, residential districts, open spaces and public buildings to be catered for and at the same time this rationalization constitutes a vital factor in architecture. In creating a new aspect of a city, the Soviet architect can adhere to a unity of design and he can prepare his schemes to conform to a prescribed form of building complex.

The building and architecture of new cities is based on the following considerations:—

(1) Maximum co-ordination between the interests of industry and residential interests.

(2) Maximum development and properly planned distribution of public institutions affecting residents' lives, such as schools, kindergartens and crèches, theatres, clubs, &c.

(3) Widespread incorporation of open spaces in the shape of wooded parks and gardens in the territory occupied by the city.

(4) Provision for best transport facilities possible between various parts of the city.

In addition to the building of new cities, the reconstruction of old ones presents an important problem. The reconstruction of Moscow may be cited as a typical example. This ancient mercantile city of Tsarist Russia with its chaotic groups of buildings and narrow streets was utterly unsuited to the requirements of a metropolis of the Soviet Union. In 1936 a large-scale plan of radical reconstruction was put in hand. It was to be completed within 10 years and provided for the retention of certain old historic features and buildings dating from the early days of the ancient city, while a number of others were ear-marked for complete rebuilding or removal. The scheme defines the character of the network of streets, provides for a number of new main thoroughfares to facilitate municipal transport, regulates the distribution of the city's public utility institutions such as schools,

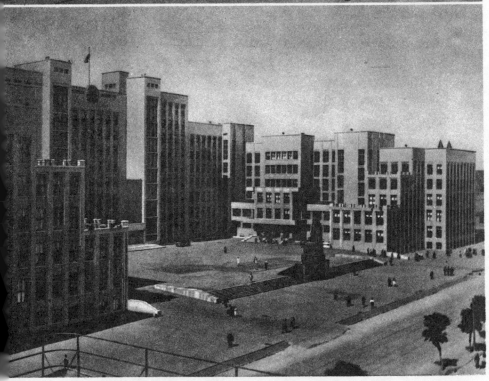

New hospital at Sverdlovsk—New government buildings in Minsk

hospitals, crèches, &c., and ensures the best possible hygienic conditions for safeguarding the health of the inhabitants. The scheme for rebuilding Moscow provides for the removal of all industrial establishments which might be regarded as inimical to the public health of the city and reserves the healthiest quarters for residential purposes. Large tracts of territory within the city itself and all round it are set aside for public parks, recreation grounds, &c. The banks of the river are to be used solely for residential buildings, as is also the new south-eastern quarter of the city which is located on high ground, amidst healthy and picturesque surroundings. A number of so-called Parks of Culture and Rest are being laid out in various parts of the city and these will provide all the necessary facilities for sport, recreation, physical culture, games and cultural pastimes.

The whole of the building work involved in the reconstruction of the city has been designed to meet the cultural needs of the population and to provide it with the most favourable conditions of life. With this object in view the denseness of the population is being kept within certain limits, while the character and type of the buildings in each residential district is being made to comply with conditions which ensure the best possible illumination and ventilation of the various buildings.

The scale of the building programme involved by the Moscow reconstruction plan may be judged from the following figures:—

Within 10 years the newly built residential buildings of Moscow will cover a total area of 161 millions square feet and during the past three years, in addition to an enormous number of houses, over 300 school buildings have been erected, together with numerous workers' clubs, crèches, kindergartens and a whole number of important public buildings.

Apart from the capital, quite a number of other large cities (Tula, Penza, Ivanovo, Voronezh and others), which were formerly backward provincial towns, have acquired an entirely new appearance. The streets have been paved with asphalt, sewage systems have been installed, tramway services provided and innumerable schools, cinemas, theatres and clubs, &c., built. Soviet architects are striving to rebuild the old cities in order to adapt them to present-day standards of life.

The reconstruction of the old eastern cities in the various Soviet republics of Central Asia and Transcaucasia presents a particularly difficult architectural problem. The regions concerned were formerly mainly agrarian, and right up to the Revolution the Central Asiatic districts, with the exception of a few places, still retained much of their feudal character, both as regards appearance and conditions of life. The radical change effected in the social life of the community, the intensive growth of industry, the industrialization of agriculture and the transformation of the latter into the collective system of farming, have completely changed the culture of these republics. The cities and towns have also undergone a transformation and what were formerly primitive Eastern settlements and so-called "kishlaks," such as were the great present-day cities of the Soviet East, like Alma-Ata (capital of Kazakhstan) or Ashkhabad (capital of Turkomenia), are now up-to-date cities of a new type. Needless to say, the architecture applied to the planning of these cities must conform to local customs and requirements arising from climatic, geographic and national considerations. In undertaking the reconstruction of an Eastern city, the architect pays the utmost regard to the forms of traditional style and appearance evolved by centuries of valuable experience, while discarding such of the old features as are merely feudal relics unsuited to the needs of the present-day Soviet East.

The main items in the architectural programme is the provision of large numbers of public buildings, such as palaces of culture, schools and kindergartens, in addition to houses for the community.

The actual types of these various public buildings represent a number of new architectural forms. For many centuries past there has been all over the world a sharp contrast between architecture intended to meet the requirements of the "chosen few" and that of the houses of the commonalty. The most modern technical methods, most expensive material and expert craftsmen were more or less concentrated on work for the needs of only the upper section of the community. The usual run of houses on the other hand was, as a general rule, built of the cheapest material available. The contrast in a modern city between the centre and the suburbs, between the luxurious residences and grandiose buildings of the central and residential quarters and the gloomy hovels of the factory districts is sometimes almost unbelievable.

Soviet architects are not only eliminating this contrast between the centre and the suburbs, but are also evolving their own new types of mass construction. A striking example of this new school of architecture is presented by the Moscow Metropolitan Railway. The underground stations of Moscow have handsome halls and vestibules, each with its own distinctive architectural style. The design of the pillars, arches and galleries, the bright colouring of the surfaces of the materials—Ural and Crimean marble—and the lighting system, are all intended to deprive the underground route of its tunnel-like character.

That the Moscow Underground Railway may justly be considered a genuine work of art is by no means fortuitous. It is symbolical of the joy of life and labour and intended for the benefit of the whole community. The same spirit has inspired the design of such purely engineering undertakings as the Volga-Moscow Canal, the locks, dams and bridges of which are designed to blend harmoniously into a unified architectural *ensemble*. Their appearance fits admirably into the surrounding countryside and man's victory over nature finds expression here in clear and attractive architectural forms. The architecture of the canal not only represents a victory of engineering over the forces of nature, but the fact that the fruits of this victory are devoted to the service of mankind, for whose sake the union of the rivers has been brought about.

This idea of service to mankind, propounded and clearly expressed by J. V. Stalin has provided the key-note for the development of Soviet architecture. It is just this idea which has inspired the building of the numerous homes of rest, sanatoria, kindergartens, pioneer houses and other public institutions for social service in the towns and villages.

Soviet architects were confronted with new problems in designing buildings such as the Palace of Culture at

The new Rostov Theatre—One of the stations of the Moscow Underground Railway

the Stalin Works in Moscow, the Gorky Memorial Art Theatre in Rostov, the Red Army House in Minsk, the Heavy Industry Commissariat Sanatorium in Kislovodsk and many workers' clubs and rest-homes. In order to apply a single style of architecture to premises of such widely differing character as club rooms, a gymnasium, an exhibition gallery, a library and observatory, children's rooms and restaurants, the architects of the Palace of Culture at the Stalin Motor Works in Moscow were compelled to have recourse to an entirely novel method of planning for the interior of the vast building. The architects (the Vessnin brothers) chose an extremely simple plan for this building. Two structures, placed at right angles to each other, contain all the various club rooms, while the intersecting point of these two structures forms the "nodal" part of the plan: staircases, unenclosed by wells, lead to the different storeys of the building and are at the same time the natural centre of the whole building. The main club premises intersect at this "staircase centre": the winter garden on the ground floor and the corridors leading to the club rooms, restaurant, children's section and library. This simple method of joining the various divisions of the plan (perpendicular intersection of the different parts of the building) is supplemented by another main entrance leading to the principal vestibule; there are separate entrances leading to the children's section and the library; furthermore, a special entrance connects the vestibule with the part which leads straight to the embankment of the River Moscow.

This plan makes the different parts of the club building very "manageable." One of the important problems with which the architect of a large public building is faced is the facilitation of entrance into the building and of circulation within it, and in the Palace of Culture this problem has been simply and correctly solved. Everything has been done to enable the visitor to find his way about the place easily, and to shorten the distance between the different parts of the building. It was this object which provided the keynote for the whole architectural plan.

The architects introduced another important element into the three dimensional design based on the ground-plan described above. They strove to attain a maximum of *unconfined* space in their building, to have open visual perspectives in the interior, to do away with the "four walled" system wherever this was feasible, i.e., wherever it was not absolutely necessary to enclose the given space within four walls. Corridors have been replaced by semi-open lobbies with side, as well as forward, perspectives; the staircases, which are not enclosed in wells, enter, as it were, into the space of each storey; finally, the flat roof-balconies form an inseparable part of the whole architectural composition and building design.

The design and construction of residential buildings naturally involved especially important problems for Soviet architects, as the immense growth of the cities rendered the provision of increased residential areas extremely urgent.

During the years of the Soviet régime approximately 650 million square feet of housing accommodation has been built in the towns and urban districts which is equivalent to 40% of that of the entire country in 1937.

In the first years after the Revolution Soviet architects evolved extremely "radical" designs for residential housing, including gigantic "communal houses" to accommodate several thousand persons, in which only a few rooms were intended for individual use, all the rest being communal. However, both the Soviet public and the Government rejected such schemes of living accommodation. The present conception of housing arrangements provides for widely organized collective cultural and public utility services, but at the same time a maximum standard of domestic comfort is laid down for each individual apartment which must be fitted up in a manner corresponding to individual and family requirements.

Soviet architects will not entertain the idea of apartment houses in the form of skyscrapers, but neither do they countenance the building of detached residences. In most cities the usual type of residential building is the five- or six-storeyed house. In the newer ones the utmost care has been taken to provide every convenience for the tenants both as regards lay-out and equipment, but at the same time the architects endeavour to give each building an attractive and artistic aspect with a certain amount of individuality.

Recent architectural activity has been largely concerned with the construction of important agricultural farming centres. Within the last few years the establishment of a large number of collective farms in various parts of the country has involved the practical problem of architectural planning in agricultural areas and the evolution of suitable building designs for residential and public purposes in the rural districts. The great size of the collective farm undertakings has enabled systematic planning in agricultural districts to be carried out and new cultural facilities for the villages in the shape of clubs, sports grounds, cultural centres, kindergartens, &c., to be provided. The country people are displaying the utmost interest in this work and to cite one example, when a special architectural conference was recently held in distant Kabarda, a mountainous region in the Caucasus, which was attended by the leading architects of the Soviet Union, the local peasant mountaineers raised a number of questions relating to buildings. This instance is by no means an isolated one.

In addition to the numerous buildings for ordinary public and residential use, Soviet architects have designed and constructed a number of monumental edifices destined to become memorials of the present age. Among such works of art is the immense Palace of the Soviets now under construction in Moscow. Its architectural design is very simple and consists of a number of superimposed cylindrical structures, which taken together give an appearance of a calm and confident upward movement. In the centre of the palace is a vast hall, a novel type of popular amphitheatre to seat 20,000 persons. The building is crowned by a huge effigy of Lenin and its total height, including the statue, is over 1300 feet.

Even a temporary building like the U.S.S.R. Pavilion at the Paris Exhibition of 1937 possessed unique and striking architectural features of its own. The simple and restrained outline of the structure, surmounted by the steel figures of a youth with a hammer and a girl with a sickle, held aloft in their raised hands, was an admirable conception of the basic theme it was intended to represent.

Soviet architects do not recognize a monopoly of any particular style of art in architecture. On the contrary, they arc developing their own work by means of the creative competition of the various current tendencies in present-day architecture, since they regard such competition as the only effective means of evolving a new style of architecture.

In the early years of the Soviet régime architecture was strongly influenced by the new schools of thought represented by the adherents of "functionalism" and "constructivism," but the situation underwent a radical change towards the end of the period of the First Five Year Plan. The improved living conditions and cultural level of the masses of the people led to a demand for a higher standard of building generally, and for a more artistic design for new buildings in particular. This caused the majority of Soviet architects to reconsider their original working methods. The principles of functionalism and constructivism were submitted to general criticism and it was pointed out that constructivism had reduced architecture to what may be described as "the fetishism of technicality." The machine had come to be regarded as an absolute æsthetic ideal, and the basic inception of all architectural creation—i.e., the man—was subordinated to the machine. The doctrine of functionalism proclaimed that the "function" of a building was the determining factor in the design of its architecture. This principle was, however, interpreted in too narrow a sense; it reduced the whole question of architecture to its technical and biological aspects and completely ignored its artistic aspect. Thus the logical outcome of this conception of functionalism was the complete denial, by at any rate some of its exponents, of architecture as an art.

As a result of lively discussions and debates between

Soviet architects in recent years, it has been generally agreed that Soviet architecture should strive not only to produce buildings of the highest technical merit at minimum cost, but also to give the architectural design of the buildings an artistic merit worthy of the great historic age in which we are now living. The architect of the present day is thus faced with the problem of utilizing modern technical science to the best advantage for the construction of buildings of the exact description required, without allowing the technical factor to become predominant. An architectural work is based on something more than the mere function of a building, since the latter is a complex unity of technical function and artistic form, this unity being organical and not merely mechanical.

Soviet architecture rejects all eclectic imitations of old styles, but considers it essential to make a profound study of the most valuable legacies bequeathed to it by classical architecture. In this respect Soviet architecture follows the teaching of Lenin who pointed out that the culture of the new social order must inherit, examine and adapt all that is best and of value in the work of humanity throughout the ages.

At the present time Soviet architects are busy seeking new forms and a new style. An architectural style embodying the spirit of our epoch cannot be evolved overnight in completed form, like the mythical Pallas Athene who sprang fully armed from the head of Zeus. A style is evolved by means of organic growth, the rate of which will be increased according to the closeness of the contact between architecture as represented by those engaged in it and the life of the people. Soviet architects realize that an architectural style is not merely a system of outline governing the whole external aspect of a structure, but its internal plan, technical basis, the details of its equipment and the manner in which it fits into the architectural *ensemble* of the city. In seeking to combine all these elements, Soviet architects are making full use of the best work of the architectural profession all over the world, of the rich architectural heritage of the peoples of the U.S.S.R. and of the highest achievements of up-to-date building technique. At the same time they are guided by a thorough knowledge of the conditions of present-day life and of the interests and needs of mankind.

XVII

THE PUBLIC HEALTH SERVICES

By Professor N. I. Propper-Grashenkov
Doctor of Medicine, Assistant People's Commissar of Public Health

The Public Health Services have always been the subject of special concern to the authorities and their policy in regard to them is based on that of the social and economic structure around which the whole life of the Soviet people is built up.

Medical attendance is not dependent on the work of private practitioners, but is entirely in the hands of the state and public authorities.

The right of every citizen to enjoy free medical attention is specifically laid down in Article 120 of the Constitution, which reads as follows:—

> "Citizens of the U.S.S.R. have the right to maintenance in old age and also in cases of sickness or loss of capacity to work.
>
> This right is ensured by the wide development of social insurance of workers and other employees at state expense, free medical service, and the provision of a wide network of health resorts for the accommodation of the workers."

Any comparison between the Soviet health services and those of Tsarist Russia is scarcely feasible. The care of public health in Tsarist Russia was practically non-

The younger generation on an outing from a Kiev nursery

existent and the country had one of the worst records in the world as regards epidemics and infant mortality, as also in respect of the small number and poor service of health centres and hospitals available. The total number of beds in hospitals and medical establishments of *every* kind—including mental asylums and lying-in hospitals—in the whole of the vast country was only 175,000 and among these only 6824 beds were available in the lying-in hospitals.

The number of doctors in Russia even during that country's time of maximum economic prosperity—in 1914—was approximately 20,000. Things were particularly bad in the so-called border regions of Russia. The annual expenditure on public health in the Central Asiatic Territories in 1913 was no higher than the equivalent of 3¾d. per inhabitant. Whereas in European Russia there was one doctor per 25-30,000 inhabitants, in the Asiatic Territories such as the former Semipalatinsk District or the Province of Ferghana (the present Kazakhstan) there was only one doctor per 120-140,000 inhabitants.

Medical training in Tsarist Russia was limited to that provided by the various chairs of theoretical and clinical medicine of the 16 medical faculties in the country. The surgical equipment of hospitals was extremely primitive and no medical or surgical requisites of any kind were manufactured in Tsarist Russia.

The Soviet Government attaches the utmost importance to all questions affecting the health of the people and the development of every branch of medical science. There are innumerable medical establishments of every kind for the welfare of the inhabitants. In the towns there are—

(1) hospitals with special departments for internal disorders, surgical cases, nervous diseases, ear, nose and throat diseases and ophthalmic ailments, mental hospitals and hospitals for the treatment of tuberculosis, venereal and skin diseases, children's hospitals as well as children's departments in the general hospitals, medico-therapeutic and X-ray establishments attached to hospitals;

(2) outside establishments comprising clinics and dispensaries with consulting-rooms and full surgical equipment, X-ray and medico-therapeutic rooms, analytical laboratories for research work of every kind, clinics and surgeries for children and special centres for the treatment of tubercular, venereal, mental and other disorders.

The outside establishments are associated with the service for the provision of medical attention in patients' homes. Each clinic or dispensary dealing with a definite quarter of the city or large industrial undertaking with a workers' housing estate has attached to it a number of medical officers whose duties include visits to patients in their own homes.

Furthermore, this organization of outside medical establishments includes a large number of health centres at various industrial undertakings for the purpose of providing medical attendance for the workers and technical staffs employed in the latter in all cases which do not actually require the services of a specialist.

Under the Soviet régime the number of beds in municipal hospitals has been increased by 450% as compared with that of the beds available in 1913. At that time the number of such beds was 89,000, whereas in 1937 it had increased 405,000. The number of dispensaries and clinics has increased nearly tenfold, and there are, at the present time, 3205 municipal hospitals and 10,055 clinics in the Soviet Union. What is more, many of these establishments are located in places where practically no hospital service of any kind was provided in the days of the Tsars. For instance, there was a total of 800 hospital beds in Uzbekistan in 1913, whereas on the 1st January, 1937, there were 13,439. In Kirgizia there were only 100 hospital beds, while now there are over 3000.

Palatial hospital buildings have been erected in many cities, as, e.g., the Metchnikov Hospital in Leningrad, the Kalinin Hospital in Kiev, the first Clinical Hospital in Tiflis, together with a series of clinical departments in Erivan, &c. All these hospitals are equipped on thoroughly up-to-date lines.

Specialized medical service is now readily available to the population and there are large numbers of special medical establishments for dealing with nervous disorders, ear, nose and throat diseases, ophthalmic maladies and ailments of the digestive organs, also dietetic centres. Treatment by blood transfusion has become very widespread, while surgery has attained a high degree of perfection. The physicians and surgeons of the U.S.S.R. have achieved some remarkable results in the treatments of diseases of the nervous system by neurotomy. A number of neurological institutes and departments exist in Moscow, Leningrad, Rostov, Gorky and other cities.

Great progress has also been made in the study of diseases of the internal secretion glands.

There are at the present time over 2500 medical stations in the various industrial undertakings, in addition to 3000 odd ambulance posts under the charge of subordinate medical personnel.

The extensive service of venereal and tubercular treatment centres has done much to reduce the number of tubercular and venereal cases, and there are now over 1000 tubercular dispensaries and treatment centres, besides 20,000 beds in the tubercular wards of the general hospitals and 42,667 beds in the tubercular sanatoria of the health resorts for consumptives.

The Moscow mortality from tuberculosis in 1936 was just half that of 1913. The incidence of disease causing loss of time among industrial workers has in recent years been reduced by 75%.

The vigorous campaign to stamp out venereal disorders has resulted in a marked reduction in the number of sufferers, more especially as regards fresh cases of syphilis; as compared with 1913, the reduction in the number of such cases is nearly 93%.

Such is the general organization of the hospital services in the cities and towns. It should, however, be noted that the specialized medical services of the latter are being used to an increasing extent by the rural populations of neighbouring districts. As regards the rural districts in general, these are primarily catered for by the district hospitals, each of which deals with a group of villages and settlements corresponding to a total population of about 25,000. A hospital of this type has three or four separate departments for the treatment of surgical, therapeutic, gynæcological-obstetric, and infectious cases. It has also an out-patients' department, which is often equipped with medico-therapeutic and X-ray apparatus and has, besides, a clinical dispensary.

Certain villages normally dependent on the district hospitals have small cottage hospitals of their own with several surgical, therapeutic and gynæcological-obstetric beds, and one or more medical officers. These hospitals also possess out-patients' departments and normally serve a population of 8 to 10,000 persons. Apart from these hospitals many villages have surgeries. The total number of rural hospitals is about 6000 with a total of 168,354 beds.

In view of the shortage of qualified medical men brought about by the enormous increase in the number of medical establishments and the difficulty of providing doctors in every settlement, some of the villages have dispensaries under the charge of an assistant surgeon. The latter are recruited from among persons with a secondary school education who have undergone a 3½-year course of medical and surgical training in one of the special colleges established for the purpose.

The district hospitals maintain a consultant service for women and children and many villages have permanent crèches for infants and young children up to four years of age.

There is a widespread organization of institutions for maternity, infant and child welfare throughout the country. These comprise—

(1) crèches in the towns and villages, women's surgeries which provide medical advice and super-

vision for expectant mothers, and infant welfare centres where new-born infants are under continuous medical supervision and obtain suitable nourishment;

(2) lying-in hospitals in the towns and villages and maternity centres in rural districts, which provide a comprehensive service for the care of all mothers in towns and of a large proportion of those in the villages and country districts;

(3) children's hospitals, both general and infectious, and convalescent establishments for children and young persons, including sanatoria, open-air schools and camps. There is also the medical service of the children's schools.

On the 1st January, 1937, there were 436 children's sanatoria with a total of 41,000 beds and 236 day and night sanatoria with a total of 15,000 beds.

There has been a large increase in the number of infant welfare centres and crèches since the government decree of the 27th June, 1936, prohibiting abortion and providing for a larger number of crèches, lying-in hospitals and similar institutions for the welfare of mothers and infants. This decree was issued to meet the views expressed by a large majority of the workers. At the present time there are over 247,000 beds in the permanent crèches of the towns and over 400,000 beds in those of the country districts. A further 100,000 beds will be added in 1938. There is a progressive annual increase in the number of beds of the maternity hospitals. The number was 76,140 in 1936, which was increased to 117,315 in 1937 and will be further raised to 141,875 in 1938; of this number 74,935 beds will be in urban and 66,940 in rural districts.

The growing prosperity of the collective farms has enabled many of the latter to establish small maternity centres of their own and at the present time the total number of beds available in these already exceeds 20,000.

The huge expenditure on maternity and infant welfare and the rising standard of living and cultural level of the people have resulted in a reduction of infant mortality by over 50%, while the returns for the first six months of the year 1937 indicate that there was an increase in the birth-rate of from 45% to 80%—varying in accordance with local conditions—as compared with 1936.

A new feature among the institutions for maternity and infant welfare is the opening of "mothers' and children's rooms" at railway stations and steamer piers. These rooms not only provide for the comfort of mothers with infants and small children waiting for trains and steamers, but have attendants who can proffer expert advice on the care and feeding of infants, &c.

The public health services include a huge number of health resorts and rest homes. The numerous chalybeate and medicinal springs of the Union have served to develop a great number of health resorts and to encourage the construction of many new sanatoria and rest homes.

Any comparison of what has been achieved in this direction with the state of things which existed in Tsarist Russia would be extremely difficult. Under the Soviet régime the health resorts and institutions cater for the working masses, whereas before they were only accessible for the privileged classes. Quite a number of former palaces have been converted into sanatoria and rest homes, and in recent years several magnificent new sanatoria have been built, such as those of the Heavy Industries and the Red Army in Sochy and the Heavy Industries Sanatorium in Kislovodsk. Many new balneological and clinical establishments and centres have also been built.

The total number of beds provided by the establishments of the above categories is 64,700. In 1937 no less than 950,000 patients passed through the sanatoria and convalescent homes and over two million persons used the rest homes.

The public health services attach great importance to the prevention of disease and their preventive service provides for both hygienic and prophylactic work in the following manner:—

(1) By means of the hygienic food research service with analysts and research laboratories at the principal food-producing establishments and the hygienic supervision—by means of qualified inspectors and analytical laboratories—of food industries, storage and distributing centres, markets, slaughterhouses, &c.;

(2) by means of sanitary inspectors and establishments for the enforcement of the statutory regulations on the hygienic and sanitary measures laid down for new residential buildings and communal institutions like theatres, clubs, cinemas, railway stations, &c., and also for the supervision of public and municipal water supplies, health resorts and housing accommodation, railway trains and stations, coastal and river port establishments, steamers, &c.;

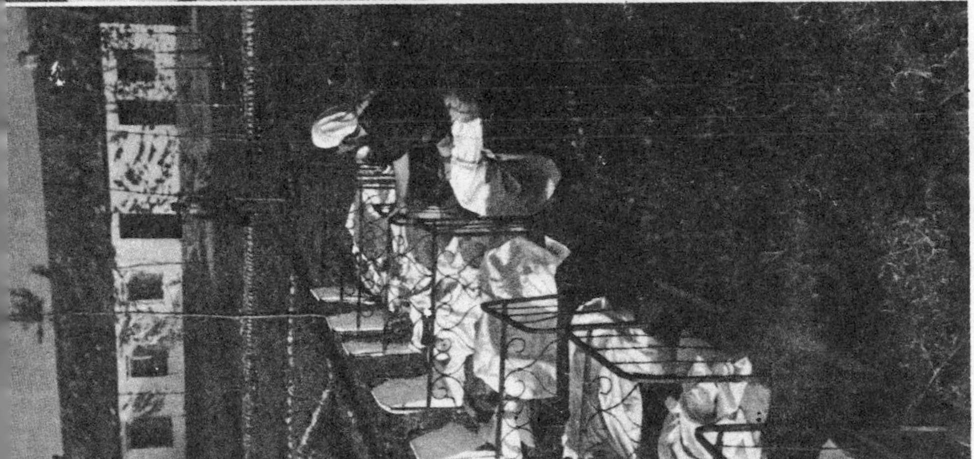

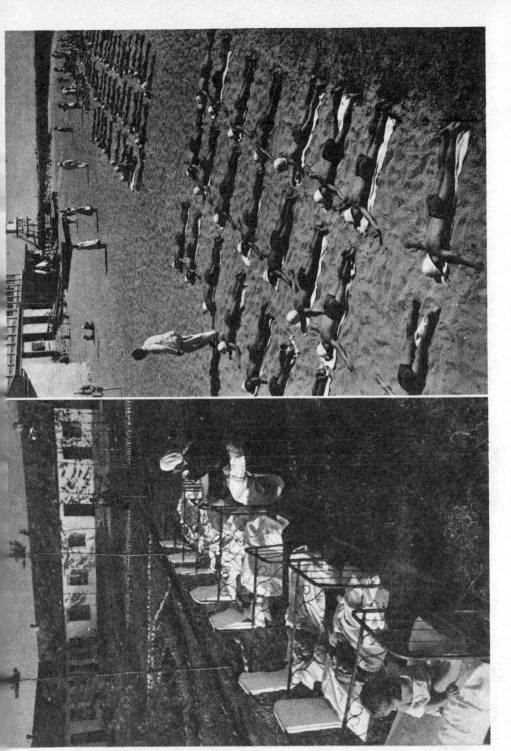

Children's sanatorium in Crimea—Crèche on a collective farm

(3) by means of sanitary inspectors and medical officers of health supervising the hygienic aspect and sanitary conditions of labour in industrial undertakings and the precautions necessary for the safety and health of the workers employed in these.

The organization for combating epidemics includes—

(1) laboratories in urban and rural districts, with expert epidemiologists whose duty is the prevention, as far as is humanly possible, of the outbreak of any epidemic, or, in the event of such outbreaks, the application of the measures necessary to overcome them;

(2) disinfecting stations and centres, with medical officers, personnel and equipment of every kind (such as disinfecting chambers, &c.) for the purpose of disinfecting, fumigating and decontaminating premises and infected articles as required. Epidemiologists and bacteriologists with disinfecting and vaccination equipment are frequently organized as mobile units which are moved about as necessary.

The work performed by the medical officers, sanitary inspectors and establishments of the above organizations, has resulted in an all-round improvement in the hygienic conditions prevailing throughout the country. For instance, in Tsarist Russia there were on the average more than 100,000 fresh cases of smallpox every year, whereas the Soviet Government have at the present time almost completely stamped out this disease, and in the first 9½ months of 1937 there were only 34 cases of smallpox in the entire country. The number of cases of typhoid fever in 1937 was 75% lower than in 1913. The child mortality from infectious diseases (scarlet fever, measles and diphtheria) has been very greatly reduced and an extensive system of preventive inoculation against diphtheria is at the present time being successfully applied, while the inoculations of a serum for the prevention of measles has produced remarkable results. These measures have led to a reduction of over 67% in child mortality as compared with the figures for 1913.

The campaign against epidemics has proved particularly successful in the national republics which, in Tsarist days, were doomed to extinction owing to the dying out of their inhabitants. Diseases such as trachoma, scabies and the like, which were the result of poverty and dirt, were widespread under the conditions obtaining in Tsarist Russia. At the present time these diseases have, to a great extent, been stamped out in the national republics. For example, the number of cases of trachoma in the Tartar Republic has decreased by 89%, in the Kalmyk Republic by 75% and in the Chuvash Republic by 61%.

The extensive system of regional and district sanitary stations has enabled a marked reduction in the number of outbreaks of typhus and other infectious diseases to be effected, as these stations are equipped with every facility for the analysis of foodstuffs and water, clinical analysis and with supplies of prophylactic vaccines and serums, disinfecting gear, &c., under the charge of qualified medical personnel.

There are at the present time over 8822 medical officers of health in the Soviet Union and some thousands of medical students are now receiving instruction in public health and hygiene in the special faculties provided for the purpose. Certain specialized secondary medical schools are established for the purpose of training thousands of sanitary inspectors as assistants to the medical officers of health. The education and training of physicians and surgeons is receiving special attention.

As previously stated, there were only some 20,000 doctors in Russia before the Revolution, and the number of medical faculties was only 16. At the present time 106,000 qualified medical men are employed in the Union and 100,000 students are attending courses at the higher medical schools. There are in all 72 colleges and schools —of which 50 are medical—belonging to the various faculties of preventive, hygienic, pediatric, and general medicine and surgery, besides 10 higher academies of pharmacy for turning out highly qualified pharmacists for industrial and dispensary work and 12 colleges of dentistry for the training of dental surgeons.

The U.S.S.R. possesses 311 medical research laboratories and institutes of various kinds. Every separate branch of sanitation, hygiene, epidemiology or other section of the science of healing has its own specialized research institute in which no less than 15,000 scientists and some 20,000 technical assistants are employed and for the maintenance of which the state annually provides a sum of several hundred million roubles.

The work of these establishments is co-ordinated with that of the hospital and other health services and is mapped out year by year to meet the requirements of current problems of theoretical and practical medicine.

In order to keep this vast organization of medical schools and research institutes supplied with professional intelligence, there are some 35 quarterly, monthly and fortnightly medical periodicals which deal not only with subjects of general medical interest, but also with questions concerning special matters like otology, ophthalmology, &c. There are also several medical publishing organizations which publish thousands of medical works every year, the editions being from 10 to 30,000 or more copies and comprising textbooks, instructions, dissertations and literature dealing with matters of biological and medical interest. The medical publishing establishments also publish classical works on biology and medicine and reports of important new developments in the field of present-day biology and medicine in every part of the world.

The colossal expansion of the industries of the Soviet Union and the importance attached by the authorities to all questions of public health has led to the birth of a rapidly growing industry connected with the preparation and manufacture of pharmaceutical products and drugs, medical requisites and surgical instruments. This industry already possesses many factories and works, with numerous drawing offices for carrying out experimental and design work in conjunction with these and certain scientific research institutes.

At the present time Soviet industry is producing every article of modern medical and surgical equipment including medico-therapeutic requisites, and quite recently it has commenced to manufacture most elaborate high-precision measuring devices (oscillographs and high-power microscopic gear) and illuminating apparatus. Optical goods and microscopes are admirably turned out by Soviet industry and the supply is almost equal to the huge demand from the numerous hospitals and scientific research institutes of the country.

The annual expenditure on the public health services is growing year by year, that in 1937 being over 7000 million roubles and that provided for 1938, 9500 million roubles.

The whole of the establishments of the public health services, including the scientific research institutes, medical schools and medical industrial undertakings, are under the jurisdiction of the People's Commissariat of Public Health of the U.S.S.R., and of the People's Commissariats of Public Health of the 11 Union Republics. The various regions, territories and autonomous republics likewise possess their own local public health authorities, as have also all the urban and rural districts throughout the country.

XVIII

SOCIAL INSURANCE

By V. Kotliar

Principal of the Insurance Department of the Central Council of Trade Unions

"Of all the world's great capital resources, the greatest and the most effective are human beings," said Stalin in the course of one of his public speeches in 1935.

The care for the welfare of humanity implied by these words characterizes the entire organization of state social insurance as one of the greatest conquests of the mass of the workers in their Revolution.

The authorities embarked on the practical realization of their programme for state social insurance immediately they came into power and while the country was still engaged in the struggle against the forces of counter-revolution and intervention and the entire strength of its people and resources was mobilized in defence of the young republic, the immense strain of the effort made in those terrible years did not deter the authorities from laying the foundations of a system of social insurance of incredibly liberal character. When the process of national reconstruction and the restoration of the country's means of production had reached a more definite stage, the programme of state social insurance was gradually extended and developed on a wider basis to embrace a larger section of the workers and to cover a greater variety of cases in which public assistance might be given them.

During the First Five Year Plan (1928-32) the estimates for social insurance already provided for expenditure under a number of votes beyond that for allowances to those temporarily incapacitated from work, including items such as infant crèches and kindergartens, milk kitchens, dietetic feeding, sick funds, &c. The annual expenditure on social insurance is increasing every year.

It is important to note that the complete and final eradication of unemployment has enabled the Government to apply a large proportion of their social insurance funds, which formerly was expended on unemployment relief, to improvements.

At the present time the benefits of social insurance are enjoyed by *all* wage-earners, i.e., by workers and employees of every description. Emphasis must be laid on the fact that not a kopeck is contributed by the worker or employee towards the cost of social insurance; the state pays the contributions for every insured person in accordance with the statutory scale laid down. In 1937 the total sum expended by the state on social insurance amounted to 6323 million roubles. This is equivalent to an average of 6.3% of the total sum expended on wages in the country. In the various trade unions the state pays the following percentage supplements to wages as its social insurance contributions: in the miners' union, 9%; oil union, 8.4%; metal workers' union, 7.1%; medical workers' union, 5.9%; pre-school workers' union, 7.9%, &c.

An important development in the growth of social insurance is marked by the transfer by the state in 1934 of its administration and working to the trade unions, who thereby became responsible for the organization of the whole of the social insurance services and the many millions of their funds. As the trade unions are established on a system corresponding to the various branches of industry with which they are concerned, this change brought about a considerable improvement in the position of individual insured persons, since the scale of insurance for each class of workers could be adapted to their special requirements. All industrial undertakings and establishments elect so-called insurance delegates at general meetings of the workers and employees and these delegates deal with all insurance matters affecting their particular establishment.

Their duties include the supervision of the scales of pensions and reliefs granted, the conduct of the various rest houses and sanatoria, &c., the visiting of sick persons in their homes and the care of the infants and children in the crèches and kindergartens, &c. These insurance delegates are obliged to render detailed reports of their work at the public meetings of the workers and employees responsible for their election.

The total number of these insurance delegates throughout the country is approximately half a million and they therefore constitute a huge army of insurance workers.

The insurance delegates nominate some of their number to serve on insurance committees, which consist of from 9 to 35 members, according to the number of insured persons represented. The insurance committees work in conjunction with the local trade union committee of the industrial undertaking or other establishment and direct the work of the insurance delegates employed there. The services rendered by both insurance delegates and members of insurance committees are voluntary and carried out in their spare time.

Payment of benefits takes place at the worker's place of employment, so that there is maximum contact between insurance service and work.

The Stalin Constitution has enhanced the importance of social insurance in the general system of welfare and cultural services organized for the workers.

Article 120 of the Constitution states:

> "Citizens of the U.S.S.R. have the right to maintenance in old age and also in case of sickness or loss of capacity to work.
>
> This right is ensured by the wide development of social insurance of workers and other employees at state expense, free medical service, and the provision of a wide network of health resorts for the accommodation of the workers."

The realization of the rights ensured by the Constitution in regard to rest, old-age pensions, sick benefit, maternity benefit and welfare, physical training of young people, the work done to ensure to the workers a well-to-do and cultured life—all these things represent an immense field for the activities of the social insurance services.

The object of these services is to afford relief to the workers in *all* cases of actual necessity and their functions are both wide and varied. They include, in the first place, the provision of relief for workers temporarily incapacitated from work, as well as for disabled workers who are at work, compensation to dependants in cases of death, payment of funeral expenses, &c. Immense sums are expended on prophylactic treatment (rest homes, sanatoria, and dietetic nourishment). Mothers and children are cared for by means of maternity grants (provision of treatment during pregnancy and childbirth, feeding and nursing for mothers and infants, supply of "layettes" for the latter). A portion of the cost of maintaining factory inspectors and of safeguarding the health of workers by the provision of safety appliances and other measures of a similar nature is borne by the social insurance funds, the balance being met from public funds.

The mutual aid funds established at the various industrial undertakings and other places of employment for the purpose of providing financial assistance to workers in temporary need by means of loans and mortgages free of interest are also administered by the social insurance services and no less than 104 million roubles has been assigned to such mutual aid funds in the 1938 estimates.

In the course of his speech on the proposed Constitution J. V. Stalin called attention to the changes which have in recent times taken place in the class structure of Soviet society, saying, "the dividing line between the working-class and the peasantry, and between these classes and the intelligentsia, is being obliterated, which means that the old class exclusiveness is disappearing. This means that the distance between these social groups is steadily diminishing. Secondly, they signify that the economic contradictions between these social groups are subsiding, are becoming obliterated."

Social legislation is endeavouring to put these principles into practice, and in 1937 all existing restrictions applied to the black-coated as compared with the manual workers of the corresponding branch of national economy were abolished as regards old age and disability pensions, sick benefit and maternity benefit.

The intensive growth of the national economic resources and the immense strides made by the country's industries during the Second Five Year Plan (1933-37) enabled expenditure on the social insurance of workers to be increased. In 1936 the total expenditure of the trade unions on social insurance was 3837 million roubles as against 2603 millions in 1935. In 1937 this expenditure rose to 5077 millions.

The year 1937 may be regarded as epoch-making in the history of the Soviet social insurance as it was marked by the introduction of important new measures for strengthening and widening its whole system. The Council of People's Commissars of the U.S.S.R. altered the social insurance contributory scales and greatly increased the expenditure of the social insurance services on the growing cultural and everyday needs of the members of the trade unions.

The 1938 estimates provide for an expenditure of 5795 million roubles on social insurance, which is 15.8% more than in the previous year.

The amounts to be expended under the different votes have been increased correspondingly, as, for example, the expenditure on maternity grants has been increased from 785 to 990 million roubles (an increase of 26.1%) and on child welfare (such as crèches, kindergartens, children's theatres, &c.) to 651 million roubles, equivalent to an increase of 36.2% to the previous 12 months' expenditure.

Pioneers' camps provide one of the best forms of healthy and cultural recreation for school children during the holidays. In 1937 a sum of 108.3 million roubles was assigned for this purpose and over 310,000 children benefited by a stay in pioneers' camps. In 1938 estimates provide for an expenditure of 139.3 million roubles under this heading (for 400,000 children). The trade unions are now building permanent pioneers' camps which will also be available for school children during the winter holidays.

There is also an annual increase in the amounts allotted to the treatment of children of insured persons in sanatoria. Some of the finest Black Sea health resorts are set apart from the curative treatment of children, as, for example, Louzanovka (near Odessa), Eupatoria, Anapa, &c.

The Soviet Government have at all times attached great importance to physical training and sport for the workers, in order to benefit their health, to harden them and to develop their creative power and ability. Sports grounds, ski courses, swimming-pools and gymnasia are now available for the workers. These amenities cost the social insurance services large sums of money apart from the grants made by "The Committee for Physical Culture and Sport," the state department of the Soviet Union. Certain items of expenditure, such as the construction of sports grounds, are defrayed jointly from the funds of the insurance services and the committee.

The trade unions possess 621 rest homes and 216 sanatoria. In 1938, 2,280,000 persons were sent to rest homes, as against 2,008,000 in the previous year, and 439,000 persons were sent to sanatoria and health resorts, as against 353,000 in the preceding year. In addition to this, hundreds of thousands of insured persons make use

The sanatorium of the Water Transport Workers at Sochi on the Black Sea

of the single-day rest homes and regularly spend their weekly day of rest in them.

The expenditure on the above institutions and other recreational amenities for the workers (travel, physical culture and parks of culture and rest, &c.) by the social insurance services may be judged from the following table:—

Year.	Cost of rest homes, sanatoria, health resorts and travelling, in millions of roubles.	Cost of physical culture and parks of culture and rest, in millions of roubles.
1933 - - -	238.0	7.5
1934 - - -	303.5	6.0
1935 - - -	470.4	11.6
1936 - - -	650.7	42.3
1937 - - -	923.1	120.4

For 1938 the social insurance services have allowed 1027 million roubles for rest homes, sanatoria, health resorts and travelling, and 200 millions for physical culture and sport.

One of the chief features of the work performed by the social insurance services of all the trade unions is the determined fight against sickness, which is meeting with a rapidly growing measure of success. The great improvement in the standard of living of the workers, the success of the Government's programme for raising the efficiency of the public health services and the great improvement in the work of the trade unions as regards social insurance, protection of labour, and prevention of disease, have all helped to bring about a further marked reduction in sickness amongst the workers. In certain establishments the reduction in the number of cases of accident and injury in 1937 was no less than 25% on the 1936 figures.

The trade unions control the powerful machinery of the Labour Inspection which enables them to exercise a close supervision of the conditions of labour in every industrial undertaking or public establishment, in regard both to high productivity and quality of labour and to the health of the workers.

The Government have striven to ensure that the worker should continue to live in comfort when he can no longer labour by the provision of a system of old-age pensions or, if necessary, by giving him lighter work. The law compels the administrative authorities of industrial undertakings and establishments to transfer workers and employees who are no longer able to work to full capacity to other suitable work of a lighter kind in the same undertaking or establishment and in accordance with the recommendations of an expert medical labour board.

The growth of the national expenditure on disability pensions and the provision of employment for disabled persons is proved by the following figures:—

Year.	Total cost of pensions in millions of roubles.	Rate of monthly pensions as compared with 1931 rate.
1932 - -	484.8	114.4%
1933 - -	639.5	146.1%
1934 - -	847.1	179.0%
1935 - -	1093.9	219.5%
1936 - -	1295.0	245.9%

The increase in the estimates under the vote for state pensioners is closely bound up with the steady improvement of the whole system of social insurance and with the continuous rise in the rate of the actual pensions paid. As may be seen from the above figures, the average monthly pension of a disabled worker (whether old-age pensioner or one who has worked a certain number of years) has increased by 150%. Pensions to families who have been deprived of their breadwinner have been increased *pro rata*—or rather more.

The above benefits under the Soviet system of social insurance do not comprise the whole measure of assistance afforded to workers when necessary. Disability, sickness and old-age pensions are paid from the funds of the People's Commissariat for Social Maintenance of the Union Republics of the U.S.S.R. and their expenditure on pensions payable in cash, on the provision of employment and on other substantial benefits for pensioners runs into thousands of millions of roubles.

The People's Commissariat for Social Maintenance of the Russian Soviet Federative Socialist Republic (the largest republic of the Union) alone possesses over 300 retreats for disabled and aged workers, of whom 33,000 are fully provided for in these establishments at the cost of the state. This same Commissariat also has 360 miscellaneous factories and workshops, ranging from metal-working establishments to toy-making shops. The Disabled Workers' Co-operative administered by the Commissariat, referred to above, embraces all the artisans and handicraftsmen for whom employment is provided in special workshops of their own, &c. Disabled workers are thereby enabled to engage in congenial labour of a nature suited to their health and degree of disability.

Special attention is paid to the welfare and medical services for pensioners. The Commissariat for Social

Maintenance of the Russian Soviet Federative Socialist Republic administers 235 hospitals and health establishments in its territory alone. These comprise hospitals, rest homes and sanatoria. There are also an immense number of mutual-aid funds for assisting pensioners and their families.

The introduction of the system of collective farming in the agricultural districts has effected a vast improvement in the position of old p ople and invalids there. The Stalin regulations for th establishment of co-operative agricultural associations provide for a *special fund* in each collective farm for the purpose of affording pecuniary assistance to old people, invalids, temporarily disabled collective farm members and indigent families of Red Army soldiers, as well as for the provision of crèches and relief for orphans. The fund is maintained by means of a 2% levy on the gross output of the collective farm. By this means an effective way of providing for the aged and disabled members of the collective farm is ensured at all times.

XIX

PUBLIC EDUCATION

By A. Likhatchev

Assistant Commissar of Education of the R.U.F.S.R.

During the 21 years of the existence of the Soviet Union the aspect of the country has undergone a radical change. A formerly backward and poverty-stricken country has now become an enlightened, cultured and strong socialist power.

Tsarism purposely maintained the people in a state of ignorance. It will suffice to recall the words spoken by that notorious reactionary of the time of Alexander III and Nicholas II, the Chief Procurator of the Holy Synod Pobiedonostzev: "Popular education is undoubtedly harmful, as it teaches people to think. . . . It is easier to rule an illiterate nation."

The Soviet authority has, from its very inception, attached the utmost importance to the matter of public education.

The new régime has awakened the creative instincts of the peoples inhabiting the Union and is enabling the hitherto inarticulate masses of these peoples to devote their creative energies to the fulfilment of their aims towards a cultural life.

The cultural structure of the Soviet Union is continuously growing. Half the population are studying in elementary, secondary and higher schools and through innumerable courses of instruction of every kind. Illiteracy, the greatest evil inherited from Tsardom, has now been completely eliminated in accordance with the law of the land. Former farm labourers, herdsmen and children of cooks have become engineers, doctors, agricultural experts, teachers, actors and scientists.

Article 121 of the Stalin Constitution reads as follows:—

> "Citizens of the U.S.S.R. have the right of education.
>
> This right is ensured by universal, compulsory elementary education; by the fact that education, including higher (university) education is free of charge; by the system of state scholarships for the overwhelming majority of students in the higher schools; by instruction in schools being conducted in the native language, and by the organization of free vocational, technical and agronomic training for the toilers in the factories, state farms, machine and tractor stations and collective farms."

This article of the Constitution, like all the others, only expresses what is already being done.

In 1930 a time limit was set to the period within which universal elementary education was to be enforced and this programme was actually realized within the minimum period of three years.

In 1933-34 compulsory elementary education was the universal practice throughout the country, while in the cities and workers' settlements a system of general and compulsory school training over a period of seven years, was in force.

All children between the ages of 8 and 11 years now

receive school instruction in all parts of the country, including the most remote districts. There were approximately 30 million children in the schools during the school year of 1937-38.

The policy of the Tsarist Government in regard to schools for the non-Russian elements of the population was to close down existing schools and prohibit the opening of new ones. In the school year of 1914-15 there were only 155,000 children between the ages of 8 and 11 years in the schools of Georgia, whereas there are now 658,000 such school children in the Georgian S.S.R. In the Turkoman S.S.R. the number of such children at school has increased 23-fold—from 7000 to 163,000—while in Kazakhstan, in which the entire population was illiterate in Tsarist days, over 60% of the people can now read and write. Nearly one million children are now being taught in the 7620 schools of Kazakhstan. In the Tadjik S.S.R.—where there were only 400 children receiving school instruction in 1914-15—there are now 199,000 children at school. Similarly startling figures can be quoted for nearly all of the remaining republics.

The building of schools is being actively pushed forward throughout the country. During the four years of the Second Five Year Plan (1932-36) 16,725 new schools were built in the U.S.S.R., 13,784 of them being in rural districts. During the entire period of the Soviet régime over 50,000 new school buildings have been erected in the country. Such new construction has been especially great in the national republics where hundreds of thousands of children have secured palatial new school buildings.

The Government have adopted a standardized classification for schools, comprising elementary, secondary and higher educational establishments. Elementary schools have four forms, while secondary schools have either seven (these being the so-called "reduced course schools") or 10 forms.

The curriculum of a Soviet school includes such subjects as natural history, mathematics, physics, chemistry, astronomy, &c. The systemized course of natural history based on evolutionary teaching serves to inculcate a scientifically materialistic view of life in the minds of the children.

The teaching of subjects like history and the history of literature is designed to acquaint students with important historical events and characters, chronological data, the masterpieces of world literature and the most important historical documents. Only concrete historical facts are utilized for the purpose of providing the scientific and historical basis of the Marxist view of history to which students are introduced.

One of the compulsory subjects in secondary schools is a foreign language—English, French or German. The study of ancient languages is confined to higher educational establishments.

Special attention is paid to juvenile physical training in schools.

The curriculum and method of teaching of all schools are co-ordinated in such a manner that any child who has completed a course of study in the four forms of an elementary school is free to enter the fifth form of a secondary school. On finishing a secondary school, students may enter a higher educational establishment, those receiving "Excellent" certificates from their secondary school being exempted from the entrance examination.

School instruction is free throughout and in the higher colleges and training schools students receive state stipends, board and lodging in hostels, textbooks and all requisites for study.

All Soviet schools are essentially secular in character. The Constitution lays down that all citizens enjoy freedom of conscience; church and state are separated in the U.S.S.R., and the schools are independent of the church. No religious instruction of any kind is permitted in the schools, which are protected against clerical influence by the law.

Teaching in all schools is carried out in the native language of the students and school textbooks are printed in the 70 different languages spoken by the various peoples and nationalities. But Russian, which is the common state language, is also included in the curriculum of the non-Russian schools. The study of the history of their native country and its literature is compulsory for all scholars and that of the Constitution is obligatory in the secondary schools.

The co-education of girls and boys is universal. In the days of Tsardom no school instruction whatever was provided for girls among various peoples like the Caucasians, the Tartars, the Bashkirs, &c., whereas at the present time *all* girls of school age, of every nationality, attend school.

Since the moral outlook of every member of society is the result of the teaching received in early life, the authorities have spared no pains to ensure that the material and ideologic training of children should make them grow up as honest workers wholeheartedly devoted to their socialist country. The schools bring up the children in a spirit of Soviet humanism and genuine love towards the workers of all countries—irrespective of their race or nationality. Respect and solicitude for public property, diligence in labour, respect for the older generation, healthy and unaffected relations between boys and girls—these are the aims of a Soviet school.

The school system is built up on discipline and the authority and guidance of the teaching staff. Corporal punishment of any kind is strictly prohibited and persons having recourse to such are not only liable to summary dismissal, but to legal penalties.

Valuable assistance in the school training of children is afforded by the various public organizations, more especially the Young Communist League.

The main object of the schools is to develop the personality of the children in every respect, to put an end to the difference between manual and intellectual labour, and to educate the future guardians of the building-up of socialist society.

The Government pay great attention to the training of properly qualified specialist workers of every description and an immense increase in the number of higher and secondary specialized colleges and schools, as compared with that of Tsarist Russia, has taken place.

In 1914 there were only 79,000 students in the secondary specialized schools, whereas in 1937 there were nearly 10 times as many, viz., 769,000. In 1914 there were 233 such colleges and schools in the country, whereas in 1937 there were 2850.

There are at the present time 470 industrial, 592 agricultural and 394 teachers' training schools of medium grade. The increase in the number of higher educational establishments is equally great. In 1914 there were 91 of these with 112,000 students, while in 1937 there were 700 with 542,000 students.

Under the old régime no higher educational establishments for the training of teachers were in existence, except for one or two maintained by private persons or public bodies. At the present time 197 teachers' training colleges are maintained by the state and the number of students under instruction in these is 137,000.

Many of the present-day republics of the Soviet Union had no secondary schools of any kind in the old days, whereas they now possess numerous higher and secondary colleges and schools for the provision of specialized training for students of the nationality concerned.

The following table gives details of the numbers of such colleges and schools and of the students attending them:—

Republic.	Secondary Specialist Schools.	No. of Students.	Higher Colleges.	No. of Students.
Ukrainian S.S.R. -	473	142,000	117	110,000
Armenian S.S.R. -	45	8,400	9	4,300
Turkoman S.S.R. -	27	4,600	4	1,400
Bashkir A.S.S.R. -	43	11,000	4	2,500
Karelian A.S.S.R. -	11	3,300	2	300
Marüsk A.S.S.R. -	12	2,700	3	800
Tartar A.S.S.R. -	43	12,300	12	9,600
Ossetin A.S.S.R. -	11	3,100	6	2,500

In addition to the above educational establishments, there are a large number of specialized courses of a novel kind known as workers' faculties, for workers in industrial undertakings and collective farms who have attended school for seven years, for the purpose of giving them a three-year course of preparation for a higher educational establishment. In 1936 there were 772 such specialized courses with an attendance of 276,000 students.

The workers, while continuing production, attend special courses for the purpose of improving their qualifications. Thus, in 1936, in the heavy industries 40% of the workers completed technical courses and 24% continued to attend them. Such technical courses are largely attended by an increasingly great proportion of both the urban and rural populations.

During the past two and a half years the People's Commissariat of Agriculture has trained about one and a half million drivers of tractors, harvesters and motor vehicles.

The Soviet authorities have done much educational work, both political and general, amongst adults. In pre-War Tsarist Russia barely 30% of the total population could read and write, while among some of the non-Russian sections of the people this percentage was only from 3 to 5. Such a thing could not, of course, be tolerated by the Soviet Government and drastic measures to combat adult illiteracy were adopted. Altogether some 40 million illiterates have been taught to read and write and, generally speaking, the whole of the adult population below 40 years of age is now literate.

The progress made in this direction by some of the non-Russian republics is especially marked. Thus, in 1920 only 3% of the population of the Kabardino-Balkarian Republic (Caucasus) could read and write,

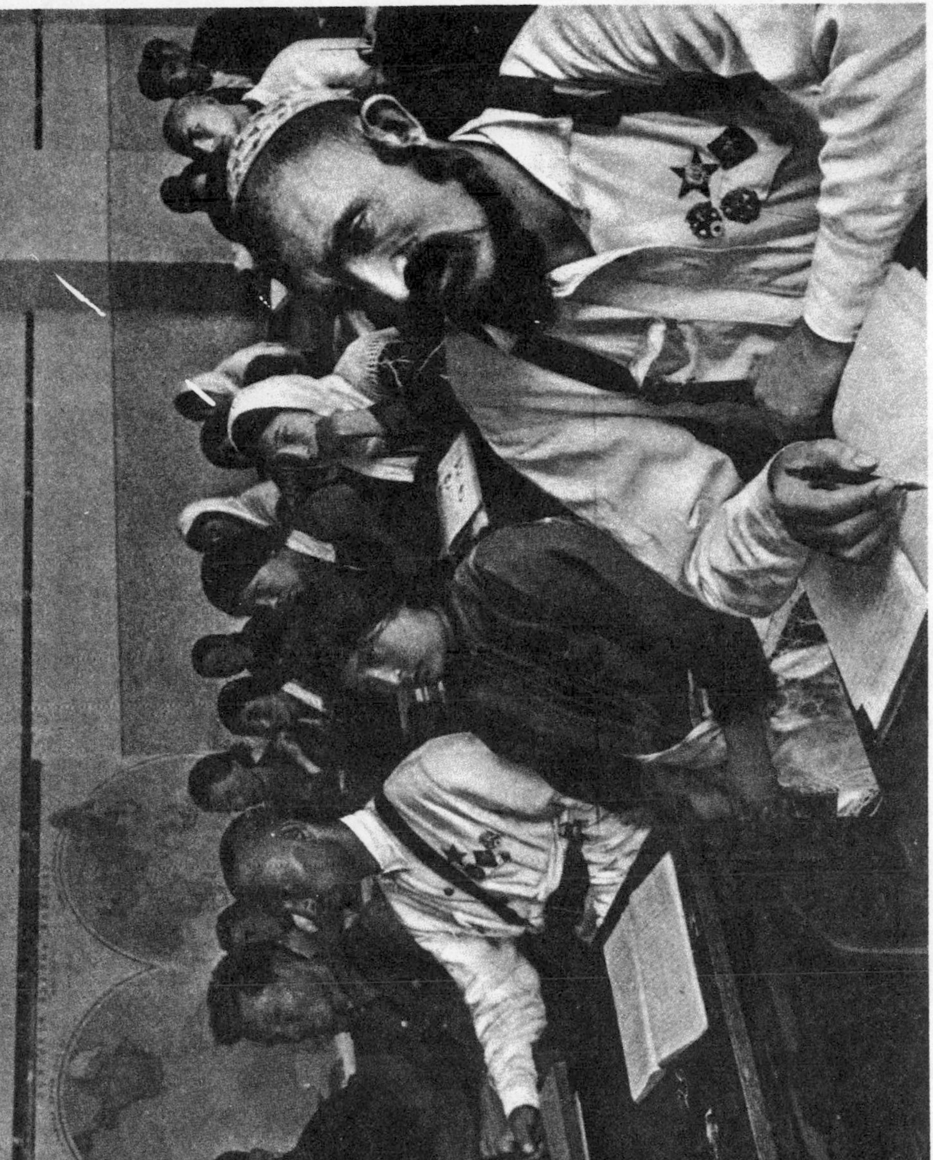

An adult school in Uzbekistan

whereas now the whole of the population is able to do so. Under the Tsarist régime only 2 to 3% of the population of Uzbekistan could read and write, whereas now the number of illiterates among them is negligible.

At the present time one of the main problems is the adequate provision of schools for persons who can only *just* read and write, in order that these may improve their education. The more advanced persons of this category can now attend continuation schools which provide a three-year course of instruction. Correspondence courses in various subjects have also been established.

Valuable work in raising the cultural level of the people has been done by the provisions of innumerable village reading-rooms, clubs, houses of culture, libraries, parks of culture and rest, theatres, cinemas, broadcasting stations, &c. In the smaller villages the village reading-room serves as a cultural centre. It provides newspapers, a small library, pictures and posters. Specially trained workers talk to the peasants, read the newspapers with them, lend them library books and arrange debates and conferences on subjects of particular interest to collective farm workers.

In the large villages and rural centres there are clubs in which theatrical performances and lectures are given and which have sound film equipment, libraries, &c. At the present time there are 81,000 rural clubs and village reading-rooms and over 36,000 libraries.

The trade unions conduct an intensive educational and cultural campaign among their members, all of whom must be literate. Special schools are provided by the professional associations for the education of the less literate members, in addition to which technical courses of instruction are available for improving the trade qualifications of members. These bodies also have their own clubs and arrange for the smaller industrial establishments to have "Red Corners," libraries, sports grounds, parks of culture and rest and similar amenities for the workers.

Welfare of school teachers is a matter of especial concern to the Government: the policy of the Tsarist Government towards them was such as to cause Lenin to refer to it in the following terms: "Russia is poverty-stricken when it comes to paying elementary school teachers. They receive bare pittances. They are compelled to starve and to freeze in unheated and almost uninhabitable huts. . . . Elementary school teachers are baited by every police inspector or village reactionary, by every self-appointed watchman or detective, to say nothing of the oppression and persecution by the authorities. Russia is poor when it comes to remunerating honest workers in the cause of popular education, but wealthy enough to squander untold millions on a parasitic nobility, on military adventures, on subsidies to sugar manufacturers, oil magnates and similar objects."[1]

Under the new régime of socialism the school teachers occupy an honourable place. The authorities devote great attention to their recruitment and training and their number has gone up from 493,000 in 1923 to 2,190,000 in 1937. This immense army of educational workers is welded together into a single great family of teachers. The former general contempt displayed by secondary school teachers towards those of the elementary schools, so characteristic of Tsarist Russia, has now disappeared.

[1] Lenin, *Works*, vol. xvi., p. 412.

The care lavished on the teaching profession by the Government is reflected in the ample remuneration which is provided for them. The total earnings of the teachers have increased 41-fold in the past 12 years—from 214.4 million roubles in 1924 to 8800 million roubles in 1937. Immense sums from public funds are spent on the training, housing, cultural recreation and medical attendance of Soviet school teachers.

The educational workers sincerely appreciate this care of the state for their welfare and scores of thousands of Soviet school teachers have given practical proof of the fact that they regard the education of the rising generation as "an honourable, glorious, noble and heroic task" (Stalin).

Expenditure on education is the first item in the financial budget of the programme of development of social culture.

In the year 1937 alone expenditure on education went up by 34.1% and there were corresponding increases in the remaining outlay on schools. The rise in the cost of each scholar attending school is illustrated by the following comparative figures for the years 1936 and 1937:—

	1936.	1937.
Elementary schools -	74.9 roubles.	129.8 roubles
Secondary schools -	292.8 ,,	356.2 ,,

Apart from expenditure on schools, large sums are also appropriated for pre-school establishments, no less than 894 million roubles being assigned for kindergartens in the 1937 budget.

The expenditure on children's homes has gone up from

671 million roubles in 1936 to 826 millions in 1937, viz., an increase of 23.1%.

Expenditure on combating illiteracy, adult education and continuation schools in 1937 was 244 million roubles, while that on cinemas, theatres, broadcasting, museums and other artistic and educational objects, including libraries and the press, amounted to 656 million roubles in 1937.

The most important item in the educational budget is the expenditure connected with the higher and secondary specialized colleges and schools (universities, technical schools, &c.). A sum of 6488 million roubles was expended under this heading in 1937, showing an increase of 35.1% on the 1936 expenditure. The appropriations for workers' and employees' technical courses in 1937 were as follows:—

	Million roubles.
By People's Commissariat of Heavy Industries -	218
" " " " Agriculture, - -	350
" " " " Transport - -	114
" " " " Public Education -	325
" " " " Public Health -	84

Immense strides have been made in the realm of scientific research of every branch of industry and study. The state expenditure on scientific research establishments in 1937 was 824 million roubles or more than 24.8% greater than in the previous year.

In addition to this expenditure on scientific work, further substantial sums are assigned for this object by the People's Commissariats connected with national economy in order to maintain or encourage the building of research institutes and laboratories in connexion with the leading factories and works, and the total appropriations for these purposes in 1937 were about 500 million roubles.

The work done in the field of public education has already yielded a rich harvest. Its citizens—workers, collective farmers and working intellectuals—have altered beyond recognition. Not only the cities and towns, but the country villages, have produced a new generation of educated men and women, among whom the school teachers enjoy a particularly honourable status.

The new culture is growing and becoming stronger. Soviet culture has inherited all that was best in the bourgeois epoch and all that was good in the 20 or more centuries' growth of human culture. Lenin's observations on the subject were unequivocal: "It is necessary to take the whole of the culture left by Capitalism in order to build up Socialism from it. It is necessary to take over all its science, technical resources and knowledge and its arts."[2]

This sentiment inspires the respect of the people for the wonderful achievements of world science, industry and art—and for the past of the peoples of the Soviet Union, for their history, literature and their national poesy. Soviet culture is essentially a culture of the people. All the schools, clubs, theatres and palaces, all the priceless treasures of science and art in the Union exist for one purpose and one purpose alone—the welfare and happiness of its people.

---

[2] Lenin, *Works,* vol. xxiv, p. 65.

XX

SPORTS AND ATHLETICS

By A. V. Zelikov

Chairman of the All-Union Committee on Physical Culture and Sports of the Council of People's Commissars of the U.S.S.R.

The part played by sports in the public life of pre-revolutionary Russia cannot be compared in any way with the mass physical cultural movement in the Soviet Union. The Tsarist Government, which subsidized a few clubs and organizations reserved for representatives of the nobility and higher classes of bourgeois society, discouraged the growth of the popular movement for cultivating athletics by every means in its power and suppressed the workers' and students' athletic associations. The Russian team of athletes at the Olympic Games held in Stockholm in 1912 returned home after a series of disastrous failures in all the events for which they had entered, which was not surprising in view of the utter lack of interest in athletics prevailing in Tsarist Russia. When the well-known Russian wrestler, Baumann, left to attend the international contest at Breslau, the "Russian Olympic Committee" voted him the princely sum of 50 roubles (£5) for his expenses! They did the same with the celebrated Russian skating champions—Strounnikov, V. Ippolitov and Naidionov.

The famous Russian scientist, Leshaft, who devoted his

whole life to the idea of the physical development of the people, was subjected to endless persecutions and molestations by the Tsarist officials. The distinguished Russian doctor, Kraevsky, who has rightly been designated the father of Russian athleticism, trained many Russian athletes, wrestlers and boxers, without any assistance from the state, but the pupils of Dr. Kraevsky found no outlet for their talents amongst amateurs and were, perforce, compelled to become professionals in the circus.

Football—that most popular form of sport—could make no headway before the Revolution. The democratic masses of the people were to all intents and purposes debarred from admittance to the football clubs and teams of workers were only able to meet and play thrilling matches on patches of waste land or in back-yards beyond the city suburbs. Many well-known Russian footballers played their first games in these suburban teams.

Athletics, gymnastics, swimming, rowing and lawn tennis were equally neglected forms of sport.

This accounted for the lamentable performance of Russia at all contests with other European countries. The only exceptions were provided by the Russian skating champions who, notwithstanding the lack of proper facilities for training, contrived to achieve brilliant results and competed successfully on the ice rinks of Davos, Stockholm and Christiania.

It was only after the October Revolution that the people of the Soviet Union were able to display their athletic gifts and place sport on a new footing.

The Soviet Government were not slow to realize the immense importance of physical training for the masses.

Vast sums of money were assigned for the purpose of laying out playing fields, sports grounds and tennis courts and building stadiums, swimming pools and rifle ranges. Numerous sports clubs and associations were formed and systematically developed, to encourage every kind of physical culture.

The Government have established a special state department to deal with every form of physical culture and sport, and this organization has done much to assist the growth of amateur athletic clubs and to foster the development of physical culture among the masses.

In order to appreciate the phenomenal growth of the sports movement, one has only to mention that, whereas there were only 20 amateur clubs in pre-revolutionary Russia, there are now over 30,000 collectives, associations, teams and clubs for sport, subsidized by the state and by the trade union organizations. During the past three years an expenditure of over 1000 million roubles has been incurred by the state and by the trade unions on the physical training of the masses and over 10 million persons are benefiting directly from the advantages it provides.

Physical culture is regarded as a matter of great national and social value and, as such, it constitutes an integral part of Communist education. Furthermore, physical culture is also being developed as a curative and prophylactic medium. It is extensively used in hospitals, sanatoria and rest-homes, in addition to the large part it plays in the life of the army, in industry, in universities and schools. Physical culture is in fact becoming an essential feature of the everyday life of the people.

The growth of the physical culture movement is in a

large measure due to the "Ready for Labour and Defence" movement, known as the "G.T.O." Millions of young girls and youths who have attained a prescribed standard of physical fitness are rewarded by the "G.T.O." Badge of Honour.

In order to qualify for the G.T.O. badge, it is necessary to pass tests in cross-country running, in obstacle racing, swimming over various distances, ski-ing, rifle-shooting, &c. In addition to these compulsory tests, there are a number of others in other forms of sport (cycling, skating, various forms of ski-ing, rowing, mountaineering, &c.).

The young people are evincing the utmost keenness in the sports prescribed by the "G.T.O." and according to the records in the hands of the All-Union Committee of Physical Culture and Sport, over four million young devotees of physical culture have already secured the "G.T.O." Badge of Honour. This movement has thereby placed the development of sport and athletic exercises on a firm foundation and has raised the standard of performance in the realm of sport.

It will suffice to remark that at the present time there are over a million football players in addition to scores of thousands of miscellaneous athletes, swimmers, rowers, tennis players, ski-ers, skaters, gymnasts, &c.

In recent years physical culture has reached the rural districts and hundreds of collective farms now possess their own playing fields and stadiums. Most of the young villagers play games and within the past 12 months All-Union competitions for collective farm football teams, ski-ers and skaters have been held.

The phenomenal growth of the sport movement has,

as a matter of course, led to a correspondingly great rise in the standard of performance of athletes as compared to that displayed by those of pre-revolutionary Russia. In some branches of sport Soviet athletes have even beaten European and world records.

The amateur athletic associations, whose membership is open to all Soviet citizens, have produced a number of exceptionally brilliant athletes and holders of All-Union, European and world records.

As an illustration of what has been achieved in this respect, the performances of weight lifters and putters are worthy of notice. The weight putter, Khotimsky, using both hands, put a weight of 116 kilograms (256 lbs.), thereby creating a world record and beating that of the former holder, Deutch, by fully 2½ kilograms (5½ lbs.). The weight putter, George Popov, who is also the holder of several remarkable records, succeeded in beating, by a considerable margin, the performance of the world champion, Walter. Brilliant results were likewise obtained by the athletes Shatov, Bojko, Krylov, Koshelev and others.

In the realm of light athletics the success of the discus thrower, Sergius Liakhov, should be mentioned. He threw the discus (with either hand) a distance of 302 feet 6 inches, thereby creating a world record. The pole jumper, Nicholas Ozolin, did a pole jump of 14 feet, beating the European record of Hoff.

Amongst women athletes, record holders include: Z. Sinitskaya, who threw the discus with the right and left hand 244 feet 6 inches; Tamara Bykova, who did 500 metres (546.5 yards) in 1 minute 16.8 seconds, thereby beating the record set up by the well-known Polish runner, Stella Volosevicz, by a fraction of a second; E. Vassilieva, who covered 1000 metres (1093 yards) in 2 minutes 58.4 seconds, whereas the world record held by Lannes was 3 minutes.

The swimmer, Simon Boichenko, is known throughout the world. His time of 1 minute 6.8 seconds, using the trudgeon stroke, proved better than that of the world champion, Higgens.

Remarkable performances have been put up by the skating champions, Jacob Melnikov, Ivan Anikanov, V. Kouznetsova, S. Paromova and M. Valova, at various international meetings, at which the Soviet entrants invariably achieved brilliant success.

By far the most popular sport among the masses is football. Every town, district and village and almost every collective farm has one or more football teams in proper training and playing regularly in matches.

It may be confidently asserted that after the October Revolution football gained a firm hold on the people and that the game has since been taken up with unprecedented enthusiasm throughout the whole country.

Russian football teams—one of which was beaten in an international match at the Olympic Games in Stockholm in 1912 by 16 goals to nil—have improved beyond all recognition. Already in 1923 a Russian football team, visiting Scandinavia, defeated representative teams from Sweden and Norway, and ever since 1924 Soviet footballers, playing against teams in Ankara and Constantinople, and also against a national team representing Turkey, have invariably proved victorious. In 1928, at the Workers' Spartacus Meeting held in Moscow, Soviet football players demonstrated their immense superiority over workers' teams drawn from every part of the world. This was further emphasized in the autumn of 1937, when the Soviet "Spartacus" team carried off the football championship of the Third Workers' Olympiad at Antwerp and then proceeded to win the "World Championship Cup" at the international meeting of workers' football teams from all countries, held in Paris.

In 1934 a Soviet footballers' team defeated a representative municipal team at Brno (Czechoslovakia) and one of the crack teams of Prague, the "Jidenitsa." In 1935 a Soviet team of players beat the "Red Star" French football team, drew with a team representing all Prague and again defeated the Scandinavians.

Some of the leading Soviet football players are well known outside their own country. They include the brothers Starostin, Butoussov, Ilyin, Semichastny, Akimov, Selin, Fedotov, Stepanov and others.

The growing popularity of lawn tennis should also be mentioned. This fascinating game was in pre-revolutionary Russia looked upon as something reserved for the privileged classes. In 1913 there were only 20 lawn tennis clubs with 850 players in Moscow, whereas last year Moscow possessed 400 clubs, not counting the tennis courts in the rest-homes, public parks, and gardens and suburban districts. The total number of tennis courts has now increased a hundredfold and the game enjoys the utmost popularity.

The growth of physical culture amongst the people has, in a large measure, been due to the creation of state institutes of physical culture and of physical training colleges for the tuition of qualified instructors and instructresses in physical and recreational training.

There are altogether six institutes of physical culture in the Soviet Union (in Moscow, Leningrad, Kharkov, Minsk, Tbilissi (Tiflis) and Baku), 25 training schools for P.T. instructors and three higher colleges for experts in all branches of sport.

These establishments provide instruction for 10,000 students who will, in due course, qualify as instructors in physical culture.

The spread of physical culture has been greatly facilitated by the construction of numerous well-equipped sports grounds and stadiums. No less than 258 million roubles has been devoted to that purpose in the last six years and at the present time the U.S.S.R. boasts 650 large and small stadiums, about 7000 sports grounds, over 350 swimming and boating stations, over 2500 ski courses, 100 physical culture centres, &c.

The largest sports stadium in the country is the "Dynamo Stadium" in Moscow, with accommodation for 100,000 spectators. It is already larger than the Olympic stadiums of Stockholm, Paris and Amsterdam, but is, nevertheless, being enlarged at the present time.

Apart from the "Dynamo," Moscow possesses 20 other sports stadiums belonging to different clubs.

A number of new stadiums have been built in Leningrad during recent years, including the "Dynamo" in memory of Lenin, the "Red Putilovets," the "Red Triangle," and stadiums at the Baltic Works, the "Bolshevik" Works and the "Red Dawn" Works.

A wonderful garden stadium with accommodation for many thousands of spectators has been built in Kiev on the high bank of the Dnieper, and the seashore stadium of Odessa, located in picturesque surroundings, is one of the most attractive sports establishments of the Ukraine. Tbilissi (Tiflis), Yerevan (Erivan), Kramatorsk (in the Donetz Coal Basin) and other cities also possess many new stadiums, sports grounds, tennis courts and swimming pools.

A whole series of still larger stadiums are now in the course of construction, including one in Moscow (at Ismailovo) for 140,000 spectators, one in Leningrad to hold 75,000 and others in Tbilissi and Kiev with seating accommodation for 50,000 persons.

Sport is now an integral part of the life of the people and the young folks of both sexes make a point of spending their leisure playing games on the sports grounds and in the stadiums.

The effect on the health of the people is correspondingly beneficial and the physical development of the younger generation is rapidly improving. This fact is eloquently proved by the returns of the medical authorities examining recruits for the Red Army.

The Soviet Union now has many millions of thoroughly healthy and physically fit sons and daughters ready for labour and—in case of necessity—to defend the frontiers of their country against invaders.

XXI

THE RED ARMY AND DEFENCE

By A. Feshankov
Regimental Commissar

The Soviet Union occupies one-sixth of the earth's surface. Its land and sea frontiers total 20,000 miles in length and in area it is one of the largest countries in the world, to defend which a powerful army, air force, and navy and strongly fortified frontiers are needed. All these were created by the Soviet Government and Bolshevik Party in a minimum length of time, and to-day all the frontiers of the Union are, metaphorically speaking, under lock and key and guarded by the Workers' and Peasants' Red Army, the Air Force and the Navy.

The Red Army is a true people's army, born in the smoke and fire of the Civil War. Its organization began with the decree of 28th January, 1918, signed by V. I. Lenin, Chairman of the Council of People's Commissars. The Government and Party exerted every effort to create an entirely new army, one that should differ in every respect from the old Tsarist army. Tsarist Russia was the prison-house of the peoples and its army served the interests of the autocratic government. The Red Army was created for the purpose of defending the conquests of the October Socialist Revolution, and served, and continues to serve, the interests of the workers and peasants.

The organization of the Red Army proceeded during the armed struggle with all the hostile forces that were attacking the country from every side. Inadequately organized and badly trained companies and divisions had to be flung into battle as soon as they were formed. Reliable cadres of Red officers devoted to their country were created in the course of the Civil War, while the example and heroism of tens of thousands of members of the Bolshevik Party helped to consolidate the newly organized regiments of the Red Army. The rôle of the military commissars in the building up of the armed forces of the young Republic was of incalculable importance. They were the soul of the army, models of valour and selfless devotion to the interests of the Revolution. The names of the heroes and participants of the Civil War, which include those of Stalin, Voroshilov, Orjonikidze, Kirov, Budionny, Chapayev, and Schorss, live in the hearts of the peoples of the Soviet Union. They have created legends about them and celebrate their deeds in song, while their heroism is a model to the youth of the land.

Notwithstanding its poor technical equipment, the Red Army was victorious on every front. It had fought for the independence of its fatherland, and had ousted the Tsarist generals and the troops of the 14 states which had organized intervention against the Soviet Republic.

On the termination of the Civil War the Government set about raising the fighting efficiency and organizational and technical level of the Red Army which was reconstructed in accordance with the heightened requirements of defence. A new system of recruitment was introduced, an extensive network of military training establishments

Part of the Soviet Air Force—A battleship at night

created and new regulations and precepts elaborated on the basis of the experience of the World and Civil Wars. While it became much stronger in its organization, the Red Army remained technically weak. During the Civil War and in the first years after its termination, the technical equipment of the Red Army was very poor—the most essential elements in it were lacking. It possessed practically no aeroplanes and no tanks. At the time of the Civil War the Red Air Fleet consisted of 200 very inferior and foreign-made aeroplanes, while for a number of years the Red Army had to be satisfied with a few enemy tanks captured during the Civil War.

A real extensive technical re-equipment of the Red Army began during the first year of the First Five Year Plan of Stalin (1928-29). This re-equipment was carried out in accordance with a well-considered plan approved by the Central Committee of the Communist (Bolshevik) Party of the Soviet Union, and under the direct guidance and supervision of Stalin. On the completion of the Two Five Year Plans the Red Army had changed beyond recognition. Large-scale industry, likewise the creation of the Soviet Government and Bolshevik Party, had provided it with first-class technical equipment. By 1934 for every Red Army man there was an average of 7.74 mechanical horse power. There was a sharp increase in the proportion of technical cadres in the army. In 1934 this proportion was equivalent to 50%, and with the machine gunners of the rifle, cavalry and other units, it was equivalent to 70% of the entire personnel. Since 1934 there has been a further improvement in the technical equipment. The policy of collectivization in agriculture has played an outstanding part in the training of technical cadres for the Red Army. An immense number of tractors, combined harvesters, and other agricultural implements worked by internal combustion engines have been assigned by the Government for use in the collective farms and state farms. Large numbers of young peasants have to be trained to operate these tractors and harvesters, and consequently, when their time comes to be called up for service in the Red Army, they come as almost fully trained tank operators and motorists, who can be prepared for military service in the minimum length of time.

The reconstruction of the army largely denoted the creation of motor mechanized troops and tank units, which it now possesses in the necessary quantity and of the required quality. These troops are equipped with every type of tank which are operated by fine men who have an excellent knowledge of their work and put all their soul into it. Thus a powerful base has been created which will be fully capable of satisfying the country's requirements in tanks in case of an attack on the U.S.S.R.

The effort to develop the air forces of the country has been crowned with success. The Red Army now possesses thousands of all the latest types of aeroplanes: high-speed bombers, fast battle planes, scouts, and attack aeroplanes, which form part of a now highly powerful Red Air Force. The standard of the air force as regards quality may be judged by the numerous international records set up by Soviet airmen—Chkalov, Gromov, Kokkinaki, Pauline Ossipenko and many others, who have all received their training in the Red Army.

Great changes have taken place in the infantry as well. Infantry equipment is now perfectly up to date, and includes automatic rifles, machine-guns of every system and other automatic arms of home manufacture.

Considerable attention is given to the artillery, which is growing and improving. At the present time the Red Army is sufficiently equipped with every form of artillery, beginning with anti-tank and tank artillery, battalion and regimental artillery, light field artillery, and anti-aircraft artillery and ending with heavy long-range artillery.

The Red Army possesses a magnificent cavalry corps, which covered itself with glory during the Civil War and has now been reorganized in accordance with modern requirements. The cavalry of the Red Army is now in a position to execute important tasks independently, as well as in combination with other corps.

Much has been done to develop the various auxiliary arms: liaison, engineers, railway, anti-aircraft defence and so on. Whereas formerly the principal means of communication in the Red Army was the telephone and telegraph, now it is wireless telegraphy and telephony. Aeroplanes, tanks, the artillery, the cavalry and the infantry all have their own wireless stations. The engineer corps are equipped with machines for the rapid construction of bridges, trenches, dug-outs, shelters, observation points, &c.

The frontiers are well protected. The western frontier from Lake Ladoga to the Black Sea and also the sections in the Far East and Eastern Siberia most open to foreign menace have been covered with a network of fortifications. There has been a considerable increase in the number of fortified regions of coast defence on the Black and Baltic Seas, in the Murmansk district, and especially in the Far East. These fortified regions are equipped with heavy artillery.

The sea frontiers are likewise well defended. The Government have achieved no small success in the technical re-equipment of the naval forces. The Soviet battleships, though they are of 1914-15 construction, have been thoroughly modernized and are perfectly up-to-date warships. Within recent years two new fleets have come into being—the Pacific Fleet and the North Fleet. The Baltic and Black Sea Fleets have been strengthened to a considerable extent, as have the Amur, Caspian, and Dnieper flotillas. The number of minor warships, naval aeroplanes and submarines, and the amount of anti-aircraft artillery, have increased by several hundred per cent. as compared with the beginning of the Second Five Year Plan. The decision of the First Session of the Supreme Soviet of the U.S.S.R. to create a special People's Commissariat of the Navy was made with a view to the further extension and development of the Navy.

All these measures taken by the Soviet Government make the Red Army equal to the most advanced armies in the world as regards technical equipment and organization. Even foreign military specialists are obliged to admit the truth of this. The following statement appeared in the German military journal, *Deutsche Wehr,* in September, 1934: "The Red Army is very well armed. It is equipped with light and heavy artillery, armoured cars, small and large tanks, chemical warfare materials, &c., in great quantities, and its personnel is well trained." In December, 1934, the following statement by Captain Maydeo, formerly Japanese military attaché in Moscow, appeared in the press: "During the period of the First Five Year Plan special attention was paid to the intensive development of the air force, the motor mechanized units, and chemical warfare materials. Immense progress has been made in each of these fields. I do not know the exact number of tanks at the present time. . . . The fact is that they possess a huge number of the newest types of tank. The mechanization of the Russian army amazes all the military attachés who attend the parades. Their achievements in aviation are especially remarkable."

At the head of the Workers' and Peasants' Red Army stands the People's Commissar for Defence of the U.S.S.R. who is responsible to the Council of People's Commissars. Since 1926 this post has been occupied by Marshal K. Y. Voroshilov, a hero of the Civil War and of the defence of Tsaritsin, under whose guidance the reorganization and technical construction of the Red Army, which transformed it into a mighty and formidable force, was carried out.

The leadership of the Red Army by the People's Commissar is effected through the People's Commissariat for Defence, which includes the General Staff of the Workers' and Peasants' Red Army and a number of Central Administrations.

The territory of the U.S.S.R. is divided into military districts under the jurisdiction of Military Councils directly responsible to the People's Commissar for Defence. All the military units on the territory of the military districts are subordinate to the Military Councils.

The principal types of troops are the rifles (infantry), which represent the main force of the army, the cavalry, artillery, motor-mechanized troops, and the air force. In addition, there are various auxiliary forces (liaison, engineer, chemical, railway, mechanical transport, anti-aircraft defence, and other corps).

In every unit, regiment, division, board and other establishment of the Red Army there is a military commissar who, together with the commander, is the immediate superior of the entire personnel of the unit, for whose political and moral tone he is wholly responsible, as he is for the discipline of the personnel from highest to lowest; for its proper fulfilment of its military duty; for the whole unit's state of readiness for mobilization and battle and for the condition of its armament and material. There are political supervisors in the companies, squadrons and similar sub-divisions.

In the divisions and other units there are political departments, and in the districts there are District Political Administrations. The entire political apparatus is under the direction of the Political Administration of the Workers' and Peasants' Red Army. The rôle and importance of the commissars and of the political apparatus in the organization of the Red Army are immense.

The personnel is divided into the commanding staff, the staff of superiors, the junior commanding staff, the junior staff of superiors and the privates.

The commanding staff consists of Red Army soldiers holding titles of rank (lieutenant, captain, major and so on). The staff of superiors consists of the military-political, military-technical, military-economic and administrative, military-medical, military-veterinary and military-juridical staffs. Every man in the army is given a title indicating his rank or special military or other qualifications, and at the present time the Red Army possesses well-trained cadres of commanders and superiors, who are devoted to the cause of socialism and stand united under the banner of the Communist Party and Soviet Government. Deep abhorrence filled the breasts of the commanders and privates of the Red Army when they learned of the small group of traitors who had sold themselves to foreign espionage services, and the death sentence passed on these miscreants was received with acclamation by all.

There are a large number of schools of various types established for the purpose of training commanders, and in them within the past 10 years thousands of commanders, political workers, engineers and technical experts have been trained for the Red Army and Navy. There are, in addition, 12 higher institutes (military academies) and courses established by the Red Army and the Navy where thousands of commanders, political workers, engineers, doctors and other military experts receive their training. The commanders continue their studies in their units where special courses are organized for them and the superiors.

The junior commanding staff is trained in regimental schools. Red Army men who undergo a year's training in these schools become junior commanders, and subsequently, when they have served their time in the army, go on long leave. Some of them remain in the army for superogatory service, while numbers of them enter military schools where they are trained as lieutenants. All roads are open to privates and junior commanders in the Red Army. They can enter any military school and, when they have finished it, become commanders and occupy high posts.

There is no antagonism between officers and privates: the former are not an isolated caste; indeed, they are closely linked up in every possible way with the rank and file of the army. Relations between the officers and privates are determined by the community of their class interests. The majority of both the officers and privates are workers and peasants, and both defend their people and their fatherland. On duty the commander is the chief whose orders require unquestioning obedience. But off duty—at meetings, in the theatre, and so on—the Red Army private and commander are comrades.

These relations not only do not undermine discipline, but actually strengthen it. Discipline in the Red Army is stern, revolutionary discipline, which is not based on fear and on blind obedience, but on the high degree of class consciousness of all the men. Both the officer and the private know perfectly well that the Red Army can never be strong and efficient without a system of firm discipline. This does not mean, of course, that those who are guilty of a wanton breach of discipline go unpunished. If every other measure (educational methods, public censure, &c.) has been tried without success, the commander is bound to punish the offender in the manner prescribed by the disciplinary statutes of the Workers' and Peasants' Red Army.

A particularly heinous crime is high treason. Article 133 of the Constitution declares: "The defence of the fatherland is the sacred duty of every citizen of the U.S.S.R. Treason to the country—violation of the oath, desertion to the enemy, impairing the military power of

V. Bluecher
Marshal of the Soviet Union

K. E. Voroshilov
People's Commissar of Defence

the state, or espionage—is punishable with all the severity of the law as the worst of crimes."

Article 132 declares: "Universal military service is a law. Military service in the Workers' and Peasants' Red Army is an honourable duty of the citizens of the U.S.S.R." Every Soviet citizen who has attained the age of 20 gladly discharges this duty. The conscription period is always a time of festival nowadays, and quite often young men who have been granted exemptions for various reasons decline to take advantage of them. In more than one case a young man has volunteered his services in place of a brother who has perished on active service. Recently a junior commander by the name of Firsov was killed at his post by an enemy. His father sent a letter to Marshal Voroshilov, People's Commissar for Defence, asking him in the name of the whole family to enter his second son Anatoli into the same corps in place of his dead son. Marshal Voroshilov complied with the father's request, and Anatoli left his home to take his brother's place.

The personnel of the Red Army is educated in a spirit of Patriotism, is well-trained, has great staying-power, is active, selfless, and brave. This was particularly striking during manœuvres and when guarding the frontiers especially during the Lake Hassan events in the Far East.

A great amount of political and cultural work is done in the Red Army by the political organs, commissars and communist organizations. The Soviet Government provide all the material requisites for the purpose. In every company, squadron, battery, &c., there is a special room for political studies known as the Lenin room. Every unit has its own club, cinema and wireless apparatus, class rooms, physics and other laboratories, mathematics rooms, and so on. The army possesses innumerable libraries containing many millions of books. Each unit issues its own newspaper. Over 150 Houses of the Red Army—real palaces—have been built, and many of them are the cultural centres of the towns in which they have been erected. The representative of a certain foreign army who paid a visit to one of these Houses declared: "I envy the soldiers and officers of an army which possesses such cultural centres as this House where the soldier and officer can study, rest and amuse themselves in a rational manner."

Political studies form a very important part of the general educational system in the army. Political classes are held every day on subjects such as the history of the peoples of the U.S.S.R., the history of their revolutionary struggle and of that of the peoples of other countries, the achievements and tasks of socialist construction in the Soviet Union and the natural wealth of the land. The life and work of the great revolutionary leaders, Marx, Engels, Lenin and Stalin, are also studied.

Every day the newspapers are read aloud and discussed, especial attention being paid to the most important events at home and abroad. The number of newspapers subscribed to in the army works out at over one copy per man. All this tends to broaden the political outlook of the men, arouses a profound interest in questions relating to home and international affairs and instils a deep feeling of patriotism and love for their country.

The commanders, in addition, study Marxian and Leninist theory and the principles of Bolshevism.

An elementary standard of general education is compulsory in the Red Army. In the old Tsarist army 50% of the soldiers were illiterate, whereas when the Red Army celebrated its 20th anniversary, not a single man in it was illiterate. Half of the men have been through six or seven classes of the secondary school, while a large number of them have finished the secondary school and university. The students and cadets of the military academies and schools study foreign languages, as do thousands of commanders on active service.

Numerous Red Army choirs, music circles and dramatic societies give first-rate performances, not only in the clubs and Houses of the Red Army, but in the ordinary theatres of the towns where they are always a great success. The Red Banner Ensemble of the Red Army Songs and Dances, beloved by the men of all ranks, betokens the vast improvement in the standard of culture of the army. The performances of this Ensemble in France and Czechoslovakia were an amazing and brilliant success.

The Red Army may, in view of all the foregoing, be looked upon as an excellent political and cultural school where those who receive instruction in it become cultured, disciplined citizens with a wide political outlook as well as well-trained military experts.

When they have completed their service in the army, the men return to their collective farms, factories, &c., and take their place among the industrial shock-workers and Stakhanovites. There they are active in furthering the militarization of the population and participate in Soviety, party and public work. In 1937 70 riflemen from one division who were discharged on long leave were utilized for work in the district Soviet apparatus and other district organizations. Not a few ex-Red Army men are now engaged in important state work, and numbers of them are well-known artists, poets, writers and actors. A. Morozov, a Mourom shepherd, was almost illiterate when he entered the army. While there he became literate, finished an art school and was sent to continue his studies under Professor Leberg, and during the 20th anniversary celebrations of the October Socialist Revolution his works were shown at the Young Painters' exhibition, where they were universally admired for the amazing mastery of their execution. N. Ostrovsky, the author of *How the Steel was Tempered* and *Born of the Strong,* who died recently in early manhood, was also an ex-Red Army man, whose brilliant gifts were highly rated by Maxim Gorky.

The Red Army does a vast amount of political and cultural work among the industrial workers and collective farm peasants. In the period before the elections to the Supreme Soviets thousands of Red Army agitators were sent to the collective farms and industrial establishments. The Red Army men afford immense help to the collective farms during the sowing season and at harvest time.

Representatives of the army are always welcome guests at the factories and collective farms. The Soviet people love their army and envelop it in an atmosphere of affectionate solicitude: the people and the army are one—they are not separated from each other by an insurmountable barrier. When a young man joins the army he does not lose his status as a citizen of the U.S.S.R. because he has undertaken the honourable task of defending his country. Article 138 of the Constitution declares: "Citizens serving in the Red Army have the right to elect and be elected on equal terms with all other citizens." They, like all other citizens, take an active part in the political life and administration of their country. In 1934 thousands of officers and privates were elected to the Soviets: 4787 to the village soviets, 9083 to the town soviets, 2972 to the district soviets, 264 to the regional and provincial soviets, and 183 to the Central Executive Committee of the Union Republics.

On 12th December, 1937, 65 officers, Red Army men, and political workers were elected to the Supreme Soviet of the U.S.S.R. At the First Session of the Supreme Soviet of the R.S.F.S.R. on 19th July, 1938, a Red Army officer, Mollayev, was elected deputy chairman of the Presidium of the Supreme Soviet of the R.S.F.S.R.

The purpose of the Red Army is not aggression. It does not intend to attack anybody. It was created in order to defend Soviet Russia against the numerous enemies who fell upon the young Republic, and on the termination of the Civil War the Red Army was organized as an army whose purpose was to defend the Soviet Union, and to secure its independence and the inviolability of its frontiers, of which it is the faithful and trusty sentinel. It keeps a vigilant watch on all the events of the day and, while it has no intention of attacking anyone, is prepared at any moment to crush the foe who dares to attack the Soviet Union, and is sufficiently powerful to defeat the enemy on his own territory.

XXII

LITERATURE

By Professor V. Y. Kirpotin

Member of the Council of the Association of Soviet Authors

Soviet literature as such is quite new, but notwithstanding this circumstances and the shortcomings thereby involved, it can already claim a whole series of successful achievements. Soviet writers, who were for many years headed by Maxim Gorky, have been able to create a novel and characteristic literature of their own. The Revolution created the peculiar conditions for its development and brought it into intimate contact with the masses of the people. Soviet literature has been built up and developed around the cultural heritage of the past; our authors learn the art of the best writers of their own and foreign countries—Poushkin, Gogol, Leo Tolstoi, Shakespeare, Dickens, Balzac, Maxim Gorky and others.

The principal novelty in Soviet literature is its subject matter as compared to that of pre-revolutionary Russian literature. The latter's principal theme was the life of the intelligentsia. The authors of that era devoted their attention to the unbelief and pessimism of the intellectual cut off from the masses of the people. Thus one of its most brilliant representatives, Leonid Andreev, endeavoured to show that everything is two-sided—that there are two sides to the human mind, that love is false and that supreme heroism may be synonymous with the depth of degradation. Leonid Andreev's entire work, which exercised a guiding influence in the minds of his contemporary readers, represents a cry of despair and the voice of a man who has reached a dead end.

The popular hero of pre-revolutionary Russian literature was the "small" man, the man occupying a humble position in the social scale, but many of the leading Russian authors—including some as great as Dostoevsky —wrote about the "small" man, not in order to inspire him with courage to fight for his right to enjoy life, but rather to convince him that the principal human virtue was the exercise of patience, submissiveness and docility.

On the eve of the Revolution the dominant tendency in Russian literature was that of idealistic subjectivism. Both poets and prose writers chose the single isolated mind as the theme rather than the boundless scope offered by the world of reality.

Soviet literature is, on the contrary, essentially concerned with everyday life. The Revolution gave power to a new class of people—workers, peasants, toiling intelligentsia—all of them strong and enterprising men and women, believing in reality, seeking their happiness on earth and devoting their common efforts to its creation.

Obviously this radical change of the social order called a different type of hero into being in the world of literature. New men had asserted their right to be masters of their own life, and the new literature, bound up as it was with reality, made such men its heroes. Interest in the new life of the country and a proper appreciation of the social lives of men and women resulted in the regeneration of novel-writing as a literary art; before the Revolution this branch of literature had gradually come to be supplanted by others.

The keynote of Soviet literature is *socialist realism*—described by the late Maxim Gorky at the first All-Union Congress of Soviet authors in 1935, as "affirms existence to be a deed, an act of creation having as its object the constant development of the individual capacity of men, for the sake of victory over the forces of nature, for the sake of their health and length of life, and for the sake of their happiness on this earth, which in accordance with their ever-growing requirements, they wish to turn wholly into a fair home of a humanity united into a single family."

The reader of a Soviet novel will find that it deals artistically with the main events of the Revolution and incarnates the basic types to be met with in the new society. Furmanov in his novel *Chapaev,* Fadeiev in his *The Nineteen,* Sholokhov in *And Quiet Flows the Don,* Serafimovitch in *The Iron Torrent,* Vsevolod Ivanov in his narratives *The Armoured Train* and *The Partisans,* have all depicted heroes of the Civil War with its leaders and humbler participants. Alexis Tolstoi's most recent work, *Bread,* is a fascinating story of the heroic defence of Tsarytsin and contains a wonderfully artistic account of the part played by Stalin and Voroshilov in the overthrow of the Whites.

Many writers have been inspired by industrialization and the latter is the main theme of Gladkov's novels *Cement* and *Energy,* of Valentine Kataev's *Days to Come* and, to a certain extent, of Leonov's romance, *The Ocean Road.*

The collectivization of agricultural means of production marks an era of special importance in the life of the U.S.S.R. For the first time in the history of humanity the divided and individual peasant farmers have, under the guidance of the working-class, pooled their resources for the purpose of performing more productive and successful work on a socialist basis. This event has wrought a radical change in the whole life of the peasant community—it has completely altered its economic, cultural and psychological aspect and it is this change which forms the theme so ably and vividly treated in M. Sholokhov's *Virgin Soil Upturned,* in Panferov's *Brousky* and in a large number of other books.

One of the subjects which is finding great favour in current Soviet literature is the rise of a new intelligentsia. A number of brilliant writers, including A. L. Tolstoi, Fedin and Leonov, have devoted attention to this theme.

The author P. Pavlenko has written an interesting novel about a future war, brought about by the deliberate attack by the jingoists of Japan on the Soviet Union. This book, which bears the title *The East,* describes the growing power of the U.S.S.R. in the Far East and its author paints a dramatic picture of the events leading up to the Japanese aggression and of their utter defeat by the Red Army.

As may be seen, therefore, Soviet novels deal with a variety of subjects. Historical romances are in a class by themselves and among them Yury Tynianov's *Kiukhla* and *Poushkin* and Alexis Tolstoi's *Peter the First* have achieved a well-deserved popularity, as have also A. Tchapygin's romances of the peasant wars of the seventeenth and early eighteenth centuries, *Razin Stepan* and *The Freemen.*

The subject-matter of a book cannot be wholly detached from its treatment and a change in the material involves a corresponding alteration of the whole artistic texture of the work.

One of the prevailing tendencies in recent world literature is the concentration on the abstract psychological universe of an individual man. Typical examples of this class of book are afforded by the works of Joyce and Proust.

The outstanding feature of Soviet literature is, on the contrary, the revival on a new basis of the epic narrative relating to events of interest and importance to the whole people. The best examples of Soviet prose are presented in the guise of an original epos dealing with some particular aspect of the life of a community, the fortunes of the masses of the people and the changing social order. The epic novel of Soviet literature was first inspired in an atmosphere of acute class warfare so that its keynote is provided by the great ideals of socialism and its usual theme by the development and growth of the individual personality.

The Revolution imbued millions of men with a new creative spirit and enabled every worker and peasant to develop his or her individuality, after centuries of political oppression and economic exploitation. This development of the personality of every worker, manual or otherwise, must be considered one of the greatest and most remarkable achievements of the Revolution and as such it was bound to influence literature and inspire Soviet writers.

Classical literature has always reflected the highest, noblest and most progressive sentiments of mankind, but it must be admitted that the classical literature of the past in every country has almost invariably been based on the ideology of individual proprietorship. In its earlier stages of development this literature laid particular stress on the latter and the father of European literature, Hesiod, actually went so far as to proclaim in his poem, *Works and Days,* that "virtue and honour follow in the wake of riches." After a lapse of many centuries and notwithstanding a totally different environment and culture, we find that Daniel Defoe, in his romance *Moll Flanders,* concurs in the view expressed by Hesiod that the acquisition of wealth must precede that of virtue and honour.

The ideology of individual proprietorship in classical literature is not always lauded in quite such a crude form and it is more usually expressed in the glorification of a bourgeois and petty bourgeois individualism based on private ownership. The Soviet Union has seen the birth of a literature which in all its essentials is directly opposed to the psychology of private property and the selfishness of individualistic egoism. The literature of the whole family of Soviet peoples is the first of its kind in being based on a socialist ideology and on a real and not verbal equality of mankind.

The release from the shackles imposed by the psychology and relation of individual proprietorship has given writers and artists true creative freedom. Authors are not hampered by any problems of sales, publishers or patrons, and the motive which inspires their work is the service of humanity.

It is this which gives Soviet literature its high degree of spiritual pathos—a pathos which is a vivid feature of the work of the great humanist, Gorky, the teacher and patriarch of Soviet literature and the classic master of Russian prose and drama. The idea of socialist humanism, the profound love of toiling humanity and the urge to build up a new and happier life on earth—these are the basic principles on which the young Soviet literature is founded.

An outstanding feature of this literature is the optimism displayed in its works, although this optimism has nothing in common with the cheap assurance characteristic of bourgeois and bookstall literature with its happy ending at all costs. The optimism of Soviet literature is buoyant, confident in its own strength and yet essentially realistic.

These distinctive traits of intense optimism and spiritual socialistic pathos are admirably displayed in the work of the young writer Nicholas Ostrovsky, *How The Steel Was Forged.*

Ostrovsky died recently from the effects of wounds received in the Civil War, which left him blind and paralysed. Yet, although he was bedridden, Ostrovsky never ceased to feel that he was fighting for the future welfare of mankind and, inspired by this sentiment, he dictated a book permeated with a lofty spirit of pathos, supreme heroism and firm belief in socialism. His book has achieved a well-earned popularity among the youth of the Soviet Union. Many millions of copies have been sold.

The awakening of the socialist personality has exercised a similarly beneficial influence on poetry. Civic pathos inspired Vladimir Mayadovsky, beloved by all Soviet readers, to write such great and sonorous poems as *Good,*

Lenin, &c. The lyrical verse of Mayakovsky is original in form and remarkable for the love of his country which it displays. His brilliant command of language enabled him to be the pioneer of a novel type of verse.

Mayakovsky's work greatly influenced a number of other poets. The outstanding characteristic of their writings is the combination of the spirit of love, of friendship, of Soviet patriotism with interesting subject-matter, and this is typified in the ballad-like poems of Bagritzsky, Tikhonov, Prokofiev and others. The poet Lebedev-Koumatch wrote a number of songs which enjoy a widespread popularity throughout the country. The pathos of the Soviet poetry is that of the harmonious co-existence of the individual and the community.

Soviet art is a return to the art of action and movement, whereby it affords wide scope for a continuous further development of the drama.

Soviet playwrights gave the Soviet theatre a number of plays which have enriched the repertory of the latter. One of these writers, K. Trenev, wrote *Liubov Yarovaya,* a play of the Civil War. Vs. Ivanov's *The Armoured Train* and Vishnevsky's *An Optimistic Tragedy* have a similar theme. Leonov writes plays dealing with everyday life in the Soviet Union (*Skutarevsky*) and Finck is a master of bright comedy. Several of Pogodin's plays depict new characters, including ex-criminals re-educated by work and Soviet reality (*The Aristocrats*). He also wrote *The Man With The Gun,* in which one of the characters represents Lenin.

An account of the growth of Soviet literature would be incomplete without some reference to the influence of Soviet critics.

The reviews of these critics frequently take the form of lively and apt discussions on the merits of the latest books, the work of individual authors and the future prospective development of Soviet literature. One of the most interesting discussions which took place recently concerned formalism and socialist realism. It included a detailed examination of the work of many writers, which proved extremely instructive and useful.

Soviet literature is not by any means confined to Russian literature. The national policy of the Government has done much to encourage the literature of all the peoples living within the borders of the Union.

The gifted and highly artistic people of the Ukraine possess a wealth of literature of all kinds and dealing with a large variety of subjects. Among the Ukrainian poets, the most distinguished is probably Paul Tychina, an academician and scientific scholar, who is a perfect master of the verse in which he deals with new themes in a strictly classical manner. The dramatist Korneitchouk in his play *Platon Kretchet*, so widely popular throughout the Union, depicts the new socialist life of the country.

In Byelorussia the two writers Kolas and Kupala, whose books, under the Tsarist régime, could only be sold in negligible numbers and in the poorest of editions, have now become the national poets of their republic.

Georgian literature has traditions which go back many centuries. Roustaveli's poem, *The Knight in the Tiger Skin,* is one of the finest masterpieces of the world's poetry. The seven hundredth centenary of his birth was celebrated in 1937 by all the various peoples of the Soviet Union. Under the Tsars the literature of Georgia was discouraged in every possible way, but at the present time Georgian writers are entirely free to act as the mouthpieces of their gifted countrymen. The leading Georgian writers are Galaktion Tabidze, Shalva Dadiani and Simon Tchikovani.

Amongst the authors and poets of outstanding merit of other nationalities of the U.S.S.R. are the Jewish writer, Peretz Markisch, and the Tadjik poet, Hassem Lahouty.

The new régime has also led to a great revival of the old art of verbal story-telling. The folk-lore of the Soviet is developing both in an epical and a lyrical sense. The Russian story-teller, Kruichkova, has created some new legends about Lenin and Stalin. The recently deceased Daghestani singer, Suleiman Stalsky, and the Kazakh singer, Jambul, were rightly described by Gorky as the Homers of the twentieth century. They adapted the harmonious brilliance and originality of the traditional forms of national poetry for the glorification of the new social order.

Soviet literature is deeply rooted in the life of the people and is pervaded with the spirit of the new patriotism. Every great and gifted writer loves his people and his country, but in the old Tsarist Russia this love was poisoned by the ever-present consciousness of the injustice of the political and social régime. The best types of Russians in the days of the Tsars loved their people and their country, but were at the same time compelled to feel ashamed of the way they were governed.

The patriotism of Soviet literature is that of a free people with a pride in their country. Soviet writers are aware that the people of the Union have no designs on the freedom and independence of others as representatives of an inferior race.

The status of an author is an honourable distinction and writers not only enjoy popularity among the people, but the support of the Government and Communist party. Many of them, like Alexis Tolstoi, Serafimovitch, Lebedev-Koumatch, Vishnevsky and others, have received decorations for their literary achievements. Some of the best authors and poets, such as Sholokhov, Tolstoi, Korneitchouk and Dadiani, have been elected Deputies of the Supreme Soviet. The sales of these writers' books are fabulous. In the twenty years before the Revolution just over a million copies of Gorky's works were sold in Russia. In the twenty years following the Revolution the sales of the Russian editions alone of Gorky's works amounted to no fewer than *33 million copies.* There were 1½ million copies of his novel, *Mother,* sold in the U.S.S.R. in the first edition.

The underlying principles of Soviet literature are a high standard of ideals, vividness, optimism, realism, simplicity and clarity. Socialist realism enables the writers to face reality boldly and dispassionately, to foresee the path of development of present-day life at its proper value and to turn out work which educates men and women in the spirit of socialism.

" Future Pilots " *by Deineka*

" At the Wheel " *by Pimenov*

XXIII

THE THEATRE

By P. Markov

Literary Director of the Gorky Memorial Art Theatre in Moscow

The leading theatres of pre-revolutionary Russia were mostly confined to the capital and great cities, while those in the provinces were always handicapped by serious financial difficulties. The actors and actresses struggling to make a living on the provincial stage were invariably overworked and even the most gifted among them doomed to eventual stagnation. The repertories were largely made up of uninspired comedy and plays devoid of real artistic value. The Russian theatre was compelled to cater for the tastes and fulfil the wishes of a distinct and relatively small section of the population and, notwithstanding the opposition of the leading theatrical directors, nothing could be done to remove the economic dependency under which the theatre was labouring. The founders and directors of the Moscow Art Theatre, Stanislavsky and Nemirovich-Danchenko, sorrowfully admitted that the theatre was passing through a critical period owing to the continual widening of the gulf which separated it from the realistic traditions of Russian drama.

In the case of the Ukrainian, Byelorussian, Georgian and Armenian theatres, the censorship, administrative repressions and limitations and excessive taxation effectively stifled the national drama at its very inception.

Notwithstanding the great reputation acquired by the Russian theatre and the fame achieved by its artistes, the results were far short of what they should have been. Even the brilliant dramatic record of the Moscow Art Theatre, the Little Theatre (of Moscow) and the Alexander Theatre (St. Petersburg), the dazzling ballets and the work of the greatest artistes in the operas could not give adequate expression to the dramatic talent of the nation.

The first important difference between the Soviet theatre and its predecessor of the pre-revolutionary era lies in the fact that the former affords ample scope for the unhampered development of the people's dramatic power.

There is, to begin with, a vast increase in the number of theatres in the country. During the years of the Soviet régime their number has been trebled and has now reached 800. The radical change which has taken place in economic conditions and the spread of culture among the mass of the people has transformed the character of the theatre, and from being an exclusive and expensive form of entertainment it has now become an essential and readily accessible spiritual necessity for the masses.

The stage is now part and parcel of the life of the citizens, who look upon it as being as natural and indispensable an adjunct of the latter as the press or books.

In addition to the municipal theatres there are a large number of collective farm theatres in the country districts, which present the best examples of classical and modern drama to rural audiences. There are about 250 of these theatres in addition to those maintained by certain units of the Red Army. Special theatres have also been established for juvenile audiences. Hundreds of amateur dramatic societies in public institutions, factories, collective farms and Red Army units, directed by experienced theatrical artistes, present plays and serve as a stepping-stone to the professional stage for new talent.

Peoples which were formerly complete strangers to the theatre are hastening to take advantage of the opportunities now open to them by developing their own drama founded on the traditions and customs of the country. Other national theatres, already possessing a high degree of dramatic culture, but cramped and distorted by oppression, such as those of the Ukrainians, Armenians, Byelorussians, Georgians and Jews, have now attained a standard comparable to that of the best Moscow theatres. Plays in 57 languages are presented on the Soviet stage.

In Moscow there is an annual season for the presentation of the national drama of the Union republics, which is always given an enthusiastic reception. These seasons include plays from Georgia, Kazakhstan, the Ukraine, Azerbaijan and Uzbekistan and each of the nationalities concerned displays the best examples of its dramatic art. This is frequently based on their folk-lore or the doings of their legendary heroes of history or present-day Soviet life—like the moving drama *Abessalom and Eteri* by the Georgian playwright Paliashvili, which in point of pathos and profundity rivals *Romeo and Juliet*, or the Azerbaijan opera *Kör-Ogly* by Hadjibekov, a typical example of heroic opera, or Mousrenov-Brussilovsky's *Kyz-Jibek* of the Kazakh theatre. The Russian stage, in its search for experience, can no more afford to overlook the

Georgian drama or the Azerbaijan opera, than can the national theatres of the Union republics neglect the theatrical quests proceeding in the capital of the Union.

A new generation of actors is developing and the very type of their work differs completely from that of their pre-revolutionary forerunners.

In former times a theatre in the provinces might have to put on 80 or 90 new pieces per season, whereas now the average number of new plays staged in a provincial town is only 9 to 12, which obviously allows far more time and attention to be devoted to each one. The old-time actor had no interests outside the narrow limits of his professional ambitions and thereby acquired the weaknesses of the worst type of stage mummer; his present-day successor is a man of wide cultural development and lives the life of the people.

The Government treat the theatrical profession with every consideration and take care that it should be adequately remunerated. Its outstanding members receive rewards in the shape of honours and marks of distinction and some of the leading actors have been elected members of the Supreme Soviet of the U.S.S.R. At the present time the Soviet theatre provides congenial employment for old-time artistes and directors like Stanislavsky and Nemirovich-Danchenko, Kachalov and Moskvin, Korchagina-Alexandrovskaya and Blumenthal-Tamarina, alongside younger players of the Soviet era, like Khmelior and Tarassova, Schchukin, Simonov and Cherkassov, and exponents of the new nationalist dramatic school, such as the Jewish actors Mihoels and Zusskin, the Georgians Khorava and Vassadze, the Ukrainians Butchma and Litvinenko-Wohlgemut, the Azerbaijanians Mamedova and Bul-Bul, the Kazakh "nightingale," Koliash Baisseitova, and many others.

The actual scope of the drama has been extended and made wider. The percentage of classical plays has been greatly increased and is by no means limited to the Russian classics like Gogol, Griboyedov, Ostrovsky and Gorky. There is scarcely a single dramatist of world-wide reputation whose plays are not staged in the Soviet theatre. Apart from Shakespeare and Schiller and the Italians Goldoni and Gozzi, Soviet theatres present works by Aristophanes and Sophocles, Ben Jonson and Fletcher, Racine and the French dramatists of the Renaissance, Hans Sachs and Kleist, de Musset and Hugo, Bernard Shaw and Oscar Wilde. The Soviet stage is the rightful legatee of the culture of the whole world and as such is bound to present the latter to new audiences in all its pristine purity and depth.

The frivolous farce and meaningless comedy which formed so large a part of the light entertainment of pre-revolutionary audiences have vanished from the repertory of the Soviet stage, which is more concerned with the realities of life and their study. The drama of the Soviet Union deals with the mental processes of human psychology, political problems, the rebirth of mankind, a better appreciation of duty, friendship, honour, labour, love and faith and with the great questions which have, at all times, troubled mankind. It possesses a wealth of concrete material in the shape of the new social and political order prevailing in the U.S.S.R., and serves to depict the characteristics of the country's people as displayed in their lives at the present time. The Soviet stage is fulfilling a difficult task in this direction and under these circumstances it is not to be wondered at that, notwithstanding a large number of interesting and great achievements, it is not yet wholly equal to the demands made on it by the rapidly growing country.

The nature of the plays varies greatly. Among those which are nearly always included in every repertory are Alexis Tolstoi's tragedy, *Peter I,* and the descriptive plays of the time of the Civil War, Vsevolod Ivanov's *Armoured Train 14-69,* Treven's *Livbov Yarovaya,* Pogodin's plays —more especially *The Aristocrats* and *The Man with the Gun* in which the author makes Lenin one of his stage characters; N. Virta's *The Earth* of the period of the anti-Soviet revolt in the villages and, above all, Maxim Gorky's last plays, *Igor Boulychev and Others* and *Dostigaev and Others.* With these two plays Gorky marked a new trend of Soviet drama—a trend towards more sincerity and a better grasp of the great philosophical problems.

Passionate and moving dramaturgy helps the theatres to produce plays dealing with contemporary life in the Soviet Union, while the stage assists the playwright by sharing its experience with him.

The stage has extended the scope of its themes and the time-honoured characters of *jeunes premiers* and gay *ingénues* have been thrust aside by figures taken from classes of society whose earlier appearances on the stage were transitory and casual. They must be represented not in a narrow empirical sense, but in the light of a deep comprehension of the basic tendencies of Soviet life.

Although they are not blind to the shortcomings and inconsistencies with which they must contend, Soviet playwrights strive to make their work reflect the same optimistic outlook and the same belief in the cause of Socialism as animates the lives and labour of the greatest men of the Soviet Union. On the Soviet stage we see *Othello* and *Hamlet, Œdipus* and *Harpagon* alongside collective farm and party workers, Soviet intellectuals and Stakhanovites, combatants of the Civil War and aviators, Red Army soldiers and engineers.

The general subject-matter of the Soviet stage may be described as socialist humanism, while its form is that of socialist realism. Its art is that of a powerful living organism, an acute sense of political values and unshakable confidence in the future. These are the sentiments which have inspired the complicated changes wrought in the mentality of the theatre in recent years. They have furnished ample data for far-reaching theoretical conclusions. The dramatic art of the Soviet does not tolerate any formal or naturalistic limitations of reality.

Soviet dramatists have, after much labour and tireless search, come to understand that their work is closely bound up with the fruitful roots of the truly popular and realistic art of their country. The people and the audiences reject scholastic schemes and have no time for a sceptical and paradoxical attitude towards reality—what they demand is the profound and serious meaning, harmonic poesy and full-blooded pulsating realism characteristic of the dramatic genius of Molière and Shakespeare.

In the early days of the Revolution a zeal for the destruction of the hateful features of a decadent stage resulted in a temporary period of formalistic experiments or naturalistic imitations, of which exhaustive use was made on the Soviet stage. The playwrights and producers responsible displayed a high degree of artistic talent and inventiveness, but the character of their work was, at best, merely controversial, as they were unable to present a new world outlook and great human characters as substitutes for the accepted features of the Philistine stage which they have destroyed. In their efforts to reform the external aspects of the stage they aped the eccentricities of the music hall and similar establishments, deliberately emphasizing the artificiality of the theatre, thereby divorcing art from the truths of real life and carrying it into the realms of histrionic trickery. All these young producers ignored the work of educating actors to become great enough and sufficiently versatile to be capable of conveying the most subtle and complex sentiments of present-day humanity to the audience. Therefore the further these producers travelled along the road to formalism, the more spiritually meaningless and dull was their presentation which even ceased to excite the curiosity of the playgoer and merely bored him.

At the present time the first place in the dramatic art of the Soviet Union must be awarded to the Moscow Art Theatre, the work of which, even in pre-revolutionary times, corresponded to the highest aspirations of intellectual democracy. This work is realistic, simple, vivid and profound and aims at achieving on the stage, what writers like Tolstoi, Turgenev and Balzac strove to achieve in the realm of literature. The Art Theatre presents both classical and Soviet plays, among which the most successful in recent times are the dramatic version of Tolstoi's *Anna Karenina,* Trenev's *Liubov Yarovaya* and Gorky's *Enemies*.

These plays are distinguished by a profound idealism

and lofty conception of morality on the one hand and simplicity and clarity of stage interpretation on the other. The theatre only presents the most important and essential features of the narratives, omitting minor naturalistic details but concentrating the playgoer's attention on the most interesting and important features, in which the vividness and beauty of each individual life does not conflict with a sober social analysis.

The subtlety and versatility displayed in these presentations constitute a proof that the Soviet stage's opposition to formalism is in no sense a neglect of form. On the contrary, the plays presented by the Art Theatre possess a high degree of formal accuracy and finish.

The Moscow Little Theatre—the oldest in Russia and the upholder of the highest traditions of the dramatic art of the nineteenth century—is now going through a most interesting process. It is endeavouring to discard the irrelevant and petty characteristics introduced into its work during the years of pre-revolutionary decadence, when its actors and actresses played in obscure pieces by minor playwrights. The Little Theatre is attempting to revert to the days of Ermolova's genius in the heroic verse of Schiller and the dramatic power of Shakespeare, and the Sadovskys' presentations of characters in Russian life.

In Gleb Ouspensky's *Rasteriaev Street* and Shakespeare's *Othello* the colourful and bold play of the actors enhances the high dramatic standard of the presentation and serves as an outlet for genuine passion.

The basic pathos of the Soviet stage of the present day is a striving for realism in all its aspects, a realism with a depth of feeling and passion which will inspire the audience with the idea of the play and the living image of its characters. This striving after realism extends to the opera and the ballet, both of which were formerly inspired by a totally different feeling and mentality. The operatic stage, standardized for many years and largely dominated by artificial characters or reduced to far-fetched æstheticism, is now engaged in a noteworthy series of experiments in the presentation of monumental realism born of the spirit of the music.

The operatic experiments of Stanislavsky and Nemirovich-Danchenko and the operatic performances presented on the stage of the oldest opera house in Moscow—the Grand Theatre—the creation of operas around the themes of Sholokhov's famous novels, *And Quiet Flows the Don* and *Virgin Soil Upturned,* by the young composer Dzerjinsky, &c.—all this indicates the penetration of the operatic stage into aspects of life hitherto inaccessible to it. When the tragedy of the simple Cossack girl Axinia (*And Quiet Flows the Don*) is staged, the entire company evokes storms of appreciative applause from the audience.

Such are the characteristic features of the dramatic art of the Soviet Union of the present day. They may be observed in all parts of the vast country, in a variety of forms, in collective farms, in small towns, on the steppes of Kirgizia, among the mountains of Georgia and on the plains of the Ukraine.

XXIV

CONTEMPORARY MUSIC

By E. Neuhaus

Professor at the Moscow Conservatoire

In pre-revolutionary Russia musical matters were the preserve of the upper classes of society. At the present time they have become a subject of national concern. Love of music, interest in musical matters and the amount of work devoted to them have increased to an incredible extent.

The achievements of the people of the Soviet Union in the field of music are, as in all branches of art, marked by a high measure of success.

The time is long since past, when the devotees of the pseudo-radical school in Soviet music considered the great musical heritage of the past from the viewpoint of their own narrow theories, rejecting the importance and the work of many great composers and discarding complete epochs. This school of thought was soon forced to give way to the pressure of public opinion and did not last long enough to inflict much harm on the development of Soviet music. The country is receptive to all that is best in the world of music and its composers are carrying on and developing the traditions of the Russian classical music of the nineteenth century bequeathed by Glinka, Borodin, Tchaikovsky, Moussorgsky, Rimsky-Korsakov and others. The masterpieces of the musical world meet with wholehearted appreciation not only among professional musicians, but among the masses of the people. Concert programmes include works selected from the musical classics and romantics of the past as well as the best of the present-day compositions.

Whereas Brahms was until recent years unpopular in Russia—a circumstance for which Tchaikovsky's antipathy to Brahms was largely to blame—he is now becoming increasingly popular. On the other hand, the great works of Bach are not played often enough at concerts and Wagner's operas are rarely given.

Socialist realism with its incarnation of ideas in art to which Soviet art as a whole is tending, represents the lodestar of musical creativeness in the U.S.S.R. A comparison of Soviet music of 15 years ago with what is being done at the present time is interesting. Some of the composers laboured under erroneous conceptions which were frequently reflected by the extreme urbanity and slightly mechanical effect of their work, with an exaggerated tendency to polytonism and atonalism and a striving to achieve "modernism at any price." These composers were also hampered by the extreme illiberality of their work which by its nature could only appeal to a small circle of friends and admirers. At the same time other composers, in their anxiety to write popular music, frequently allowed their work to degenerate into extreme primitiveness and schematic ultra-simplicity.

At the present time the effect of Soviet reality and the influence of modern thought is expressed in a return to healthy realism, a genuine endeavour to make the best use of the treasures of the national folk music and a determination to produce musical work inspired by a greater and clearer degree of everyday thought. The cult of humanism finds a ready outlet in the sphere of music.

All this has raised the standard of Soviet music to a much higher level and even if some of our younger composers' work is not wholly free from defects—due to inadequate technique and lack of thorough musical culture—the general tendency they display indicates that they are on the right road for the creation of valuable and necessary work. The language of Soviet composers is becoming clearer and easier to understand, while at the same time it is getting richer and more expressive.

The case of one of the most gifted of our composers, Dmitri Shostakovitch, illustrates the way in which our leading musical composers have developed their gifts. Shostakovitch himself in his youth came under the influence of the prevalent fashion of formal artificiality and there was a good deal of scepticism in his music. However, his present-day work, as judged by his *Fifth Symphony,* indicates that the just criticism of Soviet opinion has exercised a beneficial influence on his ability. He no longer fears to make use of profound and widely conceived thematics and his *Fifth Symphony* is a great dramatic work almost completely free from any trace of those elements of scepticism which were so marked a feature of his earliest compositions.

This departure from all forms of sophistry and eccentricity and the abandonment of the former pandering to the lovers of extravagance by our composers has been succeeded by a deep devotion to the human problems in art and is now making the Soviet music of to-day worthy of the great traditions which it has inherited from the glorious past. The ground has now been prepared for new musical geniuses and the latest developments which have been noted justify great hopes for the near future.

At the present time operatic (and other) music is tending to become more and more devoted to typically Soviet themes. We have a series of operas like *Virgin Soil Upturned* and *And Quiet Flows the Don* by the young composer, Dzerjinsky, *The Battleship Potemkin* by Oless Tchishko and others, which, like the dramatic theatre of the Soviet, reflect contemporary life in the Union. Although the earliest efforts made in this direction were not always very successful, it may now be rightly asserted that these subjects are at the present time being treated by an increasingly higher class of composer.

In regard to these last, one of the most brilliant amongst them is Serge Prokofiev, whose magnificent work is well known to music-lovers in Western Europe. His most recent compositions are distinguished by a new wave of musical inspiration, this being particularly marked in the case of the beautiful, serious and profoundly emotional music of his ballet *Romeo and Juliet.* To honour the occasion of the twentieth anniversary of the October Revolution Prokofiev wrote a specially grandiose cantata for full choir and orchestra with soloists. Prokofiev, like other composers, is turning away from his original formal tendencies and replacing them by simplicity, depth and idealist-emotional satiety in music.

Miaskovsky, the leading Soviet symphonist, has already produced 18 symphonies and a whole series of piano sonatas, quartets and similar major works. His latest compositions—the *Sixteenth, Seventeenth* and *Eighteenth Symphonies*—display greater lucidity than the music of most of his earlier symphonies, which was frequently gloomy and pessimistic, whereas it has now become brighter. It is beginning to strike a more joyous note and the standard of his art is steadily progressing.

Glier, An. Alexandrov, Shebalin, Veprik, Kabalevsky (the composer of the delightful opera *The Master of Clamecy,* the libretto of which is an adaptation of Romain Rolland's *Kola Breignon*), and the younger writers like Khrennikhov, Biriukov, Makarov and Rakitin are, year by year, enriching the music of our country with numerous symphonic, chamber, theatrical and operatic works.

In writing about Soviet music, one cannot, of course, confine oneself to the works of Russian composers only. A great deal of creative art in the world of music has been displayed by other nationalities of the various republics which are included in the U.S.S.R. Among the leading Ukrainian composers the most prominent are Revutsky, Kozitsky, Yorish (composer of the heroic opera *Shors*), Liatoshinsky and Verikivsky.

In Georgia the new generation of composers includes Mshevilidze, Balanchivadze and others.

It is only now that the operas of the recently deceased great composer, Z. Paliashvili, are becoming known. A brilliant exponent of Georgian music, his work combines the beauty and originality of the folk music of his country with a remarkable degree of creative skill, backed by a finished technique.

The works of the young Armenian composer, Khatchatourian, are very largely inspired by his native folk-lore. His music is extremely vivid, emotional and colourful. He orchestrates his work admirably and the peculiarly vivid colouring, which is his national heritage, enables him to produce work of a specially novel, fresh and unusual character. It has met with well-deserved success in the U.S.S.R. and his piano concerto is particularly popular.

The music of the remaining peoples who were the most backward under the Tsarist régime, as *e.g.*, the Kirgiz, the Kazakhs and other races, was little known in former times, beyond the interest displayed in their folk songs. These songs now constitute a treasure-house of national music and folk-lore which serves to inspire many of the most brilliant composers of the Soviet Union.

In order to popularize such music, it has recently become the practice to hold musical "decades" in Moscow and other great cities at which a special study of Ukrainian, Georgian, Kazakh and Uzbeg music is made. These musical festivals have not only familiarized the Russian section of the Union with the best of the musical achievements of their fellow-citizens of the sister republics, but they have also done much to stimulate the development of national music as an art.

The basis of Soviet music is the ingrained love of music which is characteristic of all our countrymen and which finds its expression in the widespread and active interest evinced in it by our people. Practically every factory, workers' guild, collective farm and industrial undertaking, has its musical society and at the present time there are no fewer than 30,000 amateur choirs and about 25,000 amateur orchestras. They are all directed by professional musicians and display the utmost zeal in endeavouring to improve the standard of their musical performance.

Many of these choirs and orchestras have not only

attained an extraordinarily high degree of perfection, but have also produced a considerable number of first-rate solo performers. The most gifted among them give proof of their artistic talent at musical festivals and competitions and frequently turn professional.

The workers' and collective farm orchestras and choirs often give performances of complete operas and it is not unusual to hear a workers' string orchestra of folk instruments such as balalaikas, dulcimers and lutes, &c., playing classical as well as popular music.

The best known of the national choral organizations are the State Choir of Moscow, the Ukrainian "Doumka" Choir and the Jewish Choir.

The Red Army possesses some remarkably fine musical talent, including the celebrated "Red Flag Troupe of Singers and Dancers" who created such a sensation at the Paris Exhibition a year ago and also appeared in Czechoslovakia.

The development of Soviet music is due not only to the all-round improvement in the education of the people, their natural love of music and to the vast amount of musical talent available in the country, but also to the whole system of musical training and selection of students.

The number of pupils undergoing instruction in the secondary schools of music is about 100,000, all of whom aspire to be professional musicians. There are also 11 conservatoires—in Moscow, Leningrad, Kiev, Kharkov, Odessa, Saratov, Sverdlovsk, Tiflis, Baku, Erivan and Tashkent.

As is well known, not only is education free in the U.S.S.R., but all students receive state stipends while undergoing instruction and are only admitted to the higher educational establishments by a process of competition and selection, so that only the very best among them enter the conservatoires. The latter are not concerned, as in former days, with students who can pay high fees, but solely with their musical abilities: not a single really gifted person can pass unnoticed.

The schools of music do not confine their work to the teaching of musical subjects; the instruction which is given aims at not merely giving a sound musical training, but at producing educated and cultured men and women. The conservatoires only admit candidates who have completed a course of study in a normal secondary school. In many of the towns there are 10-year normal secondary schools in which selected pupils are given special training in musical subjects in addition to the ordinary ones. Some of the most brilliant young musicians of the Union, whose performances have won them international prizes, are former pupils of the secondary school attached to the Moscow Conservatoire. Among them are the violinists Boussia Goldstein and Lisa Hillels, the pianist Rosa Tamarkina and many others.

The national competitions which are frequently held all over the country constitute a great incentive for the demonstration of unknown talent and a stimulus for the various schools whose pupils take part in them. These competitions are of value both to the students and to the teaching staffs of the innumerable colleges and schools in all parts of our immense country. The conferences held in conjunction with these competitions afford the teaching staffs an opportunity of meeting each other to discuss all sorts of important matters of common professional interest.

Valuable service to the cause of music is also rendered by the various professional conferences, debates and meetings held from time to time by composers and critics to discuss questions connected with matters of current interest, new tendencies in the world of music and similar subjects. All this provides encouragement and inspiration for the musical life of the country. Mutual criticism not only benefits those engaged in the profession, but also does much to stimulate public interest in matters of musical art.

One particularly useful institution serves to bring musicians and teachers from the more remote districts into closer touch with those of the capital and leading educational centres: this is the organization in Moscow, Leningrad, Kiev and certain other great cities, of so-called Post-Graduate Institutes for Teachers of Music, which are attended for periods of one, two or three months by instructors from remote districts for the purpose of receiving the benefit of consultations, discussions, lectures and instruction with, and by professors of, the central higher educational establishments.

The effect of Soviet activity in the teaching of music has extended far beyond the borders of the U.S.S.R. The brilliant performance of Soviet artists at various international musical festivals held since 1927 has enabled the world to discover and appreciate the merits of a number of talented persons who have won numerous first prizes and other high awards for their work. For the time being Soviet singers and conductors have deferred their entry into international competitions, but the names of such pianists as Leo Oborin, Jacob Flier, Emil Hillels, Jacob Zack and Rosa Tamarkina or of such violinists as David Oistrakh, Boussia Goldstein, Lisa Hillels and Marina Kozolupova, are known throughout the world of music.

Very successful concerts are given by all these gifted young musicians, as well as by their colleagues of an older generation who include players like the violinist Poliakin, the pianists Sofronitsky, Yudina, Igumenov, Feinberg, the writer of this article, and many others.

XXV

THE CINEMA

By V. Poudovkin
Film Director

Art plays an important part in the great and historic process of building up a new socialist order in the Soviet Union. Art reflects real everyday life and explains its meaning; it rouses the strong, supports the weak and convinces the doubtful; art can draw near and almost depict the actuality of things to come; it can recall the past so realistically as if we were actually living through it again; art likewise fulfils the supreme function of rallying all manner of men to a common cause. Amongst the various branches of art fostered in the Soviet Union, that of the *cinema* is of supreme importance.

The educative and constructive force of the cinema film is stupendous. "Of all the arts, that of the cinema is the most important for us," said Lenin at a time when the production of cinema films in the Soviet Republic was still in embryo. He was merely looking ahead and foretelling the future.

Soviet cinematography has, from its earliest days, been permeated with the pathos of the fight for the Revolution, a pathos of a new and better future for humanity. Certain people in the realms of art, having little knowledge of the truth in the Soviet Union, were, at one time, only inclined to look upon the development of Soviet art as "tendentious," and "devoid of creative freedom." The fallacy of this judgment has been demonstrated by the creation of many scores of films of an artistic merit which won the acclamation of the world. The fact of the matter was that the conditions which those people regarded as irksome and oppressive were fully understood and appreciated by Soviet artists, who themselves impose and support them.

The world's greatest artists have invariably carried out their creative work within clearly defined limits which they themselves visualized beforehand: architects, according to the size and nature of the building; painters, according to the size and shape of the canvas; poets, by the length and rhythm of the verse; musicians, by the exactness of the canon. Unrestrained anarchy has never served as the basis of an artistic masterpiece, but has invariably been the hallmark of idle dilettantism. Only a thorough and lively appreciation of necessity has served to inspire the greatest artists. Is it not natural that the limitations accepted by all artists in regard to form should be equally applicable to the most important feature of a work of art—its *subject-matter?*

The profound idealism of Soviet cinematography is merely a reflection of that which pervades every phase of the country's life. The duties imposed on the film industry as a whole and on every individual worker in it are of a vitally important character, comprising as they do a thorough appreciation and understanding of the great ideas of the age and their reproduction in life by means of the art of the cinema. It is no easy task, but much has already been achieved in this direction.

The film industry has travelled a long way from the pathetically scanty technical resources utilized for the purposes of film propaganda work during the Civil War, to the world-famous masterpieces of cinematographic art made in specially constructed film studios supplied with the best of modern technical equipment. We are entitled to some pride in enumerating the following recently produced films: *Chapaev* (Vassiliev Brothers), *We of Kronstadt* (Dzigan), *The Baltic Deputy* (Heifetz and Zarkhi), *Thirteen* (M. Romm), the two serial films *The Youth* and *Return of Maxim* (Kozintsev and Trauberg), *Peter The First* (Petrov), *Lenin in October* (M. Romm), *The Great Citizen* (Aermler) and *The Wealthy Bride* (Pyriev). This list does not include a number of successful films made by our younger generation.

The growth of the film industry in Moscow and Leningrad is being emulated by that of the national film industry as a whole. To name only a few of the outstanding producers and directors, we have men like Dovzhenko in the Ukraine, Shengelai and Tchiaurelli in Georgia, Bek-Nazarov in Armenia, Korsh and Taritch in Byelorussia and others.

All these film producers and directors handle the artistic problems with which they are faced in their own individual fashion. There are innumerable genres in Soviet cinematography, just as there are an infinite number of directions, characters and methods of producing, all of which vary according to human individuality, but there is only one style, which is not peculiar to the artist but to the people and surroundings in which he is living and for which he is working. Style is born of the epoch and subsequently determines the latter.

The style of Soviet cinematography is that of *socialist realism*. The writer of this article, when making his films, *Mother* or *The End of St. Petersburg,* endeavoured, like all other Soviet film directors, to produce a picture corresponding, as far as possible, to a truthful, complete and objective representation of the triumph of the Revolution and of the hero of the new era. Film audiences cannot fail to be impressed by the simple and profoundly realistic truth of the stirring picture *Chapaev* with its legendary hero of the Civil War and by the figure of that great citizen and revolutionary scientist—the old professor in the film, *The Baltic Deputy*.

The thema of Soviet films is as varied as life itself. Soviet cinematography will have nothing to do with the vulgar and futile films designed to pander to low tastes. The aim of every Soviet film is to present a story of an adequately high degree of idealism, but its actual nature may vary considerably. We must have drama and comedy, adventurous and fantastic films. Historical films are of special importance and the U.S.S.R. already possesses a whole series of valuable films on subjects connected with the Russian Revolution and other historical topics, such as the two films *Peter the First, The Paris Commune* (directed by Roshal), *Alexander Nevsky* (produced by Eisenstein), *Minin and Pozharsky* (directed by Poudovkin and Doller), &c. Further films of this category are in the course of preparation.

The application of the principles of socialist realism to Soviet films inevitably produced many difficulties and led to errors, confusion and irrelevance. Such defects were unavoidable if the search for the right way was to be continued and although they have now largely disappeared, every endeavour is being made to overcome them entirely.

From the film "Chapayev"—A scene from "Anna Karenina" at the Moscow Art Theatre

The difficulties involved are, broadly speaking, due to two separate tendencies.

One such fallacious "tendency"—if it can be designated as such—may be termed "naturalism." Here the artist is merely concerned with the accurate and mechanical reproduction of the external characteristics of people and things; thought and feeling are replaced by stark physiology. The naturalist represents the murder of the hero by streams of blood, cries, groans and convulsions, thereby destroying the dramatic meaning of the event for the audience by submerging it in a welter of physiological commotion. The naturalist fills his picture with a wealth of mechanically reproduced detail and he substitutes the latter for the profound generalization which his film lacks. The defects of naturalism have been noted in the work of some of our leading film artists, as, for example, the killings and the overeating with dumplings shown in Aermler's well-known film *The Peasants*. The friendly criticism of his colleagues has caused this film director to abandon his former tendencies completely and his latest work, perfect in every respect, is that magnificent film *The Great Citizen*.

The other erroneous tendency which frequently manifests itself as actually hostile to the Soviet régime may be described as "formalism." Its external characteristics are the emphasis laid on the so-called "form" at the expense of the "contents": its essence is as follows:—

The artist, cut off from actual contact with the real, burning and urgent problems of the day, remains isolated with his canvas, paper or clay. His creative spirit is dependent solely on the inanimate substance and his imagination is directed to the sphere of abstractions. The great conception of *beauty* born of real life and wholly belonging to it, is turned into a cold and barren "æstheticism" and a dreary search for a variety of possible combinations of colour, outline, form, &c. Form becomes the ultimate object of this type of artist. He is like a boy in Andersen's fairy tale, sitting on the floor of the Snow Queen's vast deserted palace, with a fragment of a fiendish mirror distorting every image in his frozen heart, vainly trying to compose the word "eternity" with bits of ice. To carry this analogy further, it will need a live person with a warm heart, a lover of life and human beings to drag him from the icy desert and to cause him to live and share the interests of humanity. Then only will his frozen heart melt and expel the fragment of mirror "which shows everything great and good as insignificant and evil," enabling him to develop a genuine ability to create.

The development of this creative ability in the film industry, as in all branches of art, is proceeding apace in the Soviet Union. Formalism as such makes no appeal, as a country in which the creative forces of society are being strained in every nerve to reach a real and visible goal, has no time for any deliberate or involuntary indulgence in stark "form" and obscure abstractions. Such indulgence only leads to the replacement of our great ideas by a number of petty, uninspired, and ultimately senseless and irrelevant considerations.

It will, therefore, be understood why the film industry is displaying vigorous and uncompromising opposition to every type of formalism. For this reason A. Romm's film, *Relentless Youth,* which dealt with vital aspects of morality from the point of view of the petty "æsthete," met with a hostile reception from the public. A similar fate befell Garin's film, *The Wedding,* a distorted travesty of Gogol's classical masterpiece evolved by an unimaginative director.

Where should the causes of naturalistic and formalistic defects in films be looked for? The film director begins his work with the scenario. In the U.S.S.R. a number of prominent authors are film scenario writers; as, for example, in Vishnevsky's *We of Kronstadt,* Alexis Tolstoi's *Peter The First,* Pavlenko's *Alexander Nevsky,* Sholokhov, Kataev, Babel and others. The actual causes of the defects, incongruities and failures from which we are still suffering, are the crude and poor scenarios. Because of these shortcomings the special "Cinematographic Committee of the Council of People's Commissars of the U.S.S.R." appointed in March, 1938, have taken immediate steps to create an adequately strong pool of authors, dramatists and film scenario writers.

A film is the product of the common effort of a series of persons working in harmony, which, in the first instance, means the co-operation of the scenario writer and film director. The film industry is endeavouring to combine the creative functions of directors and dramatists both in regard to the scenario and the actual story on which it is based. Where such a combination cannot be made at the outset of the work, creative co-ordination at a later stage is invariably insisted on.

Taking the maximum utilization of the creative talents of the actors and directors as our watchword, we are now establishing a new procedure in the making of films. We are introducing and fostering important preliminary work prior to the shooting of the film.

The actor, Cherkassov, who played the part of Professor Polejaiev in the film, *The Baltic Deputy,* so brilliantly, spent a long time over it before the picture was shot. In the end he could, as he himself stated, live as the old professor at any time and under any circumstances. While playing the part of the 70-year-old man, he sometimes went out wearing his make-up and costume, entered a restaurant and engaged in casual conversation without exciting any comment or perplexity.

The same sort of thing was done by Babochkin in *Chapaev* and by many other actors.

Vsevolod Vishnevsky and Dzingan, the authors of the film *We of Kronstadt,* spent days and weeks on end with the leading actors in various ships and submarines, living the life of sailors of the Red Fleet in order to perfect their rendering of the parts they were to direct or play.

The film industry requires the actor to possess both a high degree of technique and to play his part true to life. At the same time, in connexion with the greater demands made of the art of cinematography, he is called upon to create great typical portrayals like Babochkin's popular hero, *Chapaev;* Cherkassov's wonderful representation of a spotless and honourable man—Professor Polejaiev; Tchirkov's typical Bolshevik working man in the Revolutionary struggle of the films, *The Youth of Maxim* and *The Return of Maxim;* Shchukin, who made the first daring attempt to play the part of the living figure of Lenin and who succeeded so admirably; the magnificent likeness of the worker, Shakhov, in the picture, *The Great Citizen,* played by the actor Bogoliubov, inspired by the living example of the fiery revolutionary tribune S. M. Kirov. These examples will serve to illustrate the greatness and importance of the cultural task undertaken by our progressive film actors.

The evolution of the sound film was responsible for the introduction of new features into the art of cinematography—the spoken word and music. We attach supreme importance to music in our films and do not merely regard it as convenient background for the captions and as a means for the more or less artificial inclusion of a couple of songs in the text of the scenario. Music, as we understand it, is in the first place an ideal medium for presenting a special aspect or emphasizing the subject-matter of separate scenes and of the film as a whole (as for example, the music in *The Baltic Deputy*) and in the second place music in films is an invaluable means of spreading and popularizing musical culture among the masses of the people. For this reason leading Soviet composers, men like Shaporin and Shostakovitch, who are world-famous as such, display keen interest in writing music for films.

Despite the growth of our film industry, it obviously has not kept pace with the demands made on it by the country. We need far more pictures than we can make at present and this fact has called attention to the urgent need for the systematic training of expert workers for the film industry.

The State Institute of Cinematography in Moscow trains film directors and operators. The training of actors and actresses has been linked up with production and the film studios have dramatic schools for the instruction of young players.

Cinematography differs from other branches of art in that it calls for highly elaborate technical equipment.

Complicated photography and laboratory apparatus, the lighting system and the large number of auxiliary accessories cause the making of a picture to be directly dependent on the qualitative and quantitative merits of the technical resources available. Soviet industry is aiming at self-sustenance in manufactures in order to avoid dependence on foreign countries and this applies equally to the film industry.

The Soviet Union has, in a comparatively short space of time, organized the manufacture of essential film materials, apparatus and equipment. We possess two large factories for making films and can turn out high-grade sound apparatus. Our camera-making branch of the industry is less advanced, but it is anticipated that the difficulties experienced in this direction will shortly be overcome.

The nature of the pictures produced by the Soviet film industry is manifold. In addition to dramatic films a large number of highly successful news-reels have been produced, together with a whole series of educational and scientific films demonstrating the work of the academician Pavlov, the eugenist Mitchurin and other scientists. A special establishment is set apart for producing films for children.

Great attention is being paid to the production of composite film pictures, in which the industry excels—more especially as regards three-dimensional pictures. The film entitled *The New Gulliver* (directed by Ptoushko) is a brilliant example of this class of picture.

All the above categories of films receive the utmost encouragement from the Government and enjoy a widespread popularity.

Our film industry is expanding: its growth is primarily due to the peculiar social structure of our country. I know of no other land in which the members of the Government read film scenarios prior to production and express their views on them, and where film directors can seek the guidance and advice of persons holding the highest public office.

It is worthy of note that in connexion with the films, *Lenin in October, Peter The First* and *The Wealthy Bride,* the Soviet Government awarded decorations not only to the film directors, scenario writers and artistes, but also to the technical personnel responsible for the make-up, lighting properties, laboratory work, &c.

The object of this attention to the film industry is obvious. The cinema constitutes a powerful influence in the socialist education of the masses, the improvement of their cultural level and the enlistment of their active co-operation in the structural development of the public life of the country.

XXVI

PRESENT-DAY ART

By Igor Grabar

The material—and moral—welfare of artists of every nation has, at all times, been dependent on the good will of their customers and patrons, who were made up of royalty, the papacy, the higher nobility and the wealthy mercantile classes. The state was very rarely a patron or purchaser of works of art. Therefore when the October Revolution of 1917 terminated the hegemony of the privileged class in Russia, destroyed capitalism and laid the foundations of socialism, a new type of patron and customer became necessary. It was then that the masses of the people themselves became the patrons of art, with their ruling body, the Soviet Government, as their representative.

In the early days of the Revolution foreign intervention and the resulting chaos overwhelmed the Soviet authorities with numerous urgent problems and prevented them from dealing with that of "Art and the State," although even then they found time to issue a series of decrees intended to enhance the value of the part assigned to art in the life of the country. One of the earliest decrees was that nationalizing the principal private collections, the owners of which had fled and which were in imminent danger of being taken abroad and dispersed.

At the same time further decrees were issued concerning the preservation of historic and ancient works of art and the establishment of a Chief Directorate of Fine Arts. Painters, engravers and sculptors were given work by the state and a State Purchasing Commission was appointed to acquire what they produced.

During the 21 years which have now elapsed since the October Revolution, the creative art of the peoples of the Soviet Union has steadily developed and turned away from the formalistic trickery introduced from the West before the Revolution and which appealed in the first instance to the wealthy snobocracy and, after the flight of the latter, to a section of the Revolutionary community which fondly imagined that a "Left" inclination in politics necessitated a "Left" form of art. This play of words, which merely concealed ignorance and lack of imagination, was exposed in no uncertain fashion by Stalin's call for "socialist realism" which met with an enthusiastic reception from all Soviet artists.

The change-over was effected gradually, beginning approximately in 1922, and finally leading, in the spring of 1932, to the replacement of the scattered remnants of numerous art societies and circles by a single great "Union of Soviet Artists." Shortly after its inauguration a special code of rules dealing with the mutual relations of the state (as patron and customer) and the artist was elaborated and adopted for the encouragement of art and artists in general. All the more or less skilled painters, engravers and sculptors of Moscow, Leningrad and 10 other capital cities of the United Republics were put under contract to the state. They were granted fully adequate stipends and allowances which enabled them to devote their entire energies to art without the necessity of seeking any secondary occupation. The actual amounts paid to them varied according to the talents, professional status and experience of the different artists; in hundreds of cases they were very substantial and sufficed not only to maintain an extremely comfortable standard of living, but to allow savings to be effected. The terms of the contract only bind the artist to deliver a part of his output to the state and the greater part of it remains at his own disposal. It finds purchasers amongst the hundreds of museums, sanatoria, holiday homes and other cultural institutions.

In addition to this system of contracts, that of orders is retained. Some idea of the nature and scale of these purchases may be formed by mentioning the conditions under which the Soviet artists worked for the great All-Union Exhibition of the People's Commissariat of Heavy Industry opened in 1938 under the title of "The Industry of Socialism."

This exhibition was originally planned in 1934 by the late People's Commissar, Ordjonikidze, and it aimed at utilizing art to depict the greatest achievement of the past 10 years—the conversion of the most backward agrarian country of Europe into a great industrial state and the far-reaching effects of the change which was thereby wrought in the lives, habits, culture and mentality of the peoples inhabiting the Soviet Union.

All the artists of the country were represented and 700 of them produced over 1000 exhibits among them, the exhibition constituting a complete display of the history of Soviet art from its inception down to the present day.

A review of the best work of Soviet artists must, of

course, begin with that of its senior generation inherited by the Revolution from an earlier period. The Revolution found a number of the great masters of Russian art still living, among them being Ilia Repin (1844-1930), Vassili Polenov (1884-1929) and Victor Vasnetsov (1848-1926). The first-named was at his country home in Finland at the time of the Revolution and was, by the force of circumstances, compelled to end his days there, cut off permanently from his native country, while the other two were passing their days in retirement and did not exhibit again.

In contrast to these masters their junior colleagues, Sergei Maliutin (1859-1937) and Michael Nesterov (*b.* 1862), displayed great activity. Maliutin was one of the leading portrait painters of pre-revolutionary days and became one of the greatest masters among Soviet portraitists. With a single exception, all his portraits were in pastel, but he made use of a special technical process of his own in applying thick layers of colouring. This characteristic of his work combined with the exceptional brilliance of his tints, gives his pastel portraits the appearance of oil-paintings.

Nesterov was formerly a painter who excelled in religious and ecclesiastical themes and who carried out a great deal of mural work in churches, but after the Revolution he devoted himself solely to portraiture, in which he had also specialized. His portraits of his daughter and of Leo Tolstoi were famous masterpieces. During the past 20 years Nesterov has, year after year, exhibited a number of portraits, invariably exquisite in composition, true to life and attractive in colouring. He has been particularly successful with his group portrait of the artist brothers Korin and of his portraits of the academician, Severtsev, and of the celebrated physiologist, Ivan Pavlov. The standard of his work as a master of portraiture has improved so greatly on that of his earlier work, that there is every reason to assert that Nesterov, the portraitist, is greater than Nesterov, the painter of religious subjects.

Igor Grabar (*b.* 1871), the writer of this article, may claim to be a representative of the next generation. A painter, architect and writer, he is the author of a history of Russian art in several volumes and of a whole series of monographs on similar subjects. A pupil of Repin, he was a landscape and still-life painter prior to the Revolution, but since 1918 he has definitely reverted to his temporarily abandoned work as a painter of portraits, genre and historical subjects (*Lenin speaking on the direct wire with the Front* and *Casting iron on a foundry conveyor*).

Among his most prominent contemporaries are the landscape painter, Arkady Rylov (*b.* 1870), the xylographer, Anna Ostro'oumova (*b.* 1871), the black-and-white and mural artist, Eugène Lanceret (*b.* 1875), the painter of the countryside round Moscow, Constantine You'on (*b.* 1875) and the black-and-white artist and pedagogue, Dmitri Kardovsky (*b.* 1865). All of them are regular exhibitors in the Soviet Union and are masters of their own specialized branch of art.

Then comes a very slightly younger and more militant group of former post-impressionist artists, who have turned to healthy realism. This group comprises Peter Kontchalovsky (*b.* 1876), Ilia Mashkov (*b.* 1881), Alexander Kouprin (*b.* 1880) and Alexander Lentoullov (*b.* 1882).

Woodcut by A. Kravchenko illustrating Byron's "Mystery."

They mostly specialize in subjects which give scope to their delineation and colouring, which is always bold and vivid.

A somewhat different tendency is observed in the work of another group of artists who likewise specialize in colouring, but apply it in a more distinctive manner. There are the brilliant colourist Paul Kouznetov (*b.* 1878) and the expert epitomizer of original combinations of colours Kouzma Petrov-Vodkin (*b.* 1878). This group also included the portraitist Nikolai Oulianov (*b.* 1875) and the landscape painter Nikolai Krymov (*b.* 1884), but both these artists have now broken away from it in regard to the tendency displayed in their work.

All the above-named artists had achieved a reputation before the Revolution and joined the family of Soviet artists, earning their right to do so by working on the subject-matter of the present time. They have not remained stationary since the Revolution, but have on the contrary steadily progressed and kept in step with their younger colleagues. Obviously the knowledge and experience of the older generation of artists tend to put most of them at the head of their profession in regard to technique, but the younger generation has already produced some first-class masters who are successfully emulating their seniors.

This applies to a number of artists who were trained before the Revolution and may even have shown their work at the exhibitions of the day, but who only acquired prominence under the Soviet régime. First and foremost is the large group of artists who combined early in the 1920's to form "The Artists' Association of Revolutionary Russia," and who played an important part in the movement to break away from the formalistic ravings already referred to. Their watchword was: "Realism—not formalism!" which, in their case, was equivalent to discarding conventional representation in favour of Soviet topics. The leading artists of this particular group eventually, and not unnaturally, reached a stage at which their formula become "Down with colour; long live form!" Whereas others stressed colour, they cultivated form; the adherents of one school were primarily painters and those of the other were essentially draughtsmen.

One of the most individual and outstanding pioneers of this movement is Vassili Yakovlev (*b.* 1894), a worshipper of the old masters whom he follows not only in knowledge of form and style of brushwork, but even in regard to the yellowishness or "gallery tint" which he has adopted. A brilliant draughtsman, he dreams of immense combinations and huge canvases.

The work of his companion in arms in the fight against formalism, that of the ardent preacher of realism, Eugène Katzmann (*b.* 1890), is no less distinctive. Declining to use oil colours, he makes his pictures with special coloured crayons of his own invention which frequently produce an effect closely resembling oil-colouring. He mostly does portraits and groups and sometimes collective groups—such as *Men of the Soviet Union.* Admirably drawn and life-like, they have a characteristic style of their own, which is instantly recognizable by the public at the exhibitions at which his work is shown.

Isaac Brodsky (*b.* 1883) has won a great reputation as a portrait painter with his series of portraits of revolutionary leaders and huge pictorial groups. Millions of copies were published and enabled him to achieve popularity among the masses. Their style is more that of a photograph than a painting and they display the art of the draughtsman rather than that of the painter.

Another producer of huge canvases is Alexander Gerassimov (*b.* 1889) whose groups are painted rather than drawn. One such picture represents a group of soldiers of the First Mounted Corps. His namesake, Sergei Gerassimov (*b.* 1889), is a born artist who does first-rate landscapes as well and easily as large canvases of an elaborate nature. He excels at peasants and village life, being himself of peasant origin. His latest and best picture, *New People of a New Village,* was one of the most remarkable works on show at the Industry Exhibition.

Then come the artists of the younger generation, whose present average age is round about 40 years. Among them is the versatile romantic Fedor Bogorodsky (*b.* 1895), who has not yet finally adopted a speciality to suit his ability; George Riajsky (*b.* 1895), an enterprising and inspired genre and portrait painter; George Nissky (*b.* 1903), a brilliant landscape painter and unusually keen observer of novel features of nature themes; and Alexander Deinecka (*b.* 1899), who has a distinctive style of his own in the linear and colour simplification of nature, both in landscapes and life.

Quite recently a certain number of still younger artists have attracted attention by the brilliant quality of their work in every kind of painting, among them being Fedor Malayev (*b.* 1902), a sensitive colourist, who promises to become one of the greatest artists in the Soviet Union, Fedor Shourpin (*b.* 1904), Tarass Gaponenko (*b.* 1906) and Alexander Boubnov (*b.* 1908).

It was only in 1937 that the young painter, Vassili Efanov (*b.* 1900) achieved prominence through his great picture representing the reception by members of the Government of the public women-workers; it is a masterpiece of technique and brush-work which many an experienced artist might envy.

Among other branches of art, that of engraving occupies an important place, more especially as applied to book illustration in its various forms, such as wood engraving, lithography, etching, linotyping, monotyping, &c. Soviet artists in these classes of work have achieved world fame; those of Vladimir Fovorsky, Alexis Kravchenko, Ivan Pavlov and Peter Staronossov being familiar to xylographers throughout the civilized world.

Another well-developed branch of Soviet pictorial art is that of the cartoonist and its exponents include such masters as the three artists working together under the pseudonym of "The Koukrynixes," and the artists Dmitri Moore (*b.* 1883), Victor Denny (*b.* 1892) and Boris Efimov (*b.* 1900).

The development of the present-day Soviet sculpture has been greatly assisted by the modern tendency to assimilate architecture and sculpture. One of the finest examples of such assimilation was the Soviet Pavilion at the Paris Exhibition in 1937. One of the best Soviet craftsmen is the sculptress, Vera Moukhina (*b.* 1891), whose gigantic figure executed in stainless steel evoked such admiration in the above pavilion. There is a considerable demand for monumental and decorative sculpture in the Union due to the extensive programme of construction of public buildings, parks, &c. Relief-portraiture is also being widely used.

Apart from Vera Moukhina, the most prominent and gifted sculptors are Ivan Shadr (*b.* 1890), who adheres to austerity in the form of his work and who is an excellent portraitist; Alexander Matveiev (*b.* 1872), a sculptor of large form and simplified lines; Joseph Tchaikov (*b.* 1888), a sculptor of elaborate composite groups; Sarah Lebedeva (*b.* 1895), a sculptress of small form, a delicate portraitist and an artist of exquisite taste; Sergei Merkurov (*b.* 1881), a master of monumental sculpture; George Motovilov (*b.* 1892), the sculptor of "The Metallurgist," a work almost classical in its noble simplicity; Boris Korolev (*b.* 1885), who is responsible for a number of monuments; Matvei Manizer (*b.* 1891), a sculptor who has produced several important and elaborate monuments erected in various localities of the Union, and Leonidas Sherwood (*b.* 1871), a highly cultured sculptor producing work of remarkably fine design.

All the above-named artists, painters and sculptors represent the art of the Russian Soviet Federative Socialist Republic, the largest constituent republic of the Soviet Union. However, the October Revolution, which brought release from centuries of oppression to all the remaining peoples of the Union, gave a free scope to their latent cultural instincts and thereby enabled the creative art of the country to acquire a far wider basis.

Apart from the art of Russia, as already described, there is the rapidly growing art of the Ukraine, represented by such masters as Fedor Krichevsky (*b.* 1879), a historical painter and decorative artist of rare ability; Shulga and Shovkupenko. Among the younger artists are Dereguz, Grigoriev and others.

Georgia has also produced a number of distinguished

artists whose names are worthy of inclusion among the foremost in the Union. Such artists are Moses and Heracles Toidze (father and son), Koutateladze, Kobouladze and others.

The greatest Armenian artist is Martiros Sarian (*b.* 1880), a painter whose vivid colours and joyous life-scenes are typical of his sunny country.

The youngest republics are still in the course of developing their creative art, but it may be anticipated that before very long they likewise will produce artists worthy of ranking with those of the older republics.

The dawning of this era is already clearly indicated by the wave of so-called "amateur art" which is sweeping over the entire country and has its source in the people themselves.

Graphic by V. Favorsky.

XXVII

THE PRESS AND THE PUBLISHING AND PRINTING INDUSTRIES

By B. Magidov

Chairman of the Central Committee of the Union of Printing Workers

The Constitution of the U.S.S.R. guarantees the complete freedom of the press under Article 125, which reads:

> "In the interests of the workers and with the object of strengthening the socialist structure of the U.S.S.R., the law guarantees that citizens shall enjoy (*a*) freedom of speech, (*b*) freedom of the press. . . ."

This same article also provides for the maintenance of printing establishments, supplies of paper, &c.

In the Soviet Union there are no privately owned publishing houses or printing works. The state and the various public bodies own all printing establishments, publishing houses, paper mills and printing-ink factories, all of which are therefore under the complete control of the working citizens.

Soviet newspapers are published by the state or by public bodies (Communist Party organizations, trade unions, co-operative, scientific, sports associations, &c.). The costs of production are covered by the revenue from subscriptions, sales and advertisements. These last naturally yield little revenue, owing to the absence of competition engendered by private ownership and to the systematic planning which characterizes Soviet economics.

Immense progress has been made in the realm of the press during the years of Soviet power and in 1937 no fewer than 8521 newspapers were published with a total circulation of 36,197,000 copies (in the Tsarist Russia of 1913 there were only 859 newspapers, with a total circulation of 2,729,000 copies).

The publication of newspapers is by no means limited to the great cities and industrial towns, as no fewer than 3392 provincial towns publish their own papers, in addition to which 4605 printed papers are regularly published in various factories and works, state farms and tractor stations.

The leading newspapers are published in Moscow and among them is the *Pravda* ("Truth") with a circulation of 1,900,000 copies. The circulation of the "News of the Soviets of Workers' Deputies" or *Izvestia* is 1,600,000 copies and that of the "Peasants' Newspaper" or *Krestianskaya Gazeta*—which is exclusively read in rural districts—is 1,250,000 copies. The *Komsomolskaya Pravda,* a paper for young people, has a circulation of 600,000 copies.

The great National Commissariats—those of Heavy Industry, Transport, Defence, Machine-building, the Navy, Health, Food, the Timber Industry, Light Industry, Agriculture and Education—all publish their own newspapers.

There are also a number of periodicals devoted to literature, the arts, architecture, sport, &c. There are weekly papers in Moscow published in English and in French—the *Moscow News* and the *Journal de Moscou.*

The daily German paper, *Deutsche Zentral-Zeitung,* is the press organ of the German-speaking inhabitants of the Soviet Union.

There are in addition 1880 miscellaneous magazines with a total circulation of 250 million copies. These include a number of specialist and technical publications dealing with various technical, scientific and artistic matters and also a whole series of popular illustrated papers and purely literary magazines and reviews.

There has been a vast growth in the number of regular press publications during the years of the Soviet régime not only as regards periodicals appearing in the Russian language, but also in the case of the "national" or non-Russian newspapers. For example, the territory corresponding to the present Kazakh Republic had only 11 newspapers in 1913, whereas in 1936 there were 342—or over 30 times as many. Newspapers are published in 69 different languages spoken in the U.S.S.R. In the case of the territory corresponding to the present-day Tadjik, Kirgiz and other national republics and autonomous regions in which no literature of any kind was published in the local language in the days of Tsarism, there are now innumerable newspapers, periodicals and books published both in the vernacular and in Russian. There are newspapers published not only in the language of the peoples forming the republics and regions concerned, but also in the language of the various minor peoples living within their borders. For instance, in the Kazakh S.S.R. there are, in addition to Russian and Kazakh newspapers, periodicals in the Ouigour tongue (spoken by 150,000 persons) and in Dungan (spoken by 15,000 people).

Works and factory periodicals enjoy a widespread popularity and every large industrial establishment has its own printed newspaper for the benefit of its employees and workers. These papers are conducted by editors appointed from amongst the workers themselves. Other large establishments, colleges and army units also publish small periodicals of their own. These publications usually appear every 10 days or even once or twice a month. The costs of production are defrayed partly by the administration of the establishment and partly from the funds of the trade unions.

Where no printed newspaper is issued, there is a *wall newspaper,* which is typed or written by hand and posted up on a wall. There are hundreds of thousands of these in the Union and it would be hard to find any community of Soviet workers without a wall newspaper of their own.

A typical instance occurred in the case of the members of the *Cheliuskin* expedition, when over 100 Soviet citizens suffered shipwreck and were marooned on an ice-floe separated from the mainland of their native country by thousands of miles of icebound wastes. They were in imminent peril of death and it might have been assumed that they would have applied their entire energies to an attempt to extricate themselves from the danger with which they were threatened. Nevertheless, on the day following that on which the ship's company left the *Cheliuskin* for the ice-floe, they produced the first handwritten issue of their Arctic camp newspaper. It bore the characteristic title *No Surrender* and was probably the most optimistic and cheerful paper ever known to the world.

Who writes for all those little factory, collective farm

and institutional papers? Their editors have no need to seek the collaboration of outside help or of professional journalists, as there is no lack of voluntary contributors among the workers, engineers, technicians, employees, students, instructors, professors, agricultural experts, tractor drivers, grooms, cow keepers and dairymaids of the establishment concerned.

These people constitute the army of workers, peasants and military correspondents who write critical and technical articles and observations, short stories, eye-witness accounts, verses and narratives. The main contributors to the works and institutional periodicals are their readers themselves.

Self-criticism and criticism are a potent weapon of the local press in general. The local press attacks shortcomings in production and community life and criticizes the management, the administratives, authorities and Soviet institutions without any regard for individuals. The great daily papers do exactly the same. The extent to which the citizens of the Union appreciate the liberty of their press is amply demonstrated by the stream of "paragraphs" in the popular papers and by the "letters to the editor" in the great dailies. Every newspaper has a host of workers' and peasants' correspondents who write to it from every part of the vast territory of the Union. In 1937 the editorial office of the *Pravda* received over 350,000 letters. Streams of letters from readers also reach the papers read in the country districts.

The editors of all newspapers, from the great dailies down to the wall newspapers, are obliged to give every consideration and attention to any and every letter written to them in good faith by a private citizen. The editors may not ignore such letters and must either reproduce them in their papers or refer the particular question to which they relate to the public body or state department concerned with a view to the matter being put right or properly explained. Failure on the part of an editor to pay due regard to a letter addressed to his paper by a citizen is treated as a gross breach of trust. The writers of such letters, whether they be workers or peasants, are considered as performing a valuable social duty in putting forward their suggestions or criticisms for publication in the press. Editors enter into correspondence with the writers of such letters, invite them to call and assist them with constructive advice. There are literally millions of so-called workers' and peasants' correspondents, and any citizen may act as such if he or she is desirous of displaying social activity by writing to the press. Any attempt to suppress such letters or to persecute their authors by the persons subjected to just criticism in them, are not merely strongly resented by public opinion, but are actually punishable. There is a special press organ for the benefit of workers' and peasants' correspondents, which helps them with advice and also assists in the conduct of wall newspapers. Workers' and peasants' correspondents who display exceptional literary ability are frequently invited to become regular contributors to the papers and thereby become professional journalists. As such correspondents represent the most active social elements in the country, it is not surprising that quite a number of them have risen to considerable eminence in public life.

The entire press of the country is characterized by a rigid adherence to its principles, an unswerving support of the ideals of Communism and a genuinely ethical attitude to the problems with which it is faced. There is nothing resembling a sensation-mongering gutter-press or any literature catering for the lower instincts and tendencies of humanity. The papers never contain anything in the shape of an account of the private life of a politician or actor, &c., neither do they print detailed reports of murders or social gossip, &c.

Public opinion demands an exceedingly high standard from the press and from its contributors, both professionally and politically. At the present time there are, in addition to the many experienced newspapermen engaged in press work, a great number of young journalists, graduates of the universities and trained in schools of journalism, who are distinguishing themselves by excellent work in the field of social and political activity. The watchword of the Soviet press and of the public bodies and state establishments associated with it is "the paper must be written with clean hands," and every effort is made to ensure that no self-seekers, "Yes-men" or unscrupulous adventurers acquire any voice in its conduct.

. . . .

The phenomenal growth in the activities displayed by the mass of the people in political and social matters and their increasing cultural development is reflected not only in the unprecedented increase in the periodical press, but also in that of the book-publishing trade.

Books are published in the Soviet Union in 111 different languages, whereas in the old-time Russia only 49 languages were used. During the last 20 years dozens of minor nationalities have received the benefit of literary culture. More than 40 of these had their language expressed in writing and print for the first time in their history. The Giliak, Ingoush, Kabardin, Kurd, Lezghin, Lapp, Nain, Tunguz, Circassian, Chechen, Choukchi, and Eskimo people are among those whose language is now, for the first time, being used in printed literature.

All the 11 republics of the Soviet Union now possess their own publishing houses and produce millions of books in the languages spoken within their borders. In this respect a comparison between the years 1913 and 1937 is of interest. In the Ukraine the number of books published in Ukrainian in 1913 was 431,000 copies, whereas in 1937 it was over 65 million copies; in Georgia the corresponding figures are 443,000 and 5.3 million copies.

The largest number of books published are on social-economic and political subjects, then come works of fiction, followed by books on philology, mathematics, natural science, agriculture and art.

During the past 20 years 355.9 million copies of the works of Marx, Engels, Lenin and Stalin have been published in the Soviet Union, 300.8 million being in Russian and 55.1 million in other languages.

The number of children's books published in 1937 was more than 10 times as great as that in 1913.

Textbooks for use in elementary and secondary schools, in all 90 languages commonly spoken within the borders of the Union, were published in 1937 to the number of 1681, their actual output being 128,597,000 copies.

The sales of works of classical fiction are immense. For example, in the years 1917-37 the works of Poushkin were published in 62 languages and sold to the extent of 26,426,000 copies (23,353,000 being in Russian); the sales of Leo Tolstoi's works—in 54 languages—amounted to 15,926,000 copies; those of Maxim Gorky—in 58 languages—to 36,923,000 copies, &c., &c.

Soviet readers are particularly interested in the foreign classics and every workers' or village library now contains complete collections of the works of Shakespeare, Byron, Balzac, Dickens, Goethe, Cervantes and Zola, all of which are in great demand and eagerly read. During the years 1917-37 the sales of Dickens's works—in seven languages—amounted to 1,640,000 copies; those of Shakespeare—in 14 languages—to 773,000 copies, &c., &c.

Notwithstanding the huge issues of books made by the publishing houses, their output is nothing like great enough to meet the demands of the people. The passion for books is universal, and they are bought at sight. Some interesting observations were made in several of the largest bookshops in Moscow. It was noted that in the course of a single day one such shop sold 1000 copies of a new edition of Leo Tolstoi's *Resurrection,* while 600 copies of the works of Poushkin in a single volume were sold in under three hours. The huge demand for books calls for a further expansion of the publishing business and of the facilities for printing.

. . . .

The publishing houses of the Soviet Union have their own printing presses. In former times the latter were only to be found in the larger cities, but nowadays printing facilities in most provincial centres and in some cases the factory newspapers possess small printing presses of their own.

In recent years a number of printing works, equipped with the latest types of presses, have been established for the great newspapers. The *Pravda* has rotary presses with a capacity of one million copies per hour. Printing presses have for the first time been set up in the capitals of the Union and Autonomous Republics—in Alma-Ata, Stalinabad, Ashkhabad, Siktivkar, Cheboksari, Engels and Birobidjan. Up-to-date printing works have been established in Tashkent, Tbilissi, Baku, Minsk, Kazan, Sverdlovsk, Smolensk, Yerevan, Kiev, Kharkov, &c. During the Second Five Year Plan (1932-37) over 200 million roubles were spent on printing plant and buildings belonging to the publishing houses and during the last three years many new linotypes, offset, rotary newspaper printing machines, folding machines, &c., have been installed.

The Soviet authorities are now building their own printing machinery—a branch of industry which is new to Russia—and more than 50 different kinds of printing machines and accessories are being produced.

XXVIII

THE U.S.S.R. AND THE EXTERNAL WORLD

By Professor I. Zvavich

"The object of our whole policy and propaganda has been not to drive the nations to war, but to put an end to war."—*(Extract from Lenin's address to the Eighth Congress of Soviets on 21st December, 1920.)*

Throughout all the years of its existence the Soviet Republic has constantly and unswervingly advocated peace and set its face against war. The watchword of the Bolshevik Party, which came into power in Russia in 1917, was "Peace." At the present time, when the capitalist world is being torn asunder, it may be worth while remembering the revolutionary programme of peace advocated by Lenin in 1917, when he called upon all the belligerent powers to conclude an armistice forthwith as a prelude to a peace "without annexations or reparations." The Soviet Government published the texts of the secret treaties concluded by Tsarism, thereby exposing the militaristic aims of the imperialists. The young Soviet Republic invited all the belligerents to take part in the peace negotiations and it was only when the Allies rejected this invitation that it dropped out of the war.

The Soviet people were then compelled to struggle for five years to achieve peace and to maintain their right to set up a socialist order in their own country. Fourteen foreign powers took part in the intervention against the

Soviet Government. Germany violated the peace treaty which she had signed with Soviet Russia by invading the Ukraine and attempting to interfere on the Don, in the Caucasus, the Baltic Provinces and Byelorussia.

The Entente undertook three campaigns against Russia. The first occurred in the spring of 1919 and was a combined effort, as it envisaged simultaneous attacks by Koltchak, Denikin, Poland and Yudenitch, supported by mixed Anglo-Russian forces in Turkestan and Arkhangelsk (Archangel). The main blow was to come from the east. The Entente powers were then acting in concert and openly committed to active intervention, but the people and their army displayed a greater solidarity and resilience than their numerous opponents. The second campaign embarked on by the Entente took place in the autumn of 1919 and was likewise a combined affair, as it provided for simultaneous attacks by Denikin, Poland and Yudenitch (Koltchak having been dropped). The main force of the attack was to come from the south on this occasion. The attempt failed largely owing to internal dissensions between the members of the Entente and the protests of their own people against the policy of active intervention. The third campaign undertaken by the Entente was in the west—from Poland—in 1920. The effect of the sharp internal dissensions among the members of the Entente soon compelled them to abandon the idea of breaking the Soviet power in Russia and to devote themselves to the task of rescuing the troops of Pilsudski and his government.

The cause of peace played an important part in rallying the masses of the people to the party of Lenin and the fact that the Bolsheviks were fighting to bring peace to their country embued the revolutionary armies with the utmost enthusiasm for the defence of their fatherland. Notwithstanding the cruel privations, famine, cold and epidemics endured by the people, they successfully repulsed the invaders and drove out the White generals supported by their numerous adversaries, beginning with the hordes of the German Kaiser and ending with the Japanese Army in the Far East.

The Soviet Union had, therefore, no easy task to secure the peace born of the defence put up by the War of the Revolution.

Although compelled to recognize the existence of the Soviet State as an accomplished fact, the capitalist powers declined to renounce their idea of destroying it. In entering into normal relations with the U.S.S.R., the statesmen directing the foreign policy of the great imperialist powers expressed the hope that the establishment of ordinary commercial relations would cause the Bolsheviks to change their nature and that Soviet Russia would, in due course, resume her place in the ranks of the bourgeois states. This was not merely a pious hope, but a definite political programme. At the Genoa Conference of 1922 financial intervention succeeded armed intervention and the Soviet authorities were plainly made to understand that "the capitalistic stick" hitherto held over their heads would be replaced by the threat of "the almighty dollar." Although prepared to make considerable concessions for the sake of hastening the development of the economic structure of the country, the Soviet authorities could not entertain terms which would reduce the Republic to the former semi-colonial dependence on the Western Powers. The Government put forward a formula of "peaceful co-existence of two opposite systems," that of the Soviet socialist system and that of capitalism. At the International Conference of 1927, held in Geneva, this formula was, on the initiative of the Soviet Government, accepted by the delegates of all the countries of the world represented at the Conference.

In order to foster the economic growth of their country, the Government were anxious to improve their commercial relations with the external world. Tsarist Russia was a technically and culturally backward state and the U.S.S.R. was in urgent need of foreign-made plant for the equipment of the home industry. Despite the absence of foreign assistance and the financial blockade and boycott of the banks, the Soviet Union carried through the programme of the two Five Year Plans and became the greatest industrial state in Europe. In pursuing their objective of technical and economic independence, the Government had, however, no idea of aiming at any autarchy or separation from the outside world. The high rate at which the economic structure of the U.S.S.R. has been and is still being developed, offers a possibility for considerably increased purchases from any country prepared to offer suitable credit facilities.

The Government are quite ready to compete amicably with the capitalist powers, but this association of two opposite social orders can, as explained by Lenin and Stalin, only continue to be of a peaceful character until such time as war is *forced* on the U.S.S.R. by others. The Bolsheviks, convinced that the socialist order was better than the anarchy and aimlessness of a capitalism torn by internal contradictions, were quite ready to compete with the latter on amicable terms and the Government took advantage of the peace they had won to reconstruct their national economy on the socialist basis provided for in the two Five Year Plans. The programme of peaceful reconstruction embarked on in 1929 came just at the beginning of the greatest economic crisis which ever shook the world of capitalism. The U.S.S.R. became the second industrial power of the world and the greatest in Europe as regards output. The prestige of the Soviet Union has gone up immeasurably, helped by conditions of *peaceful* competition. The success achieved by the U.S.S.R. led to a resumption of normal relations with the U.S.A., who were considerably impressed by this remarkable economic feat.

However, even the peaceful nature of the development of the Soviet Union had to reckon with hostility from capitalist interests. The experience of the past proved that its enemies would never hesitate to embark on a policy of intervention in order to re-establish capitalism in Russia. The internal counter-revolutionary movement, lacking all support among the people, was wholly dependent on outside support. In the words of Lenin—

"We are surrounded by people, classes and governments who display the utmost hatred towards us. We must always bear in mind that our safety from attack hangs by a hair."[1]

Its external enemies are consistently supporting the counter-revolutionary elements by every means in their power.

One form taken by this support is through the activities of the White Guards. The White exiles have been conducting their anti-Soviet campaign openly and with

[1] *Lenin*, vol. xxvii, p. 117.

impunity. Their emissaries murdered the diplomatic envoys of the U.S.S.R. on two occasions—Vorovsky in Lausanne (in 1923) and Voikov in Warsaw (in 1927). In Central Asia insurgent bands, armed and financed by foreigners, indulged in frequent attacks on the lives and property of the inhabitants and committed innumerable murders, robberies and other outrages. The White Guards in Manchuria, encouraged and inspired by the imperialists of Japan, organized raids on Soviet establishments and undertakings engaged in peaceful occupations.

Another form of support given by the enemies of the Soviet to its would-be destroyers was the financing of wreckers, conspirators and spies within the territory of the U.S.S.R. The various public trials, beginning with the shakhty case in the summer of 1928 and ending with the recent trial of the spies and terrorists of the "anti-Soviet Right Wing Trotskyists" in 1938 have provided eloquent proof of the fact that these enemies will utilize any human scum if they think they can thereby inflict injury on the Soviet Union. In vain do the more hypocritical of the anti-Soviet press organs hold up their hands in horror and profess their detestation of such conduct. They omit to mention that the international secret service is constantly concerned with such nefarious activities and that many of their agents have, after exposure and conviction, made detailed revelations regarding such "heroic deeds."

Just as the Soviet Government, in their earliest days, exposed the real war aims of the imperialists and published the texts of the secret agreements, so now the Soviet courts reveal their preparations for war in the public trials of the foreign spies, wreckers, conspirators and secret agents, and in unmasking these people the U.S.S.R. is rendering a real service to the cause of world peace. Those persons beyond the borders of the Soviet Union who are deliberately or unwittingly seeking to prevent these disclosures are guilty of wilfully or unwittingly associating themselves with the enemies of peace.

Although the U.S.S.R. is relying on its own defences to repel an invasion, the Government have always been ready to co-operate with the forces of peace and with all such states and organizations as are opposed to war.

This co-operation in the cause of world peace has been and is now extremely active. At the International Disarmament Conference the Soviet representatives put forword comprehensive schemes for complete and partial disarmament. In July, 1933, at the instance of the U.S.S.R., an agreement was signed defining aggression and in 1934 the Soviet Union, by a majority resolution of the member states of the League of Nations, was invited to Join the League and to accept a seat on its Council. Since joining the League of Nations, the U.S.S.R. has given repeated proofs of its loyal adherence to all the League's proposals for the maintenance of peace and has fulfilled the terms of the Covenant. The League of Nations could certainly never be regarded as a Soviet or socialist organization. It is an international institution set up in accordance with the scheme propounded by President Wilson and the conservative pacifist, Lord Cecil, but at the present time, when a turgid wave of Fascism is threatening to drench the world in a sea of blood and mud, the League of Nations of Wilson and Cecil constitutes a definite obstacle, even though it be a minor one, to the aims of Fascist aggressors. For this reason Japan, Germany and Italy successively left the League and are now conducting a campaign against it and the principle of collective security. Without any declaration of war and in contemptuous defiance of the elementary axioms of international law, Japan is waging war on China, Italy invaded helpless Abyssinia, Germany and Italy are engaged in an armed conflict with the democracy of Spain and, finally, Hitler's Germany has hastened to seize the independent state of Austria.

The Soviet Union stands for the consolidation of all the peace forces in the world under the banner of the League of Nations; for it is convinced that aggressors will not dare to attack peaceful states if they all stand together. Unfortunately, at times a certain section of the Government circles in the Western democratic states displays a hopeless and defeatist frame of mind which the Fascist reactionaries hasten to encourage and turn to account. "If universal peace cannot be maintained, wouldn't it be better to maintain it for ourselves at least," is what these defeatists say in their endeavour to "canalize" aggression and "lead" it aside.

The Fascist aggressors merely regard this short-sighted and dangerous policy of forbearance as a sign of weakness. They make full use of the reactionary press organs in the democratic countries to raise the bogy of the "Communist Menace" and the Bolshevik danger to distract attention from their own preparations for a war of aggression. The Fascist countries, in embarking on their campaigns for Abyssinian oil, Spanish ore and the Chinese market, loudly proclaim that they are "fighting Communism." Germany, Japan and Italy have entered into a mutual pact to combat the Comintern—a convenient cloak for concealing a totally different objective, while serving to rally all the anti-Soviet elements for a conflict with the U.S.S.R.

Although the Soviet Union does not fear Fascist aggression in the slightest, it has never failed to raise its voice in protest against violations of international law on the part of the Fascist countries. At the same time the U.S.S.R. maintains normal diplomatic relations with all the capitalist states, regardless of their form of government. Its relations with Italy were consistently courteous until Italy deliberately chose to sacrifice them for the sake of the Rome-Berlin Axis. There can be little doubt that there are some unpleasant surprises in store for Italy—the appearance of her German "friends" on the Brenner Pass being the first and the forerunner of others. The Soviet Government were ready to conclude an "Eastern Pact" of collective security with Germany and offered to guarantee the inviolability of the Baltic States, but Fascist Germany rejected the offer, thereby disclosing her own aggressive intentions towards these small countries. The U.S.S.R. has, over a period of several years, repeatedly approached Japan in regard to the conclusion of a mutual pact of non-aggression, but these approaches were consistently repulsed by the Japanese Government, who prefer to retain the anti-Soviet card in their hand as a convenient cover for their policy of aggression in China.

The Soviet Union appreciates that it does not stand alone in its efforts to maintain peace. Every nation is anxious to do so and the U.S.S.R. is ready to collaborate with all those genuinely desirous of serving the cause of peace, whatever their internal political structure and ideology may be. Its sole objective is to rally these nations to the cause of peace and it aims at nothing more.

There may be difference of opinion concerning the best way of serving the cause of peace. A few reactionary politicians in the most pacific countries are so obsessed by their hatred of socialism as to be ready to sacrifice the cause of world-peace for the sake of not having to work with the Soviet to ensure it. There can, however, be no getting away from facts. The peace policy of the U.S.S.R. is a fact and the threat of Fascist aggression is likewise a melancholy fact; in the face of these, many farseeing and genuinely patriotic statesmen, who have no leanings whatever towards Communism, favour the principle of collective security and collaboration in the cause of peace.

The U.S.S.R. has concluded pacts of non-aggression with a number of countries, including all neighbour states with the exception of Japan. Pacts of mutual assistance have been concluded with France and with Czechoslovakia and under Article 49 of the Soviet Constitution the Presidium of the Supreme Soviet of the U.S.S.R. has vested in it the power "to declare a state of war in the event of an armed attack on the U.S.S.R. or in fulfilment of obligations entered into for mutual defence against aggression under international agreement, during any period between the sessions of the Supreme Soviet of the U.S.S.R." The last clause of the foregoing article was inserted in the form of an amendment by the Eighth Congress of Soviets of the U.S.S.R. at the instance of the Chairman of the Editorial Committee, J. V. Stalin. The Soviet Union honours its international obligations and is always prepared to carry them out in full.

The relations of the past 20 years or more between the Soviet Government and other countries clearly demonstrate that the U.S.S.R. has always fulfilled its international obligations. In many cases—more especially in connexion with its dealing with Eastern states—the U.S.S.R.'s policy was a deliberate departure from the traditional policy of Russian imperialism, as the former privileges exercised by Tsarist Russia in these countries (Iran, Afghanistan, China and Turkey) were surrendered. This politic action on the part of the Soviet Union was rewarded by the esteem and respect of the peoples of the East, who had formerly regarded the Western imperialists and Tsarist Russia as oppressors and exploiters striving to enrich themselves at the expense of the colonial and semi-colonial countries.

Both in the East and in the West the U.S.S.R. has ever maintained the principles of equality of rights in dealing with "small" countries. In the eyes of Fascist diplomats schooled in the worst traditions of Prussianism, "small" countries and "small" nations are to be regarded as "of inferior status." In contrast to these views of the Fascist aggressors, the Soviet Union always respects the culture and the national independence of "small" countries and nations. There has been an extraordinarily rapid development of national culture in the Soviet Union itself. The Soviet people "recognize neither Greek nor Jew," whereas the inhuman doctrine of Fascism denies "non-Aryans" the right to live.

The people of the Soviet Union are striving to acquire their lawful heritage of world culture, the best traditions and the greatest achievements of mankind, regardless of race or nationality. The destruction of the treasures of centuries of culture by barbarians in Spain, where aircraft are bombing cities, churches, museums, monuments, hospitals and peaceful inhabitants, arouses the utmost indignation.

The Soviet Union will not allow itself to be provoked into war, but it is carefully watching the anti-Soviet activities of the international reactionaries. The U.S.S.R. can rely on the support of all true friends of peace. In all the capitalist countries the question of relations with the Soviet Union constitutes the acid test for distinguishing the real enemies of peace from those who are its friends and the hesitating, neutral or thoughtless people. The U.S.S.R. is anxious to make the peaceful objectives of its policy clear to all; it has nothing to conceal; there are no secret treaties or plans for the conquest of foreign territory. The doctrine of Stalin is not that of the bourgeois states which seek to create definite spheres of interest; it is a doctrine of peace.

"Our foreign policy is clear. It is the maintenance of peace and the development of commercial relations with all other countries. The U.S.S.R. has no idea of threatening anybody, let alone of attacking any other country. We stand for peace and support the cause of peace, but we are not afraid of threats and are quite ready to return blow for blow from a warlike aggressor. Those who desire peace and business contacts with us will ever find us ready to respond, while those who may seek to attack our country must expect to meet with a formidable resistance. . . ."[2]

[2] Stalin, *Questions of Leninism*, 10th edn., p. 552.